THE BELLE ÉPOQUE

EUROPEAN PERSPECTIVES

EUROPEAN PERSPECTIVES

A Series in Social Thought and Cultural Criticism

Lawrence D. Kritzman, Editor

European Perspectives presents outstanding books by leading European thinkers. With both classic and contemporary works, the series aims to shape the major intellectual controversies of our day and to facilitate the tasks of historical understanding.

For a complete list of books in the series, see page 253.

DOMINIQUE KALIFA

THE BELLE ÉPOQUE

A Cultural History, Paris and Beyond

TRANSLATED BY SUSAN EMANUEL

POSTSCRIPT BY VENITA DATTA

COLUMBIA UNIVERSITY PRESS

NEW YORK

COLUMBIA
UNIVERSITY
PRESS

Columbia University Press gratefully acknowledges the generous
support for this book provided by Publisher's Circle members
Paul LeClerc and Judith Ginsberg.

Columbia University Press
Publishers Since 1893
New York   Chichester, West Sussex
cup.columbia.edu

Copyright © 2021 Columbia University Press
LA VÉRITABLE HISTOIRE DE LA BELLE ÉPOQUE by Dominique Kalifa
© Librairie Artheme Fayard, 2017.

Library of Congress Cataloging-in-Publication Data
Names: Kalifa, Dominique, author. | Emanuel, Susan, translator.
Title: The Belle Époque : a cultural history, Paris and beyond /
Dominique Kalifa ; translated by Susan Emanuel.
Other titles: Véritable histoire de la "Belle Époque". English
Description: New York : Columbia University Press, [2021] | Series:
European perspectives: a series in social thought and cultural criticism |
Includes bibliographical references and index.
Identifiers: LCCN 2020054764 (print) | LCCN 2020054765 (ebook) |
ISBN 9780231202084 (hardback) | ISBN 9780231202091 (trade paperback) |
ISBN 9780231554381 (ebook)
Subjects: LCSH: France—Civilization—1830–1900. | Arts, French—
19th century. | Arts, French—20th century. | France—Intellectual
life—19th century. | France—Intellectual life—20th century. | France—
Civilization—1901–1945. | France—Social life and customs—
19th century. | France—Social life and customs—20th century. |
France—History—Third Republic, 1870–1940.
Classification: LCC DC33.6 .K3413 2021 (print) | LCC DC33.6 (ebook) |
DDC 944.081/3—dc23
LC record available at https://lccn.loc.gov/2020054764
LC ebook record available at https://lccn.loc.gov/2020054765

Columbia University Press books are printed on permanent and
durable acid-free paper.
Printed in the United States of America
Cover design: Julia Kushnirsky
Cover image: Illustration by Henry Sene Yee after *Ah! La Belle Epoque!*
Palace revue adapted from André Allehaut's program on Radio-Paris

CONTENTS

PROLOGUE

Time Regained

WE ALL know something about the "Belle Époque." While the expression is somewhat impressionistic, it does evoke images familiar even to those who don't speak French. For the French, memories of school history mingle with how the era has been evoked in novels, films, and songs. The "Belle Époque" is also a term used in art history books and exhibition catalogues. And then there are period photographs, portraits, postcards, posters, advertising, certain objects, and a thousand other little things from a past that is not that distant. Let us start from that beginning and try to sketch a portrait of an era as it emerges from our most familiar representations.

"Belle Époque"—we must be in France, even if the expression was extended gradually to other languages and cultures, as if to signal the great hold, mainly cultural, that this nation had over the rest of the world at the time. When was that? Around 1900. We will see that the dates tend to float and that there are different versions of the time span, but 1900 is a round number, a "flattering date"[1] that is easy to remember and that has settled into our minds as a consensus. So we are in France at the start of the twentieth century, and more precisely in Paris, the City of Light, which seemed at the time to attract everyone's attention and to galvanize all kinds of energy.

So the "Belle Époque" is indisputably urban and Parisian; it even makes the capital something to be worshiped. But this Paris has still maintained a country charm: in the villages of Montmartre or Belleville, on the banks of the Marne River, or in the market-garden suburbs that appear just beyond the old city fortifications, the countryside is not far away. It is also a Paris of provincials "who have come up to the capital"—such as the twenty-two thousand mayors to whom the Republic offered a banquet in the gardens of the Champ de Mars in September 1900, or like a few of the nation's presidents with origins in the provinces—and the accents to go with them. In Paris, "the general tone is provincial, with a lingering flavor of the café du commerce," as the pamphleteer Pierre Dominique summarized.[2] This was also a Paris that could not exist without its various "annexes"—the seaside resorts of Deauville, La Baule, Vichy, Biarritz, Monte Carlo, and Cannes, "the chic town."[3] This last point is essential: the Belle Époque almost always evokes the insouciant and frivolous world of high society, the gay life of salons, worldliness, and the high life. Audiences frequented theaters, the opera, and hippodromes, and dined with champagne at Maxim's; the men wore top hats and carnations in their buttonholes; the women wore hobbled skirts and gigantic hats.

Nobody was naïve enough to think that this world—and the *demimonde* of the great courtesans who gravitated toward it—embodied the society as a whole, but people wanted to believe that the image gave that society its tone. The peace that had preserved Europe and the consequent growth and economic prosperity were indeed quite real, and the leisure and entertainment industries were in full flight—all of which gave a feeling of lightness and joie de vivre, implying a universe of shared pleasures. The Belle Époque was "life's festival."[4]

Some other traits are frequently associated with this sterling picture, starting with the feeling that progress was all-powerful. We commonly see the Belle Époque as positivist: the period's picture album features the marvels of science and technology. The Belle Époque is incomprehensible without the scintillations of the "Electricity Fairy" that rolled back the frontiers of the night, without

Edouard Branly's refinement of the wireless telegraph, without the work of Henri Becquerel or Marie Curie, who reinvented the physical world. This progress nourished industry and stimulated growth; it was free and nonchalant because there was no perceived downside. The optimism was expressed in the form of "exploits," those of the automobile pioneers, or better still, aviation champions like Louis Blériot or Roland Garros. It triumphed in public celebrations that seemed to captivate everybody: the automobile show that opened in Paris in 1898, the inauguration of the Métropolitain subway in July 1900, and the first aeronautics salon at the Grand Palais in 1911. The strength of both progress and technical modernity lay in their serving everybody, benefiting every citizen. The Paris Exposition (World's Fair) of 1900, which welcomed more than fifty million visitors to what was both a great industrial exhibition and an immense attraction park, made this Paris known to the whole world. The cinematograph (just invented by the Lumière brothers), purely a product of the machine and of industry, accomplished even more: in little more than a decade, it went from being a simple technology to a formidable entertainment spectacle, open and accessible to all, using a new international language that appeared to be an animated synthesis of all our representations and all our emotions.

We believe more eagerly that progress triumphed because it was conceived as the bearer and creator of freedom itself. Despite the persistence of large pockets of inequalities, the Belle Époque imaginary (*imaginaire*) agreed that poverty was retreating, that manners were softening, that well-being and consumption were increasing— bringing along with them a joie de vivre. This hard-won freedom, politically ensured by the *Triumph of the Republic* (title of a sculpture that was installed in 1899 in the Place de la Nation), was proclaimed by the French people in theaters packed to watch Edmond Rostand's play *Cyrano de Bergerac* strut its stuff in 1897; or flocking to Montmartre cabarets like the Chat Noir and the Mirliton, which launched nightclub singer (and later impresario) Aristide Bruant (see fig. 1); and at *cafés-concerts* where a variegated audience rushed after work to enjoy "Saturday night on the town." It was asserted in the gradual advance of "free" time that was starting to benefit more than the "leisure class," as theorized in 1899 by the American sociologist Thorstein Veblen.

Sport (particularly cycling) symbolized this new freedom most of all. Gradually becoming accessible to the working class, cycling signaled the moment when industrial labor ceased to be synonymous with exploitation and began to incarnate a social hope;[5] it prevailed as an instrument for conquering leisure, as well as embodying the adolescent's dream and everyone's symbol of youth. For women, the bicycle seemed to promise even more: a liberation from clothing constraints that offered movement and independence. Sea bathing, tennis, and gymnastics also played their part in the great festival of the body that was celebrated in the Olympic Games in Paris in 1900. Total freedom, insouciance, lightness, and pleasure were believed to be affecting manners and morals, so much did the Belle Époque distill a frivolous and bawdy tone, evoking "the primacy of woman," the invention of "glamour," even "sex appeal." From the simultaneously tender and sad smiles of Folies-Bergère stars emanated a discreet eroticism that was associated with their corsets and buttoned boots.

But another and decisive trait was the audacity of an era when the *"avant-gardes"* were triumphing: the Belle Époque was above all *cultural*. It relied heavily on the idea of a prodigious creative flowering that made Paris the incontestable capital of world arts and letters, which in this period witnessed a sort of paroxysm of the audacious, of experimentation and aesthetic inventiveness. A syllabus for a recent American course on the Belle Époque proclaimed: "Not only was Paris during this time the undisputed western capital of painting and sculpture, it was also the most important production site for new works of musical theater and, arguably, literature as well."[6] An extraordinary inventory could feature aesthetic dialogues between Claude Debussy's *Pelleas et Melisande* (1902) and Pablo Picasso's *Les Demoiselles d'Avignon* (1907), between the art nouveau curlicues of Hector Guimard and Alfred Jarry's play *Ubu Roi* (1896), between the scandal of the Ballet Russes (1909) and the dislocated visions of Marc Chagall's *Paris Through the Window* (1913). I could cite countless artists, movements, schools, magazines, and manifestoes that made this an era of absolute aesthetic shocks. There were also exchanges and circulation between art and industry, between highbrow culture and street culture: advertising posters reached the rank of art, and the press and popular fiction harbored inspired series and serials. For example, the *Fantômas* serial (dictated in tandem by two authors and celebrated by Apollinaire and other poets) inaugurated what the surrealists would later call "automatic writing."

Therefore everything converged to make this era an extraordinary advance in freedom, innovation, and happiness. As singer Maurice Chevalier recalled in his memoir about the start of the century: "God, but Paris seemed happy to be alive!"[7] It was a magic era of frivolity and joyous living, of *oompah* and confetti, but also of aesthetic and scientific invention and (politically) a pinnacle of democracy. But of course this fabulous picture had its shadowy aspects. Happiness and nonchalance were hedged by threats, and the "times of pleasure" were also the times of vice.[8] While the anguish of decadence did not survive the century's end, other dangers were exacerbated. Alcoholism and suicide took their toll; crime, madness, and prostitution advanced hand in hand; figures like the *apache* (thug), the anarchist, the striker, and the vagabond were seen to hinder the march of progress. The masses agitated, probably because they were in thrall to formidable utopias. On April 12, 1912, the sinking of the *Titanic*, a sort of floating Belle Époque in miniature, gave this society a tragic prefiguration of the cataclysm that was going to carry it away.

Behind the scenes, suspicions that this happiness was illusory and that everybody was refusing to see the looming perils implicitly spoiled the blithe tableau. "1900 was undermined from inside, without anybody wanting to be aware of it."[9] Everybody who recounts the history of the Belle Époque knows that it ended abruptly with the general mobilization on August 1, 1914, that quickly happiness and prosperity and carefree creation would be buried in the mud of the trenches. Despite all efforts at objectivity, our knowing what came after and how the story ends will necessarily weigh on how we understand the course of events. We know that teleology is a fearsome companion. Every historian encounters this difficulty, which he or she tries to avoid by remaining as close to the era's actors and sources as possible, by listening to and comparing witnesses' accounts. But the exercise is even more troubling in the case of the Belle Époque; the term, unlike *"fin de siècle"* (which was actually forged and used by contemporaries to depict their era), is a retrospective construction, an immediately nostalgic category that was principally designed to mourn "the world we have lost." The term "Belle Époque" was never used by any actor at the time. Thus its later and deliberate uses carry imaginary dimensions, a theatricality and even a dramaturgy that distorts historicity and thus alters its meaning.

It is just as anachronistic to speak of the 1900s as a "Belle Époque" as it is to speak of the years from 1919 to 1939 as the "interwar" period. Historians are usually prompt to flush out such mythologies, but until recently they have scarcely tried to illuminate how this term has been used, being generally content with a token caution that said *époque* was not *belle* for everybody. We may even be surprised at the alacrity with which historians appropriated this expression, naturalizing it in the ordinary mill of periodization. "A term born of nostalgia needs to be treated with a degree of skepticism," cautioned two British historians.[10]

This book is born of this caution and the questions it raises. It intends neither to correct the exaggerated representations borne by the Belle Époque *imaginaire* nor to "put an end" to a term that now belongs to French history and our language, and which will continue in any case to fashion how we grasp the era. My ambition is different: to understand when and why this denomination was born, to analyze the uses made of it, the multiple social imaginaries to which it gave rise in later decades—in other terms, to elucidate what in scholarly terms the linguists call a "chrononym," one of those "names for times" that gradually prevail in social awareness in order to define the identity of a period.[11] But naming a period is never neutral. A chrononym always carries intentions or effects—sometimes scientific, but sometimes also political, ideological, cultural, commercial—that the historian should unravel if he or she wants to grasp all the significations invested in the past. The past, far from being closed or complete, never stops being worked over by the perspectives offered and questions posed in later periods. The "real history of the Belle Époque" that this book traces is therefore only indirectly that of the actual first decade of the 1900s. We begin with the invention of the term, or rather its premises, and try to understand how the representations of this crucial period were constituted, modified, reconstituted—and sometimes even outright invented.

First we must deal with the question of the time boundaries of the "Belle Époque." French historians have often discussed this issue and proposed different dates, at least for the starting point, since the terminus—1914—is never in doubt. The start of the Belle Époque is much debated. Some imprudent chroniclers have offered categorical dates. For example: "The Belle Époque began on May 6th, 1889, when the Exposition universelle was inaugurated. The enthusiasm of the crowd was on a par with the stakes."[12] Most writers have been more prudent. While the World's Fair of 1889, which celebrated the centenary of the French Revolution and acknowledged that the Republic had at last taken definitive root, is an obvious landmark, other just as significant dates have been suggested: 1894 was the start of what would become the "Dreyfus affair," so important in the genesis of contemporary France; 1896 saw the return to a cycle of economic growth and prosperity; 1898 or 1899, when the Dreyfus affair reached its paroxysm; and of course 1900, the round number, with its abatement of tensions and the opening of the new and landmark Universal Exhibition. One more unusual (and regional) proposal makes the period start in 1876 and end in 1911.[13] Seen from abroad, things are even vaguer. For Eugen Weber, an American specialist on France, the Belle Époque represents "the nearly ten years that precede 1914," but for his colleague Charles Rearick, it is the "three decades before the Great War."[14]

Moreover, abroad and in non-French encyclopedias, textbooks, and popular history books, the term often refers to a wider time period, i.e., the years from 1871 to 1914, equivalent to the first period of the Third Republic in France and analogous to "Late Victorianism" in Britain and the "Progressive Era" in the United States. These variations, as we shall see, often tell us a lot about the cultures or eras in which they arise. Yet we should not give them too much importance; as Belgian publisher Hubert Juin subtly perceived, "the Belle Époque refers to a vague nostalgia that mixes everything up."[15] This heterogeneity had already been perceived in 1946 by the organizers of a fashion parade: "Their inspiration jumbles dates. Do not ask fashion designers for exact references! They are evoking the whole Belle Époque . . . beginning with Queen Amélie and ending with Countess Greffulhe. A half-century descends the Champs-Elysées in an enormous carriage to invade the fashion salons."[16]

The only date that truly matters to us is when the term itself was born. Research seems to be easy, since all writers agree that the term "Belle Époque" appeared just after the Great War and signified nostalgia for a world that had disappeared. Reproduced from text to text, this assertion has acquired the strength of a law. Here is how an archivist explained the phenomenon in 1972:

> The term "la Belle Époque," which in the beginning was applied to the easy and carefree life of a narrow social stratum (almost exclusively Parisian) during the first years of this century, was adopted by public opinion after the First World War to cover the whole period from 1900 to 1914. This transfer and the birth of the myth can be easily explained as the phenomenon of a generation that had known terrible suffering, lost the best of itself, along with its illusions, and tried to forget the trenches of blood and mud from 1914 to 1918 by exalting the long period of peace and stability that had preceded it.[17]

Forty years later, the explanation had not changed: "Nostalgic for the time suspended between two wars, History since 1918 has called this period the Belle Époque to stress the contrast with the Great War," writes one art historian.[18] This idea also prevails abroad; a British writer tells us that the 1920s fabricated the Belle Époque "principally to signal that France was then enjoying peace and prosperity and that Paris was the city par excellence."[19]

Of course, this explanation is plausible but has never been proved; when historians belatedly went in search of proofs that would attest to it, they did not find them. Charles Rearick was the first to express serious doubts about the authenticity of the term's birth certificate being delivered after World War One's "five years of suffering, privation, mourning." A later historian, "looking more closely . . . found no sources for this assertion."[20]

So we must begin our inquiry with a simple question: When did the term "Belle Époque" appear for the first time to depict France at the turn from the nineteenth to the twentieth century?

* * *

Two bourgeois characters are conversing in an 1892 play by Octave Mirabeau:

> "In vain you decry 'immorality,' 'decadence,' 'slackened standards,' or whatever you want. Me, I find that we are living in a *belle époque*. History will someday prove us right. There is nothing more to say. Never has France been as strong, as grand, as respected. [. . .]"
>
> "This is true! We are living in a *belle époque*, in an epoch of light. The masses are enlightened . . . education . . . freedom . . . compulsory military service."[21]

Thus in the midst of the *fin de siècle,* the friends are celebrating France's grandeur, its army, its power, and its culture, and they even allude to its being threatened. Yet here the term does *not* refer to a properly dated and identifiable period: the characters are discussing not *the* Belle Époque, but *a* belle époque. Such descriptive uses are obviously disparate: a traveling doctor in 1904 mentions "Greek works of the belle époque"; Odette in Proust's *Swann's Way* "once spoke about a friend to whose house she had been invited and had found that everything in it was 'of the period.' Swann could not get her to tell him what 'period' it was."[22] Many such uses of the phrase remain "natural"; and the same is true of its opposite: *"Sale* [foul] *époque!"* is a 1905 expletive from a pen pusher when inheritance and promotion elude him.[23]

Of course, in 1914 the declaration of war and the mobilization were perceived as the end of an era. French students know Guillaume Apollinaire's lines from *Calligrammes*:

August 31st, 1914
A little before midnight I left Deauville
In Rouveyre's little car

Counting the chauffeur we were three
We said farewell to a whole era.[24]

As if better to express this farewell, when the two companions reach Paris on September 2, they commemorate the moment by recording little films in a shop. After the war ended, such lowercase uses of the term multiplied: art historians evoke "the *belle époque* of painting in Spain and Portugal" (meaning the sixteenth century) and the "pedestal tables of the *belle époque*" (meaning the Second Empire), and the journalist Lucien Dubech celebrates in September 1924 "Georges Carpentier [a boxing star] of the *belle époque*."[25] But if we look closely, the Roaring Twenties bear *no trace* of a "Belle Époque" that was supposed to have begun at the start of the century.

Origins do became more precise when we look at the following decade, when prewar nostalgia emerges as the true prehistory of the Belle Époque. In 1930, the famous couturier Paul Poiret published a memoir in which he explains how he dressed "the epoch," while the *Poésie pur* magazine studied "the symbolist *belle époque*." Two years later, Henri Clouzot, the curator at the Galliera Museum, spoke of this *belle époque* of the aesthetic of the modern style, which for him began in 1890 and blossomed around 1900.[26] The critic Jean Valdois commented in *Cinémagazine* on a series of recent films whose action takes place around 1900; he mentions the "Maxim's of the Prince de Sagan and of Emilienne d'Alençon—the *belle époque*."[27] This is more precise, but the formula is still merely synonymous with good times. "Ah, yes, it was a good time, when people knew the sweetness of living." The singer Fréhel, now grown old, declares to Jean Gabin in the film *Pepe le Moko* (*Algiers*) by Julien Duvivier (1937): "Me, when I get the blues, I change era!"—and then she puts a song from her twenties on the phonograph.

Thus, by the 1930s the expression was "in the air"—but not yet a commonplace. In 1936 the singer Robert Burnier intoned, "Ah, la belle époque!" in the operetta *La Poule*,[28] a tune already used three years before in the film adaptation. Yet this glorified *belle époque* was not explicitly linked to the start of the century but merely used to evoke yesterday's good times, the vanished good times. It was only four years later, in October 1940, that "la Belle Époque" unequivocally came to the fore when radio host André Alléhaut inaugurated on Radio-Paris a new entertainment program titled *Ah! la Belle Époque! A Musical Sketch of the Era of 1900.* Alléhaut was obviously inspired by the 1936 refrain, but he anchored it in precise chronology and associated it with a very specific type of song: the great successes of the *café-concerts* of the 1900s. The Belle Époque was born.

* * *

In tracing in the following pages the cultural history of the Belle Époque, this book tries to account for the "historical imagination" of a reconstructed past. A question runs through it: Why did the twentieth century feel the need to celebrate and almost sanctify the first years of its existence? What mindset pushed it to cultivate nostalgia like this? What blessings and what lessons could it draw from such an imaginary? For if the history of the Belle Époque period does tell us something about the 1900s—how could it be otherwise?—it also (and maybe mainly) speaks to us about the difficult and bitter and terrible times of a twentieth century that could not forget the happy moment of its birth. The general physiognomy of the era has not ceased transforming itself. The "Belle Époque" evoked in the 1930s—which was not called so but "1900"—does not have the same face as the one that triumphed in 1950s cinema, or the one exhibited in postcard collections in the 1980s. History is constantly inflecting the representation of time, shaping images of the past for its own needs. We cannot ignore the gestures and "facts" about the past that once undeniably existed and form the framework of our lives, yet we should not be carried away by fantasy. But we must analyze like a historian the subtle reconstructions of crisscrossing temporalities in which the past is restored to us.

Let us therefore try to unravel (by going back closer to the source) the complex skein of representations that were slowly imbricated in the idea of the "Belle Époque" extending from the time of its first youth to the metamorphoses of the present day. But there is no triumphant "lesson" to be learned from this journey, nor are we aspiring to rectify the errors of common-sense understanding. We know that historical imaginaries obey laws that are not those of starchy chronologies, and that History is living—and that it always belongs (as a last resort) to the society that writes it.

Saturday, December 12, 2015, 10 a.m.

It is chilly but not raining. At the place de la Sorbonne I join forty-some undergraduate students and a young colleague. The idea is to spread out over the neighborhood in groups of three or four and ask passersby about what the "Belle Époque" means to them. We have conscientiously prepared this operation, drafting a dozen open-ended questions on what the expression signifies, possibly soliciting a key date but especially typical images, places, events, and objects that might be associated with the term. The interview should end on a more personal note: Was this a period in which you would have liked to live?

Our survey has no scientific pretentions. We agreed to interview everyone we meet, young or old, French or foreign, Parisians or provincials. It is only a sidewalk vox pop aimed to measure feelings and representations. An "impressionistic portrait," one of the students says. We know that we are in Paris, in a well-off neighborhood where students and tourists abound on Saturday mornings. But the project excites all of us, and I am happy to note the energy and vivacity of the students, whom I usually see as gloomier in the tepid lecture hall. One last briefing and we separate around 10:15. Some head to the Luxembourg gardens, others to the Panthéon and place de la Contrescarpe; most of them spread out into adjoining streets like the boulevard Saint-Michel, rue des Écoles, rue Saint-Jacques.

I meet some of them around midday for a first report, the others the following week for a complete debriefing. In total they conversed with more than 150 persons. Some students were rebuffed, but most often the response was kindly. Yet many were struck—as was I in the few exchanges I witnessed—by the reactions of people who felt caught off guard: they were intimidated, afraid of saying something wrong, protecting themselves by saying they were not historians. Though we reminded them that the study was not an oral exam, that every kind of answer was permissible, and that we just wanted to know their perceptions, we detected a strong inhibition connected with "knowledge."

Yet the "Belle Époque" did signify something to almost all of them: a happy period of peace and prosperity. Many people mentioned a carefree and agreeable time, of joie de vivre, of progress that was shared, that enjoyed freer manners, a period of luxury and leisure. "It was a time when everything was going well economically," explained one gen-tleman. A couple of young Italians talked about "decoration, flowers, color, music, and dances." But when the questions were more precise and solicited key dates, everything became vaguer and blurrier. Some cited the Renaissance, others the eighteenth century or the French Revolu-tion, others the "Thirty Glorious Years" of economic prosperity after World War Two, and a few even the end of the 1990s, the era of French President Chirac, France's winning its first World Cup in soccer, and the "period prior to the shift to the euro." An old gentleman spoke of his youth. Most people dated the Belle Époque to the early twentieth cen-tury; however, they tended to place it after World War One. While the early 1900s—its world exhibition, the legislation separating church and state (1905), and the Bateau-Lavoir artist colony—did get a few votes, most interviewees pinpointed the Roaring Twenties, the Charleston, flappers, Josephine Baker, and The Great Gatsby. *Paris incontestably dominated respondents' representations (the Eiffel Tower, Montmartre, Pigalle, the Moulin Rouge, and café-concerts) but had to contend with cities like New York or Chicago during Prohibition. Woody Allen's film* Midnight in Paris *was regularly cited, which may partly explain these recollections. In the end, the "Belle Époque" emerged as a sort of indeter-minate but happy sequence in the history of France, situated somewhere between the Second Empire (1850s and 1860s) and the 1930s crisis, an era full of "retro stuff," peopled with great figures ranging from the nov-elist Balzac to the chanteuse Mistinguett, from city planner Baron Haussmann to artist Toulouse-Lautrec, from Charles Péguy to Edith Piaf.*

PART ONE

"THE 1900 ÉPOQUE"

NEITHER MEN nor women of the 1900s ever spoke of the "Belle Époque." But words are one thing and feelings are another. That contemporaries did not know the term "Belle Époque" does not mean that they were not aware of the identity of their time. Or that a specific sentiment, a "historicity" in the widest sense that the anthropologist Marshall Sahlins gave this term ("a human community's mode of consciousness of self")[1] did not affect their thought and conversation. Were other words and other expressions used to characterize this period before this chrononym was forged? Did the Belle Époque exist in other forms, or under alternative names? This first part of this book is devoted to such questions, in a quest for what might be called a "prehistory of the Belle Époque." We start by looking at period awareness before 1914, keen as it was on introspection, perception, and "knowledge of time."[2] Then we extend our quest beyond the Great War, into those lively but troubled years of the 1920s, which nobody at the time would ever have dreamed of calling "interwar." We will not find yet the Belle Époque per se, but the term "1900 Époque" will finally surge up in 1931, already laden with nostalgia, an early "Belle Époque" imaginary that prefigures many of its later traits.

DAWN OF THE CENTURY

WE KNOW that the "fin de siècle" aroused among its contemporaries the feeling of living through a unique moment, marked by growing pessimism and cynicism, a time of decadence, moral corruption, and the "decline of the race."[1] Obviously, this fin de siècle was perceived as such only by a narrow élite of artists, intellectuals, publicists, and journalists. But the fact is that this disparate troop was the one that expressed itself and thus left written evidence, on the basis of which history is composed. Obviously, nobody would maintain that the 1880s or 1890s were *entirely* struck by moroseness or morbid excitation, and peopled with crazies and drinkers of ether, fascinated with rare orchids and refined perfumes. However, the idea of decline or degeneration did contribute to shape the *imaginaire* of the era.

But did a distinct feeling pervade the first decade of the 1900s? Did entering the new century produce a specific consciousness that nourished among contemporaries a shared sentiment of historicity? That idea has found occasional support. "This is the heart of the subject," we read in an exhibition catalogue. "The 'Belle Époque'—far from being reconstructed *a posteriori*—was affirmed from the start as an exceptional period." It is said to have connoted the experience of a sort of festival and permanent "self-celebration" that would create its own myth. But how can we be sure about such a "temperament"? How can we establish with certainty the existence of a mindset? "If you think about it," asserted French Socialist Louis Blanc in 1873, "individuals think, not whole societies."[2] This was also the view of Max Nordau when in his 1892 masterwork *Degeneration* he tried to decode "the 'fin-de-siècle' Zeitgeist," which he perceived being expressed in the French society of his day.[3] But we may reasonably doubt the existence of such collective states of awareness and inversely support the idea that only individuals think, and that they do so in the infinite variety of their differences—social, gender, age, religion, occupation, culture—in short, their "identity." And that they think differently according to the context of their thought. While in our day polling techniques, debatable as they may be, allow us to grasp something about these states of public opinion, which moreover are changeable and volatile, nothing of the sort was possible at the start of the twentieth century. Yet many contemporaries dwelled on these matters, which were magnified by the takeoff of the press and of a feeling that democracy was fragile. This was the time of the "forceful ideas" to which philosopher Alfred Fouillée, one of the quasi-official thinkers of the Third Republic, devoted three studies between 1890 and 1908.[4] It was also the era of "imitation," which sociologist Gabriel Tarde saw as the principal source of behavior and of social ties.[5] The prevailing idea was that beyond the control of individuals, collective sensibilities and systems of representations fashioned the consciousness of an epoch.

In a sense, this is the program of what we call cultural history. What back in 1828 historian François Guizot termed in his *General History of Civilization in Europe* the "moral state" of a society, which would later be called "mentalities" and then the "social imaginary," actually had an identical ambition. While the concepts forged to define cultural history have not ceased to evolve, scholars' goal and their quest have remained largely similar. In 1892, Max Nordau, who wanted to grasp the "degenerate" spirit of the fin de siècle, had no other choice than to review the enormous corpus of books and articles on the subject. Almost a century later, the ambitious enterprise of Canadian scholar Marc Angenot seemed to echo it. The scale is different since the latter tried to apprehend the whole "social discourse" of an era. While he limited his study to the single year 1889 (exactly a century earlier), made emblematic by the Exposition, in turn the centenary of the 1789 Revolution, Angenot set himself a daunting task: to consult "everything read and written in a state of society; everything printed, everything said publicly . . . everything narrated and argued over."[6] What resulted was immense and almost shapeless, a "whole cacophony" that Angenot tried to slice and cut up, to classify and reclassify, seeking convergences, patterns, or force fields able to organize or govern this extraordinary heap of texts. Of course, he could not read *everything*, but from the 1,200 books and brochures, hundreds of newspapers, magazines, songs, posters, and department store catalogues that he consulted there does emerge something that resembles a state of mind in the France of 1889.[7] Not everything is written down in a society, not everything is formulated, and the grid of "social discourse" ignores many feelings, thoughts, and unspoken things that become irremediably lost to history. Yet the remainder (whatever it is called) helps us to gauge whatever may persist of the collective imaginary. This chapter is not going to reproduce a project whose desire to be exhaustive bears the marks of its own time, the 1980s. But it is indeed the search for the discourse of an era into which we plunge now, seeking the heart of media production around the key year 1900.

ENTERING 1900

"Does our era have a style?" asked the critic Arsène Alexandre in *Le Figaro* on September 1, 1900. His question concerned the fine arts, but it carries its own response: *the* style of an era, whether called "modern" or "new," is truly impossible to find. Yet it is legitimate to enlarge the speculation to the whole of an era's society. The year 1900, which lent itself to "overviews" and "perspectives," was marvelously given to this exercise. For several years, newspapers and magazines had been keen on "opinion surveys."[8] Everything was being studied: the state of literature, various social movements, the German influence, the existence of an interior language, the state of Paris sanitation, marriage and divorce—and the methods of conducting such investigations as specified by economist Pierre du Maroussem precisely in the year 1900.[9] In Paris and other major French cities, people were carried away by a frenzy of inquiries. The formula was invariably the same: one chose a theme that was supposed to embody one of the great problems of the day, developed a questionnaire that was addressed to the nation's principal "personalities," and published the responses with great fanfare. The profusion of this type of survey, as well the small group of famous individuals who were always asked about everything, suffice to explain their artificial character. But the desire, almost the obsession, to permanently survey society, and the belief that something might be learned from such surveys, remain interesting matters from our perspective. In 1900, the intuition that an era—the fin de siècle— was coming to an end further strengthened this analytic ardor. "One epoch is unmistakably in its decline, and another is announcing its approach," Max Nordau predicted. "It is as though tomorrow could not be linked with today."[10] And for many contemporaries, tomorrow began in 1900.

The figure 1900 flattered the eye, wrote Robert Burnand; 1900 seduced the senses.[11] This round number has an elegance, a sort of arithmetic or rhetorical perfection that lent the feeling of opening a new era. "The year 1900 is not a banal year: it has a personality," asserted a journalist for the *Gaulois*.[12] Just like the "year one thousand," 1900 seemed to want to tell us something. But what? Neither the news sheets of Paris nor those of the provinces seemed capable of revealing anything about it.[13] In fact, the debate (almost the controversy) that filled the papers at the dawn of the year was quite futile: Did 1900 mark the entry into the twentieth century, or not? Starting in October 1899, Camille Flammarion had opened the debate in the *Revue des Revues*: "In what year will the twentieth century start?"[14] The question delighted the daily press. "The world is divided about the question of the nineteenth or the twentieth century," a *Gaulois* journalist remarked ironically. "On one side are mathematicians and logicians, and on the other, the sentimentalists and fantasists. Just as once there were Montagues and Capulets, Guelphs and Ghibellines, and more recently, Dreyfusards and anti-Dreyfusards, now there were nineteenth century-ists and twentieth century-ists."[15] While the Catholic daily *La Croix* soberly devoted only two articles to the matter, *Le Petit Journal* and *Le Petit Parisien* (soon surpassed by *Le Figaro*, *Le Gaulois*, and especially *Le Journal*) put this affair on the front page several times. *Le Matin*, faithful to its practice of ratcheting up an issue, dealt with this "massive question" by consulting its readers.[16] A "voluminous correspondence" followed, and the paper printed the best morsels: thirty-three readers were in favor of the end of the century, fourteen of the start. But on January 3, the Bureau of Longitudes (the institution for the astronomical standardization of time) closed the issue by affirming that "the nineteenth century will end on December 31st, 1900. The twentieth century will commence on January 1st, 1901."[17] But this scientific statement did not outweigh the evidence of social awareness, as Jules Claretie noted in his chronicle *La Vie à Paris*: "These scientific reasons will not prevail over public sentiment. The century will end for everybody on Sunday night and the twentieth century will begin, along with the coming year. I know some old men who are in a hurry to see the dawn of the next century; let us not take away their illusions and condemn them to wait another year for the new century."

No doubt most French people resembled Claretie's old folk, particularly since January 1 fell that year on a Monday, Pope Leo XIII had just proclaimed 1900 a "Holy Year," and German Kaiser Wilhelm II had officially recognized this year as the first of the twentieth century.[18] Allowing him such preemption might seem a form of patriotic crime! Content to commit a mathematical error, "opinion" supported Jules Claretie's view that "along with a new century, new ideas will rise over the world, like a rejuvenation amid this aging by a year, in this sunrise on an unknown century."[19] Moreover, this useless debate sidestepped an otherwise important modification. Starting in 1900 the Bureau of Longitudes, in an extension of the reform of 1891 that imposed a single time zone on the whole of France, would modify the way hours in the day were counted: no longer divided into two sequences of twelve hours, they were now a single sequence of twenty-four hours.[20] "We will dine at eighteen hours in order to applaud the sensational premiere at twenty-two and half hours. From now on the *five o'clock* of our charming chats will become the *seventeen o'clock*!"[21]

A RESTORATIVE YEAR

These calendar variations are merely anecdotal; almanacs and periodical reviews paid scarcely any attention to them. And so Monday, January 1, 1900, was for most French people a day like any other. More important was a desire to start afresh, to heal the country's wounds after the political tempests caused by the Dreyfus affair. The singularity of 1900, reckoned many chroniclers, was that it would be a "restorative year."[22] The prospect of the Exposition (World's Fair) that was supposed to open in April reinforced this certitude. Just as the 1889 exhibition had enabled overcoming the political crisis engendered by nationalist General Boulanger, 1900 was meant to put an end to the nightmare of the Dreyfus case; it would signify forgetting quarrels and be a "year of comfort and renovation."[23]

However, the Paris Exposition of 1900 looked more backward at the nineteenth than forward to the twentieth century. Its retrospective nature invited more of an "overview of the century" that had passed than a celebration of the advent of the new one. "The exhibition of 1900," the trade minister Jules Roche had said in 1892, "will be the synthesis and will determine the philosophy of the nineteenth century."[24] And the whole fair was planned from this perspective. The Exposition was a matter of "closing the nineteenth century with dignity," stated the 1895 law relating to its organization.[25] At the Grand Palais site, the Exposition celebrating the centennial of the Revolution offered an overview of French painting from David to Cézanne. At the Palais du Trocadéro, 130 congresses vaunted the progress—material, artistic, intellectual—achieved by humanity. Thus it was above all a celebration of the century that was ending.[26] Of course, in this context of triumphant positivism, the retrospective also involved the future; the review assumed premonitory accents: faith in the future made it an ode to progress. The Expo, explained a *Gil Blas* chronicler, was the "living and prophetic emblem of future times."[27] Celebrating the end of a prodigious century invited people to situate themselves on "the threshold of an era whose grandeur is prophesied by scholars and philosophers, and whose realities will no doubt exceed the dreams of our imaginations."[28]

The retrospective dimension of the Exposition incited many editorial committees to assess it, like the *Revue parisienne* and the *Revue bleue,* which opened a column titled "Our Century."[29] For the *Revue des deux mondes,* René Doumic wrote the will and testament of the fin de siècle.[30] Does this profusion of retrospectives give a homogeneous view of the present? Certainly some motifs were widely shared, such as belief in progress, in technical innovation, in the conquests of science. Electricity, to which each editorial rendered vibrant homage, was enlarging the space and duration of life. Everybody was expecting a promising future. People also wanted to believe in peace, even if in fact war was raging throughout 1900, foremost in the Transvaal and in China, where the Boxer Rebellion broke out. But publisher William Randolph Hearst affirmed in New York that "the twentieth century will quite probably see the end of wars,"[31] and everybody wanted to believe him. Another and more national satisfaction was that France of 1900 was crowned the "Queen of Civilization and the Arts."[32] The frightful fin-de-siècle pessimism had at last yielded to the euphoria and triumphalism that prospered in official discourse, and even more so in school textbooks. "France is today tranquil and strong. . . . In its favor stand Justice and the Law. It can expect everything from the future," wrote Ernest Lavisse in 1900 in the *Middle Course.*[33] The city of Paris, whose "capital narcissism" was reaching its height, increased its self-promotion and thought of itself as a "great cauldron of pleasure."[34] Finally, the French Republic seemed to have victoriously left behind an era of division, decadence, and moral crisis. Its success was seen as political, diplomatic, and social. The Exposition "has demonstrated to the reluctant, to the timid, to the timorous, and to the skeptics, that under the republican aegis the beloved country has lost nothing of its old splendor. Supported by documentation, it has proved that the moral level of the mass has risen by extraordinary proportions; it has shown in what high esteem our country is held in the world, what respect it commands, what effective and ideal power it has acquired."[35]

Such a celebration persuaded neither the nationalists nor the monarchists, who were both waiting for their revenge. Nor did it seduce the Catholic milieux or the conservative élites that (by contrast) diagnosed an ascendancy of crime, declining morality, menacing crowds, and corrupting mass culture. Meanwhile on the left, socialist and revolutionary milieux were no more inclined to share the government's view. "The nineteenth century is closing in a general despondency, fatigue, and apprehension about a fearful tomorrow," reckoned the socialist deputy Gustave Rouanet.[36] The same year (1900), the novelist Georges Darien published a furious and corrosive pamphlet, *La Belle France*, which painted a vitriolic portrait of a country full of lying baseness, and servitude everywhere; the cowardice, stupor, and spinelessness of an ignoble society where only the "hideous bourgeoisie" was prospering, plus the "military octopus and the Catholic vampire." While around 1900 a series of objective political and economic conditions might have signaled possible social progress,[37] this was not perceived by very many people. Beyond the self-celebratory discourse, nothing indicated a "meaning" or pointed to a clear and coherent appreciation of the present time, so divergent were opinions. Contradictions abounded. In fact, inversely, the kaleidoscope of appraisals and studies of all kinds was fracturing perceptions of the era; each person analyzed and interpreted it by the standards of his beliefs or her convictions. The dominant sentiment was of completion, and thus of openness to new possibilities, which was transposed into a multiplicity of futuristic stories and novels.[38] "We are in a melting pot, in a factory going crazy: everything is possible, anything can happen," publisher Hubert Juin judiciously perceived.[39]

The focal point of 1900 was the Exposition, which enjoyed real success (50 million visitors, 83,000 exhibitors, 350,000 electric lamps installed, etc.) and its decisive role in that year's consciousness. Once the excitement and artificial turmoil over the change of century had passed, the Exposition was the event that carried the consciousness of the moment, making it material and symbolizing its existence. Hence a strange sentiment accompanied the Exposition's closing in November 1900. "When the cannon of the Eiffel Tower announced, on Monday night at eleven o'clock, that the gates of the general enclosure were going to shut and never reopen except for the demolition crews, the crowd was dumbstruck," noted a journalist.[40] Did the singular year of 1900 end on that November 12th? Like the Exposition itself, whose plaster and stucco had been so mocked, was 1900 going to be merely a *trompe-l'oeil* year?[41] This is why the dismantling of the Expo created an initial "belle époque," with its cortege of regrets and nostalgic memories. "Long after the Exposition has disappeared, people will remember the spectacle of this city of marvels," wrote Jean Frollo[42]—unless it had been merely an illusion, cradling gentle reveries of grandeur, union, and solidarity. "Maybe we indeed thought that all people would be one. We have to wake up. This dream, like most dreams, was too beautiful! But still, it is a good thing that it lasted so long."[43]

TIME IN FLIGHT

THE PERFORMANCE continues," concluded sagely a journalist from the *Illustration* on December 31, 1900, saluting the "aurora of the twentieth century," inviting its readers to move beyond sterile periodizations. Did the following years show a clearer awareness of living in a singular time? Nothing allows us to assert this. Of course there were many enthusiastic, reasoned, or peremptory declarations claiming that people at the time were experiencing either a formidable epoch—or else a veritable nightmare. Neither newspapers nor magazines, neither artists nor scholars could offer any homogeneous representation of their era. While Matisse was painting *Le Bonheur de vivre* (1905), the nascent social sciences were diagnosing new pathologies (such as anomie, crowd behavior, the malaise of urban life) and certain avant-gardes were offering a desperate vision of the modern individual and/or an apocalyptic interpretation of the future. The ideology of decadence that had flourished at the end of the nineteenth century seemed to resurge in the following one, bearing new figures of decline and degeneration. Futurists peered downstream and saw only violence and war, and they celebrated their regenerating function.[1] Others still believed in scientific and technological progress and in civilization. The notebooks and diaries of writers that proliferated when the century began (by Léon

Bloy, Jules Renard, Maurice Barrès, Gide, Donnay, Valéry) are of no great help since all of them contain scattered, fragmentary, and personal observations. And when a writer like Virginia Woolf detects major ruptures ("in or about December, 1910, human character changed"),[2] she gives no key to the source of her inspiration.

Meanwhile, historiography has wanted to see 1913 as an extraordinary turning point. While economists have long considered it the benchmark year of international production, historians of culture saw a sort of *annus mirabilis* of literary and aesthetic creation. This thesis is not lacking in evidence. In 1913, Proust published the first volume of *In Search of Lost Time* and Valery Larbaud published *A. O. Barnabooth*, Blaise Cendrars and Sonia Delaunay composed *Prose du Transsibérien*, Apollinaire celebrated cubist painters and published *Alcools*, Copeau founded the Théâtre du Vieux-Colombier, Stravinsky had *Le Sacre du printemps* performed, and Schönberg his *Pierrot lunaire*. The list of aesthetic innovations could be extended indefinitely. This prodigious vitality involved not just continental Europe. England, where the Bloomsbury Group writers were settling their accounts with Victorian thought, was simultaneously seized by vorticism, a sort of British version of cubism and orphism. In New York, the photographer Alfred Stieglitz organized in February the famous Armory Show, where Marcel Duchamp exhibited his *Nude Descending a Staircase*. The whole Western world—if not the entire world (the Nobel Prize for literature was given that year to the Indian writer Rabindranath Tagore)—seemed borne along tracks of innovation. But it was also tormented, almost haunted, by a presentiment of destruction and death. The lightning strikes of the "1913 moment" were best crystallized by futurism: suspended above the void, animated by a sharp awareness of the abyss, 1913 would be the matrix and "expressive form" of the nascent twentieth century. It would incarnate all its paradoxes.

Many books have insisted on this extraordinary abundance, breaks with the past that opened up unprecedented fields of artistic exploration: abstraction as aesthetic evidence, the abandonment of the tonal system, the visual and aural dimensions of poetry, and the "psychological adventure novel" that Jacques Rivière theorized in a luminous article in the *Nouvelle revue française*. In *The Banquet Years*

(1958), the first book to offer a tableau of the Parisian arts and avant-gardes of this time, the American writer and historian Roger Shattuck discerned them as the inevitable climax to such a long period of intellectual and aesthetic stimulation.[3] Such ideas were taken up in the 1970s and developed in exhibitions and conferences.[4] Yet few of these later critics wondered how contemporaries, within and outside the burgeoning avant-gardes of the time, actually considered such phenomena. Certainly some of those writing in 1913 were seized by the nature of the moment: "We are at the end of one of those moments when suddenly people perceive that something has shifted," noted Rivière in 1913. "We are now living in a present wholly stripped of its past and overcome by the future. Once again, it is morning."[5] But we also know that such audacious formal experiments were most often ignored or rejected. Gone was the time when Gérôme, herald of academic art, when taking President Carnot around the Palais des Beaux-arts at the 1889 Exposition, could dissuade him from visiting the impressionists' room by exclaiming: "Monsieur le Président, here is the dishonor of France."[6] The "modern art front" that had challenged the dominant arbiters became autonomous in the 1880s, and by the end of the century it had won the battle: there was now a modern field of artistic "secessions." But this victory also shut down the way art was validated, which after 1900 triggered an explosion of new generations of avant-gardes that would engage in ferocious competition with each other, exacerbating the requirement to be innovative.[7] The general public could ignore (or jeer at) these artistic experiments. We should remember that Proust's first novel—he was an author considered to be a snob and a socialite—was rejected by every publisher and was printed at the author's expense; that the cubists (the term appeared in 1911 with malicious connotations) were unanimously rejected by influential critics at the time, who by contrast favored the sentimental art of salons and society portraitists like Boldini, Jean Béraud, or Jacques-Emile Blanche. Painters such as Forain and Maurice Denis denounced them as enemies of French art. The evidence does point to 1913 being an extraordinary laboratory of aesthetic modernity, a "critical epoch" in the sense given this term by followers of Saint-Simon. But that it was perceived as such *at the time* is much more

uncertain. Nowadays this epoch is evaluated by the standard of a culture that was marginal in its day. The modernity of 1900 was not yet
that of the "Belle Époque." "1913 was what one later thought that 1924
had been," explained Claude Roy in 1949. "There were usurpations in
the chronology too."[8]

Obviously, history needs such dates and such markers for putting
events into perspective and for constructing intelligible time
sequences. But when the goal—both more modest and more ambitious—is to understand how men and women inhabited their time,
such overview readings do not help very much. In *The Crisis of the
Mind*, published in 1919, Paul Valéry admitted the immense difficulty
he would have had "to define the intellectual situation in Europe in
1914." Someone who did hazard that definition, moreover, would
merely be seeing "nothing but a perfect state of disorder."[9] Everything leads us to believe that the situation must have been the same
for someone who tried, in 1913 or in 1910, to paint a portrait of
the era—perhaps except for one aspect, which concerns precisely the
relation to time. There was a diffuse sentiment that events were
unfolding differently, not necessarily faster but more inexorably, that
the relation to time was distended and it even sometimes vanished
in a myriad of unique events. Not all contemporaries read Henri
Bergson or attended his popular lectures at the Collège de France,
but we do know people were fascinated by his thought.[10] Many were
fascinated by a philosophy that, contrary to the idea of time being
mechanical, valued perception, intuition, the lived experience of
time as "grasped by thought." "Maybe days are equal for a clock, but
not for a man," Proust remarked in *Le Figaro*. "There are horrendous
and difficult days that one spends infinite time in surmounting, and
sloping days that let one descend at full tilt, singing. To pass through
various days, those with nervous disposition possess 'different
gears.' "[11]

Diffuse or explicit, linked or not to Bergson's thought, such ideas
were in the mindset and affected conceptions of time. Futurism, so
prized at the time, amounted to a reverie on notions of space and
time. Some went further and tried to put them into practice. Not by
painting a portrait of their age (a futile operation, because social or
collective time always proves diffracted and plural) but by trying to

fix time in flight by mooring it to spaces that might give it form. Marcel Proust and Eugène Atget, although contemporaries, did not know each other, but they both testify to the same meticulous and patient desire to restore this strange articulation of space and time.[12] Atget limited himself to Paris, which he photographed from 1895 to the middle of the 1920s—streets, gardens, house fronts, "odd jobs"— providing an album that continues to serve us to conceive the city as it was at the beginning of the century. Proustian space was broader and more variegated, involving Paris, of course, but also Balbec and Combray, not to mention the sinuous and mobile topographies of the narrator's interior life. But the gazes of both Atget and Proust helped tint with an indefinable melancholy their grasp of their space and time. Many other projects were analogous in spirit: Albert Kahn was a great friend of Bergson, and in 1908 he began (with the help of geographer Jean Brunhes) to "fix once and for all the aspects, practices, and modes of human activity whose fatal disappearance was merely a matter of time." The numerous photographers and film cameramen whom he sent out to traverse the world would collect more than 4,000 black-and-white photographs, 72,000 *autochromes* (a 1903 color process patented by the Lumière brothers), and 183,000 meters of film.[13] More or less at the same time—June 1911—the linguist Ferdinand Brunot inaugurated "the speech archives" he had cofounded with Charles Pathé. A precursor of the Phonetics Institute the Sorbonne was calling for, this project aimed to set up an immense data bank to conserve the greatest number of traces of the spoken language: timbres, rhythms, accents, vocabulary.[14] About 300 recordings were made up to the war, some at the Sorbonne, others in the provinces of Ardennes, Berry, and Limousin.

These various initiatives were not coordinated, obviously, and therefore linking such studies today is the result of a retrospective illusion. However, they did express an anxious relationship with time that tells us more about the immediate prewar years than does the idea of an aesthetic "clap of thunder" said to have struck in the year 1913. Actually, the deafening thunder came later, due to the shell shock that was unleashed starting in August 1914. Even if this war had been dreamed of, anticipated, and even desired by some people,[15] its rupture would mark minds as well as bodies. For the men who went off, as for all those—women, children, the elderly—who watched them leave, an era had undeniably come to an end. Like the friends Apollinaire and Rouveyre, many were saying "farewell to an era" that suddenly appeared, as if by default, to be endowed with the traits of peace and security that now seemed dearer. It did not take long for the singularity of the prewar years to be perceived. On August 6, 1914, the painter Jacques-Emile Blanche wrote in his diary: "If ever my novel *Louis Aymeris* is published, the reader will find the atmosphere of the prewar era; the malaise that resulted in the suicide of a man of my age, an artist who saw it too clearly and was too old or too young to bear the slow disintegration of his *people.*"[16] Always, it is only afterward that individuals and societies become aware of the singularity of any moment or era. And the more abrupt the break, the more clearly this awareness emerges. The "Great War," a moment of frightful intensity, necessarily carried within itself the representations of what it had put an end to.

"NOTHING MATTERED AS LONG AS WE WERE DANCING"

MOST BOOKS tell us that it was only after the war ordeal, in a France now devastated and in mourning, that what is called the "Belle Époque" was born, out of nostalgia for what had come before.[1] The true story is quite different. Still, the war indeed marked a major rupture, "like an equator that traverses time and divides it," wrote André de Fouquières.[2] The enormity of what had happened, the scope of the casualties and destruction, were enough to convince everybody that civilization had been shipwrecked, particularly since to the East had risen the "great glimmer" of Communism that represented new hope for many. Psychiatrists spoke of "dissonance," an irrepressible rupture that left profound scars in souls as well as on bodies.[3] The fracture caused a profound upheaval in sensibilities. "From that point onward, we must date a new era," wrote Jean-Richard Bloch to Romain Rolland on September 1, 1917.[4] And we know the famous phrase of Paul Valéry in *Crise de l'esprit* (1919): "We later civilizations, we now know that we are mortal." In Vienna the same year, Karl Kraus published the first installments of what would become *The Last Days of Mankind*. Movements as different as Communism, Dada, surrealism, and the Catholic antimodernism of the *Revue universelle* (founded by Henri Massis and Jacques Maritain in 1920) reached the same tragic diagnosis: a failure of the old world, a major crisis in understanding and representation, and the absolute necessity of inventing new forms to give hope back to a society in ruins. Rarely has a postwar period been perceived as so overwhelming. Now almost everything would have to be rethought since everything had changed; so everything must be transformed, proclaimed the champions of cultural demobilization. "When after the war people wanted to resume their places, it was perceived that the rhythm of life had changed," remembered André Warnod in 1930. "The break was clean between what now existed and what had previously existed."[5]

Yet such an observation did not invite people to seek refuge in "the world of yesterday," whose confusion and blindness had led to the disaster. Indeed, the opposite happened. While intellectuals on all sides tried to rethink and re-enchant the world, most people opted to forge ahead, unencumbered by prewar memories. "An internal joy filled everybody because we had been the victors, or at least that was what we believed," continued Warnod. "Optimism reigned."[6] André de Fouquières, who before 1914 had been one of the great organizers of high society life (and who intended to remain so) was just as categorical: "After the Great Bloodshed, people rushed to enjoy all life's pleasures."[7] Cafés, theaters, music halls, and other festivities of "*la vie parisienne*" quickly resumed their predominance—and they rarely played the nostalgia card. The venues had changed too. Montparnasse, which had already begun to shine before the war, assumed preeminence, to the detriment of the outmoded Montmartre or Latin Quarter. The rue de la Gaîté and the Vavin crossroads, which Henry Miller described as the "navel of the world," supplanted the old streets of Montmartre, rue des Saules, or rue Ravignan. In 1921 the bar-cabaret Boeuf sur le toit opened, a "sort of academy of snobbery," wrote Léon-Paul Fargue, and it quickly dethroned Maxim's as the epicenter of Parisian life. Far from replaying prewar music, the new frenzy for pleasure that gripped the city was oriented to the present day. "Paris, as soon as the war was ended, was seized with folly. A brutal cynicism and a desire to seize pleasure at all costs marked this era, with crazes for dancing and female nudity, and a taste for getting money without working," explained Warnod. "People rushed into pleasures with a fanatic craving."[8]

The period exhibited a very lively momentum, symbolized in everybody's eyes by a fury for dancing—now even more popular because it had been banned during the war. *Les dancings* (dance halls), seen by the more upright as places of perdition, opened almost everywhere. There were a hundred of them in Paris, half of them located in upper or lower Montmartre, and the other half around Montparnasse and the Champs-Élysées. And the dances that were all the rage—the Charleston, the foxtrot, the two-step, the black bottom, the tango, "Negro" dances, etc.—were far removed from what had been favored at the start of the century.[9] These dance venues succeeded each other at the pace of an imperious fashion imposing its successive "crazes."

Dancing (the English term was used) brought along with it other novelties: cocktails, short dresses, cloche hats. Those who did not dance were passionate about films that featured the era's new stars: Mary Pickford, Douglas Fairbanks, Rudolf Valentino. The war had left French cinema in a disastrous state, so foreign films hugely dominated the market: from 1924 to 1929, more than 70 percent of films distributed in France were American and 12 percent were German.[10] The economic recovery and general enrichment stimulated the advance of cultural consumption and the continual democratization of mass entertainment. At the time there were 4,200 cinemas and 580 theaters that, like the principal music halls and *cafés-concerts*, were often completely full.[11] While the radio still remained the prerogative of wireless listeners, the possession of phonographs was spreading; in 1929 more than ten million phonograph records were sold.[12] Sports events were diversifying and also attracting growing audiences. Spectators rushed to rugby and soccer matches, and the Olympic Games were held in Paris in 1924. The boxer Georges Carpentier and the *tennis-woman* Suzanne Lenglen became veritable icons. In short, it was a "happy period," wrote the British journalist Sisley Huddleston, who was passing through Paris in the postwar years.[13] As peace was restored, which diplomatic efforts tried to guarantee permanently, and economic growth attained record levels—7 percent per annum from 1919 to 1924, then 3 percent in the second half of the decade—an appetite for living surged, along with a frivolity that may have exceeded the prewar years. "Dans la vie faut pas s'en faire, moi je m'en fais pas! (In life you shouldn't worry, and me, I don't)," sang a sardonic Maurice Chevalier in the famous operetta *Dédé* by Albert Willemetz and Henri Christiné, created in 1921 at the Théâtre des Bouffes-Parisiens.

The Moulin Rouge, a major symbol of prewar life and entertainment, had burned down in 1915 (see fig. 2). But it was rebuilt and reopened its doors at the start of the 1920s, at first below ground in the form of a dance hall, then in 1924 as a music hall. But not the slightest nostalgia was expressed in the new shows, which looked unhesitatingly to the present. The show that accompanied the relaunch in December 1924 was proudly titled *New York—Montmartre* and offered audiences a discovery of the hectic life of New York, its *girls*, its "Negro quarter," Wall Street, and Chinatown.[14] Of course some still said, "We miss the epoch of the Moulin Rouge and even the innocent *quadrilles* (balls)," as the playwright and popular novelist Marcel de Bare regretted in 1925.[15] Yvette Guilbert, who published her memoir in 1927, also mentions the early days of the Moulin Rouge—she had appeared onstage as an English nurse in 1890—yet with no nostalgic tone.[16] The new management of the music hall tried to combine the old and the new. In 1925, the *Mistinguett Revue* began with a prologue that evoked Toulouse-Lautrec and the Moulin of earlier days. There was a brief tribute to cancan stars La Goulue, Grille d'égout, Valentin, and Jane Avril before the orchestra quickly switched to frenzied *jazz-band* music. The Mistinguett years as produced and staged by the new artistic director Jean Charles were resolutely "modern." *This Is Paris*, the 1927–1928 revue, or *Allo Paris* that followed in 1929, substituted *jazz-bands* and sung tangos, multicolored lighting, and acrobatic fantasies for the outmoded cancan.[17] The traditional quadrille, "danced every day," as the 1922 program asserted,[18] was better preserved in the Moulin Rouge ball, but many saw it as merely a "melancholy spectacle," "a moribund tradition." The quadrille dancers, according to Léon Werth, "resemble dried flowers between the pages of a book."[19]

Contrary to commonplaces about the Great War causing the "end of a world," the French aristocracy actually maintained its solid position, its wealth, and its values.[20] It also continued to lend its tone to worldly society, whose vitality was unabated. At the theater, at the

Opéra, in the salons, the golden age of high society kept spinning. Aviation "aces" succeeded the prewar sportsmen and assumed the same aura of celebrity. People were intoxicated by the speed reached by the new automobiles, whose number shot up (from 156,000 in 1920 to 1,109,000 in 1930),[21] and they planned their voyages in *sleeping cars* or aboard transatlantic liners. Paris kept its leadership in matters of luxury, elegance, and sophisticated entertainment just as before the war—perhaps even more so. In 1920 the magazine *Vogue* launched its French edition, and the new generation of fashion designers—Jeanne Lanvin, Jean Patou, Coco Chanel—continued to embody that quasi-organic relation that linked Paris, fashion, and femininity.[22] Maurice de Waleffe and André de Fouquières, two of the principal society figures of 1900, after the war pursued their struggle for "beauty" and lofty French taste.[23] As apostles of masculine elegance, the two men competed for all the twenties prizes: selecting the loveliest "Amazon" and awarding the most beautiful women of France, the fifty best-dressed actresses of Paris, etc. Worldly pleasures had not stagnated after the war, and their effervescence continued to emanate a shimmering mirage in which the ancestral values of the aristocracy mingled with the cachet of *la vie parisienne.*

The same was true of all aspects of cultural and artistic life. The avant-gardes that paraded around Cocteau, Dada, and the surrealists even outshone those of the prewar era, of which they were the natural heirs. Moreover, many of the old artists were still there, starting with the poets and painters of the 1910s, who began to benefit from commercial success. But they had been joined by a troupe of new arrivals—novelists, painters, sculptors, photographers—whether exiles, émigrés, or quite simply creators looking for a propitious location. As at the start of the century, Paris continued to attract artists from around the world, and thus the phenomenon became accentuated throughout the decade: Russians, Poles, Hungarians, Germans were fleeing the troubles and instability affecting their home countries, and Americans, whom the war had familiarized with France, became increasingly numerous.[24] The "very profitable agitation" (André Warnod's expression) that brought so many different creators to Paris even intensified and prolonged, with no apparent break, the attraction to the city that had reigned before the war. This diverse group of artists, who did not necessarily share the same aesthetic inspiration but whose innovations turned painting upside down, was christened by André Warnod in a January 1925 article in *Comoedia* as the "Paris School." The group was eclectic, including painters like Chagall, Soutine, Kisling, Pascin, Modigliani, Foujita, and Zadkine, but also art dealers (Kahnweiler, Léopold Zborowski) and collectors (Wilhelm Uhde, Peggy Guggenheim, Leo and Gertrude Stein). "This crowd of foreign artists from all corners of the world are coming to breathe the air of freedom among us . . . [and they] provoked by contact with our own artists a very important movement in painting."[25] For Warnod this constant and extraordinary emulation was crucial. That is why this period remained for him inseparable from the one that preceded it. Many of these artists had actually arrived in Paris before the war, as proved by his own memories, running from 1902 (date of his arrival at the Butte de Montmartre) to the end of the 1920s.[26]

But the painters of the Paris School were not the only ones to enjoy the freedom of the capital. We have to add surrealists from all over the world; composers like Martinu, Mihalovici, and Conrad Beck; and American writers of the "Lost Generation" like F. Scott Fitzgerald, Dos Passos, Cummings, Hemingway, and many others. The magazine *Paris Montparnasse,* edited by Henri Broca, became the platform of this movement starting in 1929. Paris was more than ever the international capital of the art scene, though this was deplored by those like Camille Mauclair who denounced *Les Métèques contre l'art français* (Immigrants versus French art).[27] From this intense artistic life (which had now migrated to Montparnasse) there emanated the same bubbling creative freedom, independence, and sexual permissiveness as before. For Gertrude Stein, who had lived in Paris since 1904 and around whom gravitated many from the cultural élites, the city continued to be the homeland of arts and letters. "So Paris was the national background for the 20th century."[28]

Paris attracted not just artists and intellectuals but also tourists and students; among those who flocked there, many chose to settle permanently. Americans were particularly numerous: 40,000 by the end of the 1920s. Of course there were many eccentrics, dropouts, wealthy heirs, and bohemians who were drawn by the city's cultural radiance, but also businessmen and executives of various American corporations, and government officials.[29] Exchanges were also intense between Paris and Central Europe.[30] In 1928, 24 percent of the 16,750 students in France were foreigners. In 1925 there was built for them, on a site freed by the demolition of fortifications, the Cité internationale universitaire, a sort of rejuvenated phalanstery that it was hoped would give rise to universal collegians. Intellectual exchanges likewise increased. A Commission for International Cooperation had existed since 1922, presided over by Henri Bergson. Four years later came the International Institute for Intellectual Cooperation. An International Exposition of the Decorative Arts and Modern Industry, initially planned in 1915, finally took place from April to October 1925, with 150 pavilions representing 21 nations. Of course, it was not as lavish as the 1900 Exposition, but its "new spirit" attracted almost sixteen million visitors to the esplanade between Invalides and the Grand Palais. This time, though, the extraordinary effervescence would dissipate by the decade's end. Explained André Warnod in 1930, "Paris resumed a life that was calmer, more stable, less feverish, less excessive. The postwar tumult was gone. Everything returned to its logical place."[31]

We can understand in these conditions why the teeming twenties, with rediscovered peace and prosperity, were scarcely tempted to look back with nostalgia to the period that Léon Daudet in 1920 was already calling "interwar"—referring back to the 1870 Franco-Prussian War.[32] Nor were novelists and filmmakers, usually prompt to offer retrospectives, given to such nostalgia. In vain do we look among an impressive cinema output during the 1920s for films that reconstruct a lost world. Obviously, many novels and theater plays from the end of the nineteenth century were adapted for the cinema, and some were even very successful, like *Chapeau de paille d'Italie (An Italian straw hat)*, a comedy written by Labiche whose plot was transposed by director René Clair to the 1900s. But no fundamental tendency or noticeable desire to look back on the prewar years tinged the cinema with regret and melancholy. The same was true of novels.[33] Not that they ignored 1900, far from it. Many novels published after the war were explicitly set in France at the start of the century: for example, *Simon le pathétique* by Jean Giraudoux (1918);

the volumes of Marcel Proust's opus published after 1919—whose *Within a Budding Grove* won the Goncourt literary prize in 1919; and then *Chéri* by Colette (1920); the first volumes of *The Thibaults*, Roger Martin du Gard's saga that began to appear in 1922; *Silbermann* by Jacques de Lacretelle, which won the Prix Femina in 1922; *L'Ecole des femmes* by André Gide in 1929; and so on. Escapist fiction and genre novels did not lag behind, as witnessed by Maurice Leblanc's serialized adventures of the gentleman burglar Arsène Lupin, which continued through the war and well after it: *The Countess of Cagliostro* went back to the hero's youth and was published in installments in *Le Journal* in December 1923; *The Height Strokes of the Clock* appeared the same year, and *The Barnett & Co. Agency* in 1924.

All these novels, diverse in both form and intention, had in common the locating of their action in the "era that preceded the war."[34] All of them depicted social worlds that were anchored in France around 1900 and sprinkled their stories with temporal markers (the Exposition, the first automobiles) and political events like the Dreyfus affair, the assassination of Gaston Calmette, and the extension of military service to three years. Some writers like Charles Morice signaled the absolute break caused by the war: "Today begins a new epoch in the history of the world."[35] Others like Félicien Champsaur stressed transformations in bodies and/or in appearances, and missed "the type of prewar women, from between 1910 and 1914."[36] But such asides did not suffice to inscribe their narratives in recent history or make them evocations of a lost "past" that was duly identified as such. The only exception was Proust. The appearance in the summer of 1919 of *Within a Budding Grove* produced reviews that clearly evoked the tale's historicity. "Shadows pass, an era takes shape, we are dealing with the end of the nineteenth century; no doubt initiates may recognize many of the characters described," wrote Camille Marbo. The novel, whose plot is set between 1895 and 1897, mentions many actual events: the Dreyfus affair and the visit to Paris by Tsar Nicholas II (nicknamed Theodosius), which took place in October 1896. Most commentators were critical of this focus on "lost time," on an outdated era. "Old-fashioned and outmoded," deplored Fernand Vandérem in *La Revue de Paris*. Binet-Valmer was ironical: "Before the war, there existed in Paris a civilization that was rich in sensibility; it was incarnated in a sick man who was imprudent enough to take tea with his friends, to promenade along avenues, and try to make love to girls in their flower of youth."[37]

We can also point to Blaise Cendrars's *Moravagine*, published in 1926.[38] This feverish and convulsive novel traces the journey of a "human beast," a violent schizophrenic whom a fascinated psychiatrist helps escape from the asylum where he is interned. There follows a hallucinatory voyage through a chaotic world, punctuated by horrible crimes, madness, revolutions. For Cendrars (born in 1887), could this be the deeper significance of the prewar years when he had hung out with the cultural avant-gardes? The novel's first part is titled "the spirit of an era" and opens in August 1900; it ends at the start of 1917, when Moravagine, again interned, dies after having scribbled thousands of pages on the war, the end of the world, and the language on Mars. Cendrars was not the only writer to transmogrify the feeling of a world that was lost into violence and destruction. Younger ones, born like Robert Desnos "under the insignia of the Universal Exposition," struggled to talk about lost time. What could they say, those whose youth had been cradled in an "impatient desire for love, revolt, and the sublime"?[39] Everything had exploded with the war. What remained were crime and destruction, Dada, the mythical criminal Fantômas—or just the will to forge ahead regardless.

But Proust's and Cendrars's novels were unlike all the others. For publishers and most critics, the bulk of the stories that evoked the years before the war were merely "contemporary novels": portraits of manners or tales of adventure whose primary function was neither to celebrate nor to mourn the world of yesterday. Jean Prévost, reviewing in 1929 the progression in the six volumes of *The Thibaults* by Roger Martin du Gard, thought they were "becoming a treatise of what is contemporary."[40] In 1929, Maurice Leblanc published *The Mysterious Mansion*, a new Arsène Lupin adventure story whose action was explicitly situated in the postwar years.[41] Nevertheless, except for the length of skirts and the speed of automobiles, nothing differentiated it from the preceding volumes, nothing actually "dated" it.

But we should not conclude that no voice spoke up to mourn the good old days. Some genres paid it tribute, most often out of tradition. Popular song, which as we shall see would become one of the liveliest forms expressing the imagined "Belle Époque," had long cultivated nostalgia for yesterday's world. Popular song has long been ambivalent: on the one hand, it features well-worn refrains with sentimental, frivolous, or slightly bawdy choruses; and on the other, the somber face of the "realism" in ballads and tragic couplets traces the story of pimps, bad guys, and prostitutes. Long fixed in this duality, but now taking advantage of sound recording, these two registers amply contributed to maintaining and cultivating the atmosphere of the first decade of the 1900s. But whereas the oompahs and happy harmonies of the former maintained the illusion of an enduring popular festival, the raucous accents of the "realistic" *chanteuses* wallowed in its filth and mud. Moreover, this genre of popular song was increasingly recognized as such, and it triumphed in the 1920s. Starting in 1918, a major music hall like the Olympia in Paris was practically devoted to it; song recitals predominated in many other theaters. The great prewar figures who were still performing garnered immense success. Aristide Bruant (see fig. 1), the grand master of the genre back in the heyday of Montmartre, gave his last concert in 1924 at the request of the director of the Empire Theater. It was his apotheosis, with numerous curtain calls for a career that "as a *grand artiste*, he was not trying to extend."[42] But most of the other great pre-1914 stars continued to sing throughout these years, on the stage or in front of the camera: Yvette Guilbert and Eugénie Buffet despite their age (they were born in 1865), and Fréhel, younger but wasted by alcohol and cocaine. Others took over, like Damia, the "tragedian of song," Marie Dubas, Lucienne Boyer, Lys Gauty, Léo Marjane, and Yvonne George, muse to the surrealists. All these women's voices, some of them idolized, tried to plunge to the heart of a world always anchored in tragedy, whether social or sentimental. The "realist convention" that governed them favored the register of the ballad to deliver a "complaint" of desolation.[43] They emanated a tragic inspiration that almost mechanically tipped into fatalism and a retreat into nostalgia.

Here the prewar years are indeed construed as a golden age, either of "truthful reality" or the "pretty songs of yesterday": in many respects here is where the myth of the Belle Époque takes shape. Fréhel played a particularly important role. After ten years' absence from the stage and having suffered physical deterioration, she returned to the Olympia in 1925.[44] Her body and her face were almost unrecognizable, bespeaking the cruel marks of time, while her voice tried painfully to resuscitate the vanished horizon of the prewar era. From out of the depths! Was it Montmartre, Paris, or her past love affairs that Fréhel was mourning in "Où est-il donc?" (Where is it now?), the song that André Decaye and Lucien Carol composed for her in 1926?[45]

Another type of nostalgic gaze also tended to focus on images and representations of Paris. Again, the genre was not new; it belonged to a long tradition. The last third of the nineteenth century, after the urban renovation of Baron Haussmann, was marked by a multiplication of picturesque works authored by chroniclers, reporters, and serial writers, who at length cried over a Paris that was disappearing: *Paris qui s'en va, Paris qui s'efface, Paris qui passe* (Paris that is vanishing, disappearing, passing away).[46] Like the contemporaneous photographs of Marville, thousands of written pages tried to fix the real or fantastic vestiges of the old capital for all time. A new genre took shape, with its own style and authors, where meditation on loss was combined with a focus on the picturesque and a penchant for lamentation. The 1923 *Paris qui meurt* (Paris is dying) by Elie Richard was in the same vein.[47] But what changed in the 1920s was the identity of the Paris that was being lamented; it was no longer the Gothic city of the days before Haussmann, but that of the 1900s. This shift, which would assume major importance in the following decade, was still only at its beginning. It shone through the memoirs of certain stars like Yvette Guilbert, Mayol, and Fursy, who emotionally evoked the prime spots of prewar Paris.[48] But it became full-blown with the first memoirs about Montmartre. Francis Carco published in 1926 (at age forty) the first volume of his memoirs, describing the happy times at the Butte that he spent in the company of Utrillo, Mac Orlan, Dorgelès, and Max Jacob, and the lively soirées at the Lapin Agile; then he mourned "this bitter lightheadedness that comes to us from the past."[49] Yet Carco had arrived in Paris only in 1910 and ought to have recognized that the city had hardy been transformed at all: "Nothing had yet changed about the place or its aspect—nothing except the decade of our twenties and our loves, which as they died were resuscitated and just as quickly erased."[50] Carco was offering a hymn more to the lost drunkenness of his bohemian youth than to the city.

Moreover, this type of retrospective began to proliferate. In 1929, the cabaret singer Henri Fursy's memoir movingly evoked the happy years "when the Place Pigalle was a garden."[51] The same year, the magazine *Crapouillot* published a long feature on Paris in which nostalgic views predominated. Some writers tried to maintain that "its aspect has scarcely changed" but then went on to bemoan the disappearance of the former Paris, the Paris of yesterday, a prewar Paris in which it was delightful to live. The tone was unremittingly nostalgic, as were the accompanying photographs by Atget. Today there are too many automobiles, they complained, too many buses, too many tarred roads, not to mention all these metro-building sites that are disfiguring the urban landscape. Paul Fuchs looked back on what the Latin Quarter had been like around 1890, Mac Orlan recalled Montmartre, and André Salmon did the same for Montparnasse. Another writer exclaimed that "Belleville, Auteuil, Montmartre, and Montrouge were once villages outside the city." There was pronounced melancholy for rustic Paris, Paris without cars, with little gardens and gazebos, village pubs, and the "old country-style outskirts"—a Paris where grapevines grew and that was redolent of manure. This kind of representation developed at the end of the decade and undoubtedly contributed to nourishing the prewar *imaginaire*. But as with the popular song, it was in the very nature of these productions to lament the vanished world of yesterday—or of the day before yesterday. That was already true in 1900, when inside the Exposition were built reconstructions in miniature of a town from the Middle Ages, and when a municipal commission for old Paris was created,[52] which still existed in 1960.

Therefore, (with very few exceptions) there existed no "Belle Époque" in the 1920s. The days of *la grande nostalgie* had not yet arrived. Almost the opposite was true, in fact, because after the

1914–1918 ordeal the country was rediscovering the beneficent traits of the preceding period: peace (which the pacifist movement was trying to sacralize) and a recovered power in the world that gave France back its due weight in the concert of nations. This was combined with prosperity, cultural influence, and a burgeoning cultural life, the desire to live fully and enjoy the present, and even a growing sexual freedom that was described as "bubbling libido."[53] This is why so many people today confuse the "Belle Époque" with the "Roaring Twenties." Many of the passersby who were interviewed in December 2015 by the Sorbonne students thought the Belle Époque meant the twenties, i.e., dating from the armistice of November 1918 to the crash of October 1929. One woman even confidently excluded any other possibility, since for her the frenzy and the "retro" dimension of the twenties embodied the whole spirit of the "Belle Époque." In fact, as Léo Malet wrote, weren't the 1920s actually the "second *belle époque*"?[54]

Wednesday, October 14, 2015

"*Nostalgia lies at the heart of this history,*" *somebody remarked after a lecture I gave that sketched the outlines of the present book. But the feeling of nostalgia itself has a history: its forms, its rhetoric, its effects have changed over the course of centuries. There was a time when one could die of nostalgia, another when it was merely a metaphor, and it subsequently became a rather vague uneasiness, which it was thought could be tamed in the shared intimacy of psychoanalysis. More than twenty years ago, I suggested to a young doctor (who has since become a brilliant scholar) that he undertake such a study. He thought about it, published a first article, then abandoned the subject because of its extreme difficulty. Since then others have carried the flame, but no long history of nostalgia has really come forth. The task may be impossible. For if we know what nostalgia is—"a dream of space fabricated by time," as Sylvain Venayre wrote, "a reaction against the irreversible," according to Jankélévitch— its modes of expression, and thus in part its nature, have proved to be astonishingly changeable.*

The Belle Époque that I am tracking is obviously a daughter of nostalgia. But not all nostalgias resemble each other. The war—the Great War and its consequences—have no doubt profoundly modified its face. Some writers and observers talk about the acceleration of life, others of a world that is from now on augmented, enlarged, and spilling out of its usual frameworks (the village, the nation, the continent). The frenzy for speed and movement exhibited in these years was propitious for lamenting about evanescence. And there is a lot to say about the aggravation of nostalgic sensibilities produced by photographic and cinematographic images. "Their profusion and implacability change the quality of our dreams and haunt our judgment," wrote Louis Chéronnet back then. Nostalgia comes to chill the present by telling us: memento mori. There, one is young for eternity—but already dead. We will also refer to the dolorous acuity induced by recording technologies. But nostalgia has lost its clinical connotations; it is no longer the visceral need for the home country that could kill young soldiers sent to Algeria in the 1830s, but it is not yet this "culture" of roots, of the retro, of "vintage" that we saw arise in the 1980s. It is a kind of suffering, especially in the quest for youth, for a lost unity. I think more than ever that we need a history of nostalgia.

THE INVENTION OF "1900"

I**T WOULD** take several more years for the 1900 imaginary to prevail as a major motif in the nation's culture life. The decade that opened in 1930 was decisive in this respect. While the world horizon was darkening, the longing for the past grew and its tone changed. Reputable writers began to reflect on the nature of the beginning of the century: Had it been *blasé* or fundamental? Backward-looking memoirs, novels, and songs multiplied, while the sensations of 1900 were being adapted for stage or screen. There was a veritable fascination for a period in French history that everybody now agreed should be called the "1900 era."

ANDRÉ WARNOD AS PRECURSOR

André Warnod, who had been fifteen years old in 1900, published in 1930 *Les Visages de Paris* (Faces of Paris). This was not really a memoir or recollection: the author, at the time a recognized literary figure (he had a byline in *Comoedia*), had simply noted his wanderings around Paris. The meandering promenade included snatches of dialogue and sayings and was accompanied by almost 600 illustrations, engravings, prints, and especially photographs. The book was also historical: Warnod claimed he no longer recognized Paris and was bent on exhuming all those places that for him incarnated the capital. While he devoted long passages to old Paris, the core of the book dramatized what Paris looked like "before the war," to which he composed a hymn. "One of our most cherished and intimate and profound joys was to have known the period before the war, and at an age when we were able to taste all its delights. Perhaps we found this time so beautiful because we were at that age ourselves."[1] He found everything about this Paris of 1900 charming: the theaters, the balls, the cabarets, the pleasures of the street. The artistic world predominated in his account, particularly the pictorial: therefore in Montmartre, to which Warnod had already devoted much writing. But the poets and artists of the Butte de Chaumont did not saturate the story: the world of newspapers, and of theaters and *cafés-concerts*, the elegant people of the Bois de Boulogne, the old-time fairs, the confetti at fifty centimes the kilo—all aroused his enthusiasm. What Warnod was dramatizing was the sweetness of living in an era unlike any other. Let us listen to him assemble fundamental images:

> Before the war, there had been that beauty—negative, it is true, but enchanting—of being able to live in Paris, almost without money, without working—not living well, of course, but living. This was due to the country's prosperity. The golden age? Oh, no! But it was a singular and prodigious age, still attached to tradition by a thousand ties, but also possessing formidable new forces. Paris before the war? A city where the past remained living, but which welcomed new times harmoniously and so it could evolve gently.[2]

Everything was enchanting: the electricity that gave the city a new luminosity, the advertising posters that decorated it, the Moulin Rouge and its "gas-lit ramp," even the *zone* (city limits) and its rag-pickers, and above all an atmosphere of peace and prosperity that seemed to promise that the current happiness would be eternal. "We spoke of war as it had always been, as a distant myth that lay totally outside reality. Basically everyone was persuaded that problems would eventually be sorted out."[3]

Warnod concluded that since then Paris had lost many of its charms, although he did love the Champs-Elysées, where he sensed the heart of the city of tomorrow. But everything in his writing favored the city of his youth, not without contradictions, though, because many photographs illustrating the book were taken by his friend Germaine Krull, who arrived in Paris only in 1925. "It does not really matter because Paris—the true Paris, that of the little streets and faubourgs, the one that is ignored by tourists and foreigners—is scarcely concerned with fashion and so it changes less than people believe."[4] Despite these ambiguities, Warnod's book had limited impact, though favorable critics focused on his portrait of the prewar era. "The hearts of 'old Parisians' are full of gratitude on reading these pages," noted the reviewer for *Paris-Soir*, who rambled on in this vein: "It was a charming era, a bit mannered, a bit traditional, brilliant but unconscious of the irreversible drive of progress."[5] And this was what struck most critics: "M. André Warnod has given the Paris of these happy years a large place in his book. The happy years . . . that preceded the war."[6]

The same year, the famous fashion designer Paul Poiret had just retired and published his own memoir. Unsurprisingly, it is a success story about becoming one of the great figures of elegant and luxurious Paris. Poiret relishes depicting the time of its splendor. "What a *belle époque!*" he exclaims regarding his visit to the 1889 Exhibition, confusing it with his memories of the succeeding Expo.[7] In his prose, an enchanted world takes shape: a world

where women were beautiful, the residences sumptuous, and talent rewarded. . . . It was a blessed era when the cares and vexations of life, the annoyances of tax collectors, and the menace of socialism had not yet crushed thought and joie de vivre. Women could be elegant in the street without being offended by road workers. The familiarity that reigned between ordinary people and the powerful of the earth was charming and good-natured. The great gentlemen who frequented the rue de la Paix could respond to the smiles of the *midinettes* (young seamstresses). A jolly camaraderie flourished in the street.[8]

"THE PAUL MORAND EFFECT"

As the 1900s were returning to favor, one book had the effect of a bomb. Written by a fashionable author, Paul Morand, it appeared in May 1931 under the unequivocal title *1900*. Morand, aged forty-three, was at the time a writer most appreciated for his *Ouvert la nuit* in 1922 (translated as *Open All Night* by Ezra Pound). He was also a figure of Parisian high society, a scion of the cultivated *grande bourgeoisie* (his father was director of the School of Decorative Arts and had long mingled with Parisian poets, artists, and sculptors), a diplomat, and an editor at Gallimard publishers, who had married a rich Romanian princess a few years before. All of this meant that his book *1900* was awaited and would be widely reviewed.

The length of a pamphlet, it was a violent attack on an age Morand judged to be stupid, ridiculous, inappropriate; it unforgivingly described a year of "apparent truce" during which the government tried to deal with virulent nationalism, anti-Semitism, and social unrest. The 1900 Exposition? It had been merely an illusion to "veil the face" of a hypocritical world.[9] Cultural life had been a vulgar facade. The "stifling atmosphere" of the theater was incapable of offering anything other than "pallid, unhealthy, vicious, and neurotic" plays.[10] The supposed upheaval in ideas was nothing but a permanent recycling within the "vast hospital of the *fin-de-siècle*" of nihilism, Nordism, sensualism, internationalism, and a "fetishism of underclothing, boots, and furs."[11] Literary life was even worse. Morand railed against a revolting prose style ("Never has writing been so pretentiously bad"), against an "artistic" inspiration in which every character was neurasthenic and had an aristocratic surname (with a *particule*) and a ridiculous first name (like Yanis, Éginhard, Ysolde), as well as against snobbery, affectation, punning, and awkward word plays. Truly nothing could redeem such a pathetic era: "1900: this golden age fools itself blatantly, blinded by its monocle. It believes in nothing but it swallows everything."

Morand's diatribe was severe and, in many respects, deliberately provocative. The author was settling accounts, perhaps with the era of his adolescence, which had been prematurely broken off by the war, but above all with the previous generation, that of his father and mother, as Morand admitted rather abruptly in one of the closing sentences of the book: "Why did you give birth to us, one evening, after the show?"[12] It was the book of a tyro, ambitious and peremptory, who wants to get himself noticed. As he much later admitted in a 1970 television interview: "It was the reaction of the child against the father. I was probably influenced by Léon Daudet's *Le Stupide XIX siècle* and so I started writing that the people of 1900 did not wash their feet, etc. . . . Still, it is rather ludicrous to have done a portrait purely from the outside. The book is out of print and I have never reissued it. . . . But I was amusing myself with a kind of young boy's reaction. . . . You always detest those who preceded you by ten or twenty years."[13]

But what matters is not these psychological considerations but rather this little book's decisive impact. Despite its excesses, it was the first book to identify clearly a "1900 moment" with its own traits, emblematic figures, and singular characters, the first book to sketch the portrait of a moment explicitly named "1900." As Morand noted in passing: "Nobody talks any more about '1900' and it is not yet written about."[14] In other words, this period was over, no longer current but not yet history, so one might wander around it "like in the Musée Grévin, lost among the waxworks." But for that precise reason he helped bring to life "those distant folk who wore beards and went around in hansom cabs."[15] Morand opened up a space that made this reification possible and thereby inaugurated the posthumous life of 1900.

A second major effect concerns the reception of *1900*, both in 1931 and later. The many contemporary reviews mostly testify to Morand's visibility aboard the literary juggernaut of the day. The publishers had carefully prepared for the book's publication. As early as February 14, *Le Journal* announced its prepublication in installments in *Les Annales*. On May 1 it signaled its release as a single volume: "The whole world is talking about this astonishing voyage to the land of top hats and whalebone corsets." Other ads were inserted into most of the daily newspapers as Morand was sailing to New York to promote the book. The reception was very favorable and reviews often tipped into pure fawning. Henri de Régnier complimented Morand on his style and his way of making the era come alive.[16] Germaine Beaumont spoke of a "delicious book" with "witty chapters."[17] Many reviewers were content with descriptive accounts, as if they could not take the risk of starting a debate with such a famous writer. Some overcame the dilemma with a pirouette, joking about the "young Paupaul Morand, child prodigy" or imagining that Morand's son would publish a *1931* in 1962.[18] In *Comoedia*, Eugène Marsan evoked a "brilliant and brisk tableau, elliptical and enjoyable," but thought that Morand did not venture far enough in denigrating this despicable era: the book "is delicious but not sufficiently severe."[19] Others went moderately in the opposite direction: Edmond Jaloux found the book "amusing and caricatural"; Jean Vignaud recognized it as piquant, stylish, and fanciful, but noted that the author had chosen extreme examples. "He is a little like a 1900 figure, a worldly man who takes over the hearth at cigar time and tells stories."[20] By associating Morand's book with that of Warnod and Atget's photographs, *Les Nouvelles littéraires* proved more perspicacious, stating that the time was ripe for a return to the "frilly days."[21] In a long article published in the *Nouvelle revue française*, Benjamin Crémieux best expressed (in measured tones) the feelings aroused by the book: "It is a personal book, not a history book. Above all, *1900* is the first chapter in the memoirs of Paul Morand, the chapter about his Parisian 'infancy.' And then it is a reportage about time." Its tone tries too hard to be amusing: "*1900* is facile Morand, gay Morand . . . who declares himself an antisnob and thereby risks fostering a snobbery about antisnobbery." But the review's conclusion spares the author: "This is good Morand, with liveliness, zest, and felicity of expression, and an alacrity in the satire that can be overlooked." If Morand must be congratulated for stressing the ridiculousness of the era's fashions and obsessions, "it is necessary to stress the existence of another 1900, one that will last and take its place in history."[22]

The most interesting reactions came later and from those who wanted to defend the start of the century, which they thought Morand had distorted and travestied. Thus the literary and artistic magazine *Les Marges,* founded in 1908 by Eugène Montfort, decided to launch a vast inquiry devoted to "the value" of the 1900s. Explicitly targeting a recent "showy book in which 1900 was superficially criticized and ridiculed," and not hiding his own feelings about a period "of prodigious fecundity ... astonishing invention and creation," Montfort invited forty-some personalities in the world of arts and letters to answer the following questions:

> In arts and letters, did the 1900s present characteristics of a low or
>   a high period?
> Were its manners and public taste worth more than today's, or less?
> Was the life of yesterday fuller and more intelligent, or emptier and
>   more materialistic?[23]

In June 1932, one year after Morand's pamphlet appeared, the magazine published the results of its survey. Despite its tendentious questionnaire, it had received answers from twenty-seven writers, including famous figures like Henri Barbusse, Henry de Jouvenel, Léon Hennique, Hans Ryner, Paul Valéry, and Léon Werth. The presence of a sole woman, Rachilde, testifies to the kind of cultural heritage that was being promoted. Yet the responses are interesting. If we set aside those who did not play the game and instead addressed something else (Barbusse on Communism, Louis Dimier on France's decline, Léon Werth on relationships between technology and the mind), most of the contributors agreed on the broad picture: 1900 undoubtedly had its peculiarities and ridiculous aspects (like any era), but it was also a time of exceptional literary creativity, aesthetic innovation, and scientific and social progress. That almost all respondents had lived through the years being evaluated was obviously a major bias. "It was the era of our youth. How could we not find it superior to all others?" admitted Jules Bertaut. Some responses indulged in simple panegyric. "An immense era, almost unique, an era of intense intellectual fever ... an era vertiginously stretching toward the future!" exclaimed one. Others saw it as the heart and matrix of all French modernity. Moreover, Morand's book—that "paltry, caricatural, superficial, and botched volume" (Maurice Le Blond)—did not emerge unscathed. Indulgent critics like Fernand Laudet pointed out its "attitude [that is] appropriate only to unexperienced youth." "Young people who despise the year 1900 sin out of either pride or ignorance," Georges Delaw concluded. Still, by seizing on 1900, Morand had initiated this return to favor. Paul Valéry wondered in vain: "1900 . . . why this date? I see it as nothing worth more than 1899 or 1902. It is a word in time, like a letter in the alphabet." But henceforth "1900" would exist in people's memories, endowed with singular traits and characteristics. Morand and those who contradicted him together helped give it life—as well as give it form.

This existence was quickly acknowledged by journalist and art critic Louis Chéronnet when he published in September 1932 a glossy book titled *A Paris . . . vers* [around] *1900*. Sixty-some photographic plates representing objects, places, and personalities from before the war (principally focused on the world of arts, fashion, and entertainment) were accompanied by a rather long preface in which the author tried to delineate the nascent "1900" phenomenon.[24] Chéronnet asserted a need for generational considerations: "1900 will be at once the cause, the stakes, and the field." This debate would especially concern people who were still young, born a little before 1900, and whose destinies were brutally overtaken by the war. They had aspired to a life, had perhaps sniffed its perfume and savored its premises, but all that was suddenly snatched away before they could truly enjoy it. For them, 1900 was "a lost paradise, a heaven from which they remember falling down to a planet in torment, a promised land they no longer had a right or could manage to enter; the hopes and dreams they were going to achieve were never accomplished." Hence this melancholy, this disquiet, this torment over the past, this "tragedy of the century," which Chéronnet saw as the modern form of Romanticism. For the "germ of any Romanticism is the powerlessness of a dream to be realized." Morand's pamphlet had merely revealed this tension, so we should be grateful to him. He was a witness to an unquiet time that found it hard to envisage the future since it could scarcely believe in its present, and this pushed some contemporaries to turn in despair "to the past, to their own past."

The rest of the book, essentially composed of captioned photo-graphs, was less ambitious but did show that what was at stake was the reinvention of a nearby past. Chéronnet contributed some new elements to the portrait of the 1900 era, singling out three traits: the reign of absolute positivism, the primacy (even "worship") of woman, and the invention of art nouveau, which could be criticized but was capable of giving form and a coherent aesthetic to the era. The plates were exclusively of places, key figures, and spectator events. The Moulin Rouge lies next to the Grande Jatte and the beach of Deau-ville; at Maxim's the champagne flows and Sarah Bernhardt and the famous courtesan Liane de Pougy cross paths with comic actors like Dranem and Foottit, and the former Queen of Madagascar, Ranava-lona. The imagery was conventional, of course, but *Vers 1900* admira-bly fulfilled its role. Thanks to it, "1900" recovered its reputation, rank, and honor.

"1900" FASHION

A vogue had been launched that would assume different forms throughout the 1930s. The reverberations of Morand's book invited journalists and publishers to take advantage of its success. "1900" became a sort of label with strong value added; forgotten authors could be resurrected to feed this appetite. For example, a series of arti-cles called "A Woman a Day" by Jean Lorrain (which had appeared in the *Echo de Paris* in 1890 and 1891) was reissued in 1932 under the now-trendy title *Femmes de 1900* with commentary by Pierre-Léon Gauthier. The cinema, which had previously not bothered with 1900 other than as an obsolete fantasy, also changed its view. The same year (1932), Alexandre Korda shot *La Dame de chez Maxim's*, adapted from the famous vaudeville play by Feydeau (1899). The film was an example of "potted theater" (which had a bad reputation), and it lined up the cli-chés: the cancan (two scenes), a horse-drawn double-decker bus, a phonograph with cylinders, ambulant workers who lit gas lanterns, and frilly bathing suit (thought by the actress Charlotte Lysès to be too "daring"). Sound films were still a novelty and could popularize the famous refrains from the songs of 1900: "Frou-Frou," "La Petite

Tonkinoise," "Tout ça n'vaut pas l'amour." Above all—and this is the important thing—the staging itself fashioned the nostalgia for 1900: Korda's film opens on a shot of the actress Florelle humming "C'était hier" (It was yesterday). Then she tells the audience that thanks to the cinema they will experience the world that existed "thirty years ago." A few archival images precede the plot's takeoff, which is unusual in films of the time. Korda also uses "newsreel" images, especially during scene changes in a film entirely shot in the studio. Finally the last act ends with a poster for Feydeau's play, which proudly bears the date: 1900.

Of course, Alexandre Korda and screenwriter Henri Jeanson were not the first to draw on theater or literature from the start of the century. The previous year, Marcel L'Herbier had adapted the two detective novels by Phantom of the Opera author Gaston Leroux (The Mystery of the Yellow Room and then The Perfume of the Lady in Black). In 1931 Henri Diamant-Berger had shot the subtler Tu m'oublieras (You will forget me), a musical film set in two periods: first the heartrending farewell to the stage in 1910 of the beautiful Estelle de Pressendi, a famous music hall star who abandons everything to follow the man she loves; and then the return twenty years later of Yvonne, Estelle's daughter, who tries in vain to reanimate the romance of former times. Despite Damia's performance of the title song, the film was not noteworthy. Korda and Jeanson's The Girl from Maxim's, on the other hand, not only was successful but also testified to the desire to make a "Belle Époque film" before this became a popular marketing concept. Moreover, Korda soon settled in Great Britain and began his career there with an English version, The Girl from Maxim's, which was released in 1934 (see fig. 3). There was no reason this 1900 imaginaire that was starting to seduce France could not be exported across the Channel.

The British journalist Jose Shercliff, who at the time was working for the Daily Express, interviewed Jane Avril (Toulouse-Lautrec's model) and started to write a book about her that would only appear twenty years later.[25] But this initiative gave Pierre Audiat, a reporter for Paris-Midi, the idea to use the famous cancan dancer's memories himself. Installments appeared in April 1933. Jane Avril acknowledged, as did others, the strange vogue for 1900 that was seizing the country: "People are starting to recognize the charm of our era, once so mocked, but which people insist (I don't know why) on locating in the year 1900."[26] For her, the most "splendid" moment actually lay slightly earlier, corresponding to the early days of the Moulin Rouge, which she admitted extended into the first years of the twentieth century. There was a unique atmosphere: "Since then I have never found anywhere that sensation of collective yet respectable gaiety."[27] Her story, which paraded all the expected clichés about the Moulin in its glory days, also invited other actors of the time to mobilize their memories to respond to Morand's attack: "Appeal to your recollections (they cannot help but be spicy), especially today when certain writers, too young to be well informed, try to criticize and denigrate and ridicule that happy era that we experienced at the end of one century and the start of another."[28] The playwright Claude-André Puget, although he had not known the period (having been born in 1905), heard that call and wrote *Valentin le désossé* (Valentin the boneless), a light comedy tracing the origins and debut of the Moulin Rouge, a play that opened in October 1933.[29]

But most former celebrities were not yet in a hurry to publish memoirs. As in the 1920s, some books did go back to the prewar years, but few truly showed a desire to return to a lost era. Most of them were written by music hall stars (Caroline Otero, Yvette Guilbert, Eugénie Buffet)[30] or by society figures like Elisabeth de Gramont who had a family literary tradition, or else were commissioned by editors. The memoirs of Boni de Castellane had come out in 1925, "earning him 200,000 francs, at a time when the 1914 war had deprived him of the luxury jobs he lived on since his marriage collapsed."[31] Others who were more hesitant may have been striving to follow the example of writer Georges Duhamel, who announced in the *Nouvelle revue française* in September 1933: "I will not write my memoirs."[32] In fact the vogue for memoir just came a little later. Marie Scheikévitch, daughter of a rich Russian collector, published in 1935 her *Souvenirs d'un temps disparu* (Memories of a vanished era), in which she evoked her friendships with Proust, Reynaldo Hahn, and other personalities of the arts and letters elite who frequented her salon.[33] The same year, Jean Cocteau, who had previously also refused to write his memoirs, agreed to publish his *souvenirs*, published by *Le Figaro* from January 19 to May 14, 1935. Gathered into a single volume shortly after, his *Portraits-souvenir* identified explicitly not just the date 1900, but henceforth the time span 1900–1914. It was the time of his childhood—he was born in 1889—but more especially a time peopled by phantoms and ghosts: "The *grandes cocottes* (courtesans) no longer exist . . . the Elks [a famous clown duo] are dead, dead are Chocolat and Footit, dead the Nouveau-Cirque . . . Claude Casimir-Perier, dead. Alain-Fournier, dead. Péguy, dead."[34] A whole generation had vanished. At Maxim's and at the cinema and theater, he encounters only shadows that feed his nostalgia. Regrets are even more pronounced in the case of Roland Dorgelès, whose look back at Montmartre appeared in 1936.[35] The writer, born in 1885, dedicates a veritable hymn to his twenties. What he laments of course is the time of his youth, and his friendships, encounters, and love affairs, but as Alfred Sauvy later remarked, "it is not presented as youth per se; it was the era itself that was happy."[36] Places are also mourned, particularly in Montmartre—"the real one, all at the top, not the Montmartre of ladies of the night and champagne bars"[37]—where all memories are gathered. Like Carco and Warnod before him, Dorgelès contributed to the patient edification of the Montmartre imaginary as an essential component of what was now on its way to becoming *the* "Belle Époque." "Was it *the* good time!? Hey, if you wish. We are becoming more convinced of this as we age."[38]

The same "picturesque and sentimental journey through a Paris that is no more" was undertaken by Léon-Paul Fargue in *Le Piéton de Paris* (The Paris pedestrian), a follow-up to his *D'après Paris*.[39] Here again it is a matter of sniffing the "particular odor of the prewar years."[40] Fargue "naturally" focuses on the literary and artistic life and he denounces (as did others) the imposture that Montmartre has become: "Montmartre is like those little nations from before the war that served only for confecting operettas"; all the authentic places have disappeared "and been replaced by cafés, bars, and grills."[41] Hence the need to offer a counterpoint view of the true "*grande époque*." But Fargue is less interested in the *era* itself—he presents nothing on the Exposition, for example, nor on other events, not even from his personal life—than the memory of, and suffering caused by, *lost places*. This is what is specific to nostalgia. He recalls the quays along the Seine where young people would perambulate in the hope of coming across novelists, near the Ourcq canal ("glazed like an aspen leaf") and near railway stations, with their poetry of expectation. He even embraces the gloomy suburbs, far from the noise of the city. And of course he lingers in the cafés of Montparnasse and Montmartre, where so many memories lay. Memories of space, but ultimately also of time: "Parisians at that time did not experience anxiety." As for Montmartre, it "still exists because it represents youth itself for most of my contemporaries."[42] Here 1900 is almost reduced to a stage set, expressing unfathomable nostalgia, meditating on loss, as the writer takes a sorry and melancholic (sometimes even harrowing) journey through the "vanished years."

But Montmartre did not exhaust the memory bank. Other places and other activities diversely nourished the backward gazes of memoir writers. The Lyon illustrator Louis Bourgeois-Borgex evoked "the end of a century" that for him was dominated by the personality of Aristide Bruant and the first film projections by the Lumière brothers.[43] The British writer Bryher (pseudonym of Annie W. Ellerman), who had spent her childhood and adolescence in France, would revisit it in *Paris 1900,* which was translated and published by Sylvia Beach and Adrienne Monnier in 1938. Viewed by a child subject to the rigid rules of the British bourgeoisie, this 1900 certainly differs from that of other writers, but here are the same themes that mark the whole 1900 imaginary: the important visit to the Expo, the "geographic emotions" that a city can arouse, and the feeling of becoming European amid the cultural and social effervescence of prewar Paris.[44]

This imaginary also triumphed in concert halls, where the vogue for the great realist *chanteuses* reached its apogee. Henri Varna produced in 1934 a revue in the "old style" at the Alcazar;[45] meanwhile Fréhel, Damia, Lys Gauty, and their numerous imitators continued to celebrate what was tragic about the prewar years. Lyrics like "Où sont-ils donc" (Where are they now?), written by André Decaye in 1926, and "La chanson des fortifs" (Fortification song), by Georges Van Parys in 1938, drew upon nostalgia for Paris. "Prewar refrains" were so enormously successful that some critics began to mock the merchandising of downbeat ballads and the banalization of the genre. "Pale imitators who cannot really be called song 'interpreters' are tapping into the market," Francis Carco was soon remarking. "The realist song, stupid enough to make you cry, has invaded and submerged everything, and unfortunately (except for Fréhel, Mistinguett, and Damia), underneath the black sheath dress and scarlet scarf of the ladies and the flat cap or bowler hat of the gentlemen, eight times out of ten only clichés are to be found."[46] This fascination accentuated the gradual legitimation of a suburban culture, that of bad boys and prostitutes in the 1900s. Fréhel, who in *Algiers* wept over her lost youth, as we recall, contributed greatly to this phenomenon. The following year (1939) we find her in the movies *L'Entraîneuse* (The barmaid) by Albert Valentin and *Une Java* by Claude Orval. The cinema too profited from this current. André Berthomieu directed *La Chaste Suzanne* in 1937, inviting audiences to the Moulin Rouge to experience a "Gala 1900." Others tried to play the game of harmonies in time. In *The Tender Enemy* (1936), Max Ophuls brings up from the past (specifically the turn of the century) the former lovers of Annette Dupont. The phantoms have the noble task of rescuing Annette's daughter from a terrible fate (being forced to marry a man she does not love). Thus 1900 could be served up with any kind of sauce.

HISTORICIZING FICTIONS

Literature, as so often, contains the best expression of social phenomena and supplies the keys to them. I have mentioned the many novels that up to then had been set before the war. Precise, diverse, and well documented though they were, none was explicitly devoted to describing a vanished world. This "historical" dimension would surge up in the 1930s.[47] Roger Martin du Gard, author of the *Thibaults*, embodied this new twist. Since 1920, this novelist had been methodically following the serial plan he had announced at the start, producing one volume after another with great regularity (six volumes had appeared between 1922 and 1929). But things got scrambled in the following years. Personal complications as well as his concern over the international situation led him to rethink the architecture of his oeuvre, and hence the significance of his "long-term novel." Immobilized in 1931 after a car accident, he decided to radically change his plan for the saga, to make it "more historic": the destiny of the characters should chime with the era to which they belonged. The saga of two brothers that initially was to be followed into the 1920s would now end with *Summer 1914*, a major break as well as a somber premonition. Narrative time both accelerated and melted away. "The France of 1900, the France after the [Dreyfus] affair"[48] became the sole time horizon of the *Thibaults* saga. The final volume appeared in 1936 (it was followed four years later by an *Epilogue*), written while political and international crises were intensifying. The looming world war was obviously a subtext, but du Gard dates the first steps toward war back to a time in the past. "No moment, perhaps, brought home to him more vividly than this the rupture between his past life and the days to come."[49]

The upheaval symbolized in the *Thibaults* serial was also being perceived and dramatized by other 1930s novelists. Jules Romains's *Les Hommes de bonne volonté* (Men of good will), another multivolume saga, was published starting in 1932. It draws almost as clear a fresco of another era. The first fourteen volumes, centered on the years from 1908 to 1914, follow the destinies of multiple characters tied together by the familiar and recurrent figures of Jallez and Jerphanion, two graduates of the elite École Normale Supérieure. Romains's intention was complex, both psychological and social, but also focused on depicting a very clearly circumscribed period, from the "time of the Exposition" to that of World War One. "War. Since his childhood, Jerphagnon had lived under the curse of war."[50] Each novel marched inexorably to the war, each imprisoned the narrative (and the freedom of the characters peopling it) within the closed historical time of "before the war." The same atmosphere permeated *La Chronique des Pasquier* (The Pasquier chronicle), in which Georges Duhamel describes the family saga of Raymond Pasquier and his five children. The plot begins in 1889. By 1939, when World War Two was breaking out, Duhamel had just published the eighth volume, *Le Combat contre les ombres,* which ends with the departure for the front in August 1914 of Laurent, one of the Pasquier sons.

But no doubt *The Real World*, Louis Aragon's novel sequence, is the most exemplary case of this inscription of fiction in history. After difficult relations with the Communist Party, by 1933 most of the surrealists (led by André Breton and Paul Éluard) had been thrown out. Only Aragon remained, proclaiming allegiance to the Third International and denouncing the "drifting" of the surrealist movement he had left behind. His resulting conversion to the social realist novel, a genre he conceived as a contribution to political and social struggles, was a riposte to the "close clamors of the foreign war." More than a single novel, he undertook a whole cycle, as had the other writers I have mentioned. "I must give these books a general title, and it will be in memory of a long inner conflict I have been through, and of that cloudy work I am leaving behind me: *The Real World*," he wrote in the preface to the second volume, *Residential Quarter,* published in Paris in 1936.[51] Two years earlier, *The Bells of Basel* had opened the series. Aragon traces the intertwined journeys of three figures whose destinies are joined on the eve of the war. "With *The Bells of Basel*, Louis Aragon offers a vast fresco of the prewar days," noted a reviewer.[52] Aragon mingles into the plot several real events (the attacks of the anarchist bandit Bonnot, the taxi strike of 1911–1912, the Basel Congress, the extension of military service) and many real historical figures (Libertad, Jean Jaurès and his murderer Raoul Villain, Clara Zetkin). He drew on his own memories, but also on ample documentation, particularly from back issues of the Communist newspaper *L'Humanité* and of *Bataille Syndicaliste.*[53] Some critics reproached him for this partisan stance: yes, the text "makes you relive that era, illuminates it, situates it in time, in history," but his characters are merely lifeless marionettes. Aragon needed "men of flesh, whereas they are only the animated illustrations of an era."[54] But such criticisms did not hinder his determination. *Residential Quarter*, appearing in 1936, and even more so *Passengers of Destiny* (completed in August 1939 but published in 1942) accentuate this inscription of the narrative inside a historical framework. Aragon the novelist interweaves individual destinies, those of characters onto which he transposes both part of his personal history (or his father's) and a collective destiny. Within this shortened twentieth century that ran from 1889 to the war, both would advance together toward the abyss.

Novelistic representations of the pre-war era seem by the mid-1930s to have reached a point of no return: that era was henceforth historical and belonged to a circumscribed past that was fair game for criticism—but also for nostalgia. Retrospective evaluations tended to become more complicated: some continued to perceive it as a world of pleasure and parties—"The Paris of 1912. Balls, balls, balls," wrote Cocteau[55]—or as an Areopagus that mingles artists, high society personalities, and music-hall stars. Meanwhile others, like Céline in *Death on the Installment Plan,* rose up against these images of an insouciant and idyllic era before World War One. The Paris of 1900 that Céline depicted is a dirty, ignoble, infected place, peopled with failures, traversed by the "numberless legions of thirst."[56] But within this historicizing trend, the clearest shift was to push back into the past that which not long before had been merely "yesterday." This was well expressed by Jean Cocteau: "1934–1935. A curtain falls, a curtain rises. Life is dead, long live life! Dead is an age that I lived to the full, regretfully and with all my strength; a new age begins."[57]

Among the reasons for this shift are the various writers' ages, almost all having been born at the end of the previous century. Growing old almost mechanically modifies the view of what had been their childhood or their youth. "We understood that we were saying farewell to our youth,"[58] Dorgelès lucidly remarked. On top of this came anxiety about crises affecting the country: an economic crisis (which affected France more than it was long thought), but also a "moral" and political crisis. These issues especially prospered on the Right and extreme Right, with Charles Maurras, Drieu la Rochelle, and others among the whole generation that had grown up in the shadow of the monarchist movement Action Française, which constantly deplored France's spiritual debacle and the loss of its soul.[59] But the anxiety was also expressed by Paul Valéry, who in 1939 warned against the loss of the "freedom of mind"; it also found a powerful echo among "nonconformists" and various ranks of the Left. This anxiety was accentuated by political instability, corruption, and scandals, all of which swelled in the mid-1930s. Some people saw correlations between the present day and the start of the century. Portraying the Paris of 1900 in the mid-1930s, the British writer Bryher remarked that "that era, with the deep current of political intrigues, can easily be related to that of 1935."[60] But disastrous images of the present time, experienced as being on the brink of unprecedented moral crisis, if not of collective suicide, also nourished a sharp historical pessimism, which by contrast chose to refer back to an idealized past, to a "nostalgic representation of the world from before."

Such reactions were not limited to France. From Berlin, where he was living while witnessing the world's agony, Robert Musil published in 1930 and 1932 the first two volumes of *The Man Without Qualities*, in which he describes a "fever" that spread across Europe at the turn of the nineteenth to the twentieth century: "Nobody knew exactly what was on the way, nobody was able to say whether it was to be a new art, a New Man, a new morality, or perhaps a re-shuffling of society."[61] In October 1931, the British playwright Noël Coward premiered at the Theatre Royal in Drury Lane the play *Cavalcade*, in which we follow the destiny of a bourgeois family confronted with all the social upheavals that had accumulated since the death of Queen Victoria in 1901. Its success was so great that performances ran through September 1932. The following year, Frank Lloyd produced a film adaptation in Hollywood. In 1937, the writer Osbert Sitwell published the novel *Those Were the Days*, which offered a nostalgic panorama of the Edwardian bourgeoisie. Analogously, the United States was valorizing its "Gay Nineties" through the drawings and engravings of the illustrator Richard Culter and the novels of Thomas Beer, who coined the notion of the "Mauve Decade."

But signs of impending war were what caused most anxiety. Back in 1932, Henri Barbusse was already insisting on the "eventuality, which escapes only the blind, of new imminent wars."[62] The drums of war resonated constantly in a France that since 1918 had been marked by a profound pacifism: Manchuria in 1931, then Abyssinia and Ethiopia in 1935, Spain in 1936, and especially faced with a Germany that was rearmed and aggressive. Suddenly the term "before the war" had become simultaneously the past, the present, and the future. To the French of the 1930s, people from the 1900s could come back to recount a history that was both very distant and very close by. Above all, people did not want to be victims of the same illusions that had cradled their predecessors. This is why the figure of Jean Jaurès, the Socialist leader who was assassinated on the eve of World War One, haunts the novels of the 1930s. Jaurès appears in the narratives of Aragon, Jules Romains, and Roger Martin du Gard, a Jaurès invoked as a prophet and the despairing conscience of pacifist France. "At this exceptionally grave moment through which humanity is passing, I wish, without vanity, but with gnawing disquiet in my heart, that my books about 'Summer 1914' may be read and discussed, and that they may remind all of us—the old who have forgotten, as well as the young who either do not know or do not care—of the sad lesson of the past," declared Martin du Gard in his 1937 Nobel Prize acceptance speech.[63] Obviously, the writer is alluding to the fact that Jaurès was assassinated on July 31, 1914, the day before the war broke out.

* * *

The import of the 1900 imaginary was so strong in the two years 1935 and 1936 that the expression "*belle époque*" was finally ready to arise. Already in 1930, Paul Poiret's memoir had spoken of "dressing the *époque*." Commenting in 1933 on a series of films adapted from vaudevilles of the 1900s, including *Gaîtés de l'escadron* by Maurice Tourneur and *The Girl from Maxim's* by Alexandre Korda, the critic Jean Valdois evoked in *Cinémagazine* "the good times" of hansom cabs, the Exposition, the Moulin Rouge, "the Maxim's of the Prince de Sagan and Emilienne d'Alençon, the *belle époque*. . . ." This is a more precise use of the concept, but the phrase is still not yet synonymous with yesterday's good times. "Ah! yes, those were the good times, when we knew the sweetness of living."[64] In *Algiers*, directed by Julien Duvivier in 1936 (the film came out in January 1937), as we recalled in the prologue, there is a memorable scene in which the singer Fréhel, grown older and fatter, puts a record on the gramophone and hums a refrain from the time of her splendor: "Me, when I get the blues, I change era." The most tangible trace of the origin of "Belle Époque" comes from the operetta *La Poule* (The hen), performed at the Théâtre des Nouveautés from January to April 1936.[65] The scenario is based on a novel by Henri Duvernois published in 1931, adapted for film by René Guissart.[66] This is a "delicious comedy,"[67] amiable and pleasant, about retired artist Adolphe Silvestry and his five daughters, one an aspiring painter, the others a student, a model, a reader, and a typist. Touched by the grace and modesty of this sympathetic family, an Argentine millionaire invites everybody to his villa on the Côte d'Azur. Obviously, there the five girls find five young men, and it requires all the diligence of the eldest, Guillemette, and the doting father ("papa hen" in French) to watch over the flock. Happily, despite many twists and turns, everything ends in weddings. "This is the French spirit at its purest and most amusing," wrote Henri Lhemens in *Le Petit Journal*. Duvernois's scenario was adapted by André Barde, one of the masters of musical comedy of the 1900s; the songs were written by a composer from the same era, Henri Christiné. Among the refrains that struck the audiences and critics was a "pretty song in the old style" titled "Ah! La Belle époque." This lively number evokes the ritual of asking for a hand in marriage and expresses the regret that today this custom has lost all its charm and civility. But the *"belle époque"* that it celebrates is not explicitly linked to the beginning of the century, just to generic good times, the good time of yesteryear, "old-fashioned days," when one "called on a girl by first putting on white gloves." Still, while the *"belle époque"* was not precisely identified with the 1900s, this expression was becoming attached to it, if only through the careers of André Barde (born in 1874) and Henri Christiné (born in 1867), both clearly associated with musical theater at the turn of the century. *La Poule* was to be their last collaboration.

Thus on the eve of World War Two almost everything was in place for the emergence of the definitive "Belle Époque." The 1900s, which everyone understood as lasting until the summer of 1914, now constituted a clearly defined period endowed with specific traits. From appearing low and silly in Paul Morand's description, it had gradually risen to become the tragic prewar period that spoke to the men and women of 1939. There some observers could seek answers to the perils that currently threatened, but most were content to throw nostalgic backward glances, or else draw from that era a little of the gaiety and lightness for which they longed. This complex representation was grasped by director Abel Gance in a remarkable film, *Le Paradis perdu* (Paradise lost), which he shot precisely in 1939 (see fig. 4). The scenario merits a close look. The painter Pierre and the young milliner Janine meet in the spring of 1914; an enduring passion is born between them. But their marriage lasts only a few days. The war tears Pierre from his happiness; in the trenches he learns of Janine's death giving birth to their daughter Jeannette. Pierre is broken and suffers terrible depression, to the point of not wanting to know the child responsible for killing his great love. Much later, once he has become a rich *couturier*, he overcomes his pain when he finds in Jeannette the beauty of her mother Janine (actress Micheline Presle plays both roles). He decides to marry a very young woman, whose brother is Jeannette's lover. The latter obliges Pierre to give up the idea and he agrees reluctantly. Finally he dies at his daughter's wedding.

This film, which Gance did not like and considered hack work, enjoyed immense success. He was offering an exemplary fable of the "Belle Époque." The action, which takes place in the high society milieu of fashion, spins a very transparent metaphor: Pierre, who rejects the postwar present, has withdrawn into nostalgic depression. He rediscovers life only when his daughter has assumed the face of the lost Janine and when he himself is going to marry "youth." But this illusion will kill him: paradise when lost is never regained. When the film was released in December 1940, it was wildly successful with audiences, which adds to its interest.[68] For by this date the "Belle Époque" had become a reality.

PART TWO

AH! LA BELLE ÉPOQUE!

IT WAS not until 1940, as I hinted at the beginning, that the expression "Belle Époque" came definitively to designate what for a dozen years had been known as the "1900 era." This *imaginaire* would be triumphant for about twenty years. Each cultural event and artifact—theater, music hall, cinema, history books, memoirs, and recollections—converged to celebrate a period thought to be the apogee of French power and French culture as well as a French style, an "art of living," that was envied by the entire world. Nostalgia certainly shaped these representations, but perhaps less than it seems, and less than in the evocations of 1900 that proliferated in the previous decade, as we saw in Part One. Other reasons and other intentions are intermingled now: the desire for escape, the need to find refuge in a lighter and more gratifying past, the desire to make use of nostalgia to contend with difficult current situations, and the desire to reinvigorate the national energy. As we shall see, though born in the Paris of the Nazi Occupation when it was put at the service of the German army, the Belle Époque would have no difficulty adapting to the Liberation context, which recognized some of its other virtues. During the Fourth Republic, the Belle Époque would experience its greatest glory—and forge the enduring traits of its identity.

OCCUPIED PARIS, "BELLE ÉPOQUE" PARIS?

O**N JUNE 14,** 1940, German troops entered Paris, which had just been declared an "open city" by the Vichy government. The occupying force raised swastika flags over public buildings. In the afternoon, the troops of General von Bock paraded along the Champs-Elysées; in the evening, a curfew was imposed on a city that had lost two-thirds of its three million inhabitants. Starting the next day, all the city's clocks were advanced one hour to conform with German timekeeping. On June 18 Hitler came to Paris for the first time and reviewed the Wehrmacht detachments. He came back on the 23rd for a second day of visits and photographs. The day before, the French delegation led by General Huntziger had signed the armistice (in the Compiègne forest, where the truce ending World War One had been signed) that placed the country under the domination of the enemy. The Occupation of Paris would last until July 25, 1944.

In the city, which lost its status as capital but would be headquarters of the German military command in France, life gradually resumed. Following the example of *Le Matin*, which published an issue on June 17, most newspapers resumed publication, and starting in July many of them came back to Paris, to the satisfaction of German authorities, who wanted the country to quickly resume its habits. Many Parisians who had fled, fearing combat, gradually returned to the capital. The "*vie parisienne*" came back into its own, particularly because economic demand was high from both Occupation troops and privileged spectators and consumers. The Alcazar Theater, renamed the Palace (paying respect to the Falangists and Franco cadets fallen in September 1936 inside the Alcazar of Toledo), reopened its doors on July 6, 1940, rapidly followed by the Casino of Paris and the Folies-Bergère. By August, all the Parisian music halls had resumed operations.[1] Starting in mid-July, the newsstands offered *Der Deutsche Wegleiter für Paris*, a guide to shows and restaurants with a circulation of several thousand among Occupation troops.[2] Now nothing limited the "frenzy for entertainment" of which Paris was the theater.[3] The *café-concerts* and music halls, the emblematic sites of "Gay Paree," were packed with both German officers and ordinary soldiers; entertainment enjoyed a spectacular rise in patronage.[4] At the end of 1940, more than 100 cinemas, 25 theaters, 14 music halls, and 21 cabarets in Paris were fully functioning.[5] "Revues" were particularly appreciated by the Germans and dominated almost all venues. While the Moulin Rouge had been transformed into a cinema, shows and balls did continue at the Robinson-Moulin Rouge, which organized an international amateur striptease competition. All the other venues wanted to offer revues, but the principal difficulty was how to update that kind of spectacle. The prestigious stars were less numerous and hence less available, and the previously prized British *girls* were suddenly lacking.[6] Hence the recurrence of identical old shows—and the audience's sense of déjà-vu. It was almost always the same headliners who came back: Maurice Chevalier and Mistinguett as the prestige duo, followed by lesser stars of the day (Georgius, Suzy Solidor, Tino Rossi, Lucienne Boyer) or by younger ones coming up (Charles Trenet, Django Reinhardt, Edith Piaf, and her rival Léo Marjane). To vary the bill, some directors of revues added burlesque and slapstick acts, as did Gilles Margaritis in his *Chesterfollies*. But producers mostly resorted to surefire crowd-pleasers, often featuring Paris itself: shows titled *Amours de Paris*, *Toujours Paris*, *Bravo Paris*, *Paris en fleurs*, *Paris-Printemps*, *Paris fredonne!* (Paris hums) or even *Soyons Parisiens!* (Let's be Parisians!), the title of a revue staged by Albert Willemetz at the Théâtre des Nouveautés.[7] This kind of show had the advantages of drawing on an easy and familiar repertoire, of satisfying the Occupiers without any fuss, and of being a cheap way to demonstrate a certain kind of French patriotism. Therefore it is no surprise that the "1900" repertoire, though worn down to a thread, was mobilized for good profits in a "very French vein" at all the capital's theaters and *café-concerts*.

This type of entertainment was also fodder for the radio, whose landscapes and programs were considerably reduced during the war. In July 1939, as the war approached, the Daladier government had created by decree a French national radio administration that would have a state monopoly. The Occupation obviously changed the situation.[8] Radio, the most sensitive medium at the time, was to be strictly supervised by the Propaganda-Abteilung Frankreich established in Paris in mid-July. It oversaw technical installations and the powerful transmitter of the Poste Parisien, admirably located at 116 Avenue des Champs-Elysées, and there set up a new station under the authority of Doctor Böfinger, formerly of Radio-Stuttgart. The goal was to create German-style radio broadcasting but in French, whose mission would be pure propaganda. Böfinger chose to retain the station's name ("Radio-Paris") in order to keep the existing audience; in fact this had been the name of the first private station, founded in 1922 and nationalized eleven years later as the Poste National. This station was widely listened to, and the Germans' evident intention was to recover its reputation and win back its listeners. Endowed with considerable financial resources, the new Radio-Paris began transmission on July 5, 1940; as of 1943 it became the sole radio station authorized in France. But as the principal organ of collaboration and collaborationism in France, the station management quickly realized that it had to avoid ostentatious propaganda and find other ways of pleasing audiences. Hence the primary place—two-thirds of its programming—given to music, songs, and entertainment. Much effort was given to recruiting a "Grand Orchestra" of ninety musicians, conducted by the respected Jean Fournet, but also "lighter" ensembles like that of Jo Bouillon, who had accompanied Mistinguett and Josephine Baker, and groups led by Raymond Legrand and Richard Blareau. In addition to the public concerts that it regularly organized, Radio-Paris offered many "popular" programs; even news bulletins and political programs—all of them to the glory of the new Hitlerian order—were interspersed with long stretches of variety entertainment, principally music hall shows and light comedy.[9]

So it was on the airwaves of Radio-Paris that the young director André Alléhaut (he was born in 1910) inaugurated in November 1940 a new program called *Ah! La Belle Époque!—A Musical Sketch of the 1900 Era*. This was a 45-minute program, broadcast at the start of the evening, at first at 19:15 and later on at 20:00, composed of two distinct sequences. First, a host evoked a picturesque or pleasing aspect of the 1900s (an evening at the theater, a promenade along the boulevards or the banks of the Marne River, a tour on the double-decker railway belonging to the Compagnie de l'Est). Then the orchestra conducted by Victor Pascal segued into some of the hits of those old days like "Les Bas noirs" (Black stockings), "Fascination," "Viens Poupoule," and "Caroline."[10] The program enjoyed immediate success, as the radio magazines tell us.

Alléhaut was not a novice, having made his start in the theater in 1930–1931, then turned to the cinema, playing notably in *Laurette ou le cachet rouge,* a historical film by Jacques de Casembroot, in 1933. But this acting career did not last long, no doubt due to his partial deafness.[11] Then Alléhaut went into radio, which did bring him fame: starting in 1937 he became producer and "head of theatrical productions at Poste Parisien," where he was in charge of all musical variety shows. In 1938 he hosted the last show at the Folies-Bergère[12] as well as several radio concerts or "sound films" like *Capitale-Symphonie*. So naturally enough, when he was demobilized in the autumn of 1940 after the Battle for France, he asked for a job with Radio-Paris, which gave him a post close to the one he had enjoyed at Poste Parisien. One year later, in October 1941, master of ceremonies Alléhaut described in the magazine *Les Ondes* how he conceived and organized his program:

Ah! La Belle Époque! It seems like a cry from the heart, doesn't it? For us who saw it only from the arms of our nannies, it has become a time of fairy tales, like a poet's dream. . . . I tried to reconstruct it, partly out of dilettantism, and also for making a living. This is why I started to stuff myself—that is the term—with everything that evokes this happy 1900, and, by extension, the whole era that preceded and followed the start of the century. Do not think that I am using only my imagination! Each allusion is conscientiously studied, refined with the aid of period documents. Thus when I describe how elegant people were dressed at the theater, a *café-concert*, or a great restaurant, or else when I allow myself to watch a pretty girl along the grand boulevards, I am looking at fashion plates of the very year where I am situating my action. . . . We were merely lacking the style, the *je ne sais quoi* that testifies to any era, represents its soul, and faithfully reproduces its essence. I sat down to re-read the novels of the time, all the Paul Bourgets, the Marcel Prévosts, the Theuriets, in order to imbue and reconstruct for myself (and naturally for you) the dreamy Castle in Spain where I am going to take you. Shall I take you to a party, a gala at the time of the Exposition? So I study the old newspapers, the society pages, theater and literary reviews. I instruct and amuse myself. I admit that I am passionate about this little game.[13]

Very popular, *Ah! La Belle Époque!* gradually enlarged its scope, dedicating evening outings to later years (1920, 1922, etc.). Then it evolved into *La Chanson de notre époque* (The song of our era), then *Le Bon temps* (Good old times), and finally into *Quarante ans de songs* (Forty years of songs), but it always worked on the same principle: a "presentation by André Alléhaut" and then a concert of popular old songs.[14] On the occasion of the hundredth program in 1942, the magazine *Les Ondes* accorded a long laudatory article titled "Here comes the Belle Époque!"

All the gay choruses of our youth—all the charming tunes that make us smile indulgently or make us hearts beat a little faster—are going to come out of the magic box, invade the room, the street, the boulevards; recovering intact their former freshness.

Here is the *belle époque!*

With skill and good taste, André Alléhaut fabricates a dream for us. He leads us in turn to the banks of the Marne, to Nogent; to a prize ceremony in the provinces, to the Eldorado, to the countryside, to a church mass. What is found is always happy, the pretext is

never banal, and by the force of one's imagination, we find ourselves quite naturally in 1901 at the Scala or in 1905 on the boulevards. Then, under the talented direction of its conductor, Victor
Pascal, the orchestra brings "Les bas noirs," "Fascination," or the
exquisite "Reviens" back to life, followed by "Viens Poupoule" or
"Caroline."[15]

The program's success led Alléhaut to organize a live-on-stage series
of public evenings and concerts. Thus he presented the first grand
gala of the Orchestra of Radio-Paris on November 9, 1942, which was
a "Belle Époque" variety show that closed with the much-anticipated
appearance of Maurice Chevalier.[16] More such events were produced
in 1943 and continued up until July 1944, encouraged by the station,
which saw them as a good means of dressing its propaganda in a
musical and popular veneer.[17] This choice appeared all the more natural because most of the cabarets and music halls were increasing
their turn-of-the-century spectacles. In September 1940, director
Michel Francini led the way by offering a *1900 revue* at the Théâtre de
l'Etoile,[18] and by November 1941 every producer seemed to be at it.
While the Thés-Spectacles du Ruhl offered *La Belle Époque: An Evening at a Ball in 1900*[19] as a matinée starting on November 10, an analogous show, *Paris 1900 Songs: Memories of Youth*, was given on
November 26 at Théâtre des Actualités.[20] And on the fifteenth of that
month, Georgius launched at his Etoile theater on the Avenue de
Wagram (pompously dubbed the "Music Hall of Modern Times") a
new show titled *Paris 1900 (the Hansom Cab Days)*. He stated his
intention in *Le Petit Parisien*, which offered an enticement:

1900 again! Say what you want, this year has led a hardy life.
   A veritably prodigious number of paperbacks, articles, songs,
shows, and films have been devoted to it. Yet the curiosity and
nostalgia it arouses among those who pronounce its name (four
numbers) remain the same. . . . Today 1900, aged forty-two, in gray
frock coat, flower in the buttonhole, monocle, and coiffed in top
hat, stands up, arches his back, still jovial, continues to get himself
talked about as the finest time of youth. He has taken to the bot-
tle, but he is still quite attractive. There is nobody like him at

whispering tender words into women's ears. He is still the master of the slow waltz; nobody else explains romance with so much art and charm. When people say that 1900 was a blessed year, you can believe it.

It was a golden year.[21]

Georgius's revue was immensely successful, playing at the Etoile until the end of December, then brought back in January 1942 to the Théâtre Antoine.[22] It was "an amusing retrospective of yesterday's songs produced with good taste and good humor,"[23] a "potpourri of 1900s tunes," combined with a portion of a *café-concert* that featured Mimi Pinson, Paulus, Dranem, La Belle Otero, and Aristide Bruant, "souvenirs of [entertainer Felix] Mayol," and a version of *Les Fortifs 1900*, and it closed with a *quadrille*.[24] A version renamed *Un soir à la Grande Roue* extended the run until the end of March. Transposed to the stage, it operated on the same principle as Alléhaut's radio programs and was mostly praised in newspaper reviews. Marcel de Livet in *Paris-Soir* spoke on behalf of enthusiastic spectators:

> How can one not give way to tenderness when revisiting the time of hansom cabs, whose atmosphere brings a little warmth to the cheeks of those over forty (which we are!) who still remember the lights of the Alcazar in summer, the statue of the Parisienne, and Grün's posters? For others, the new spectacle at the Etoile will bring the surprise of an era of good-natured gaiety, when people amused themselves a little—and with grace.[25]

"Paris 1900—made fun of ever since then—how much we regret not having known you!," added Roger Sardou in *La Semaine à Paris*.[26] Only some grumblers were not convinced: "For all those who have known this era, there is always some disappointment at seeing it reconstructed; I wonder if the fault lies in our memory, either unfaithful or too precise, or if we simply imagine memories that are more beautiful than the reality."[27]

Such success led Alléhaut, whose program was continuing on Radio-Paris, to try to give it a lease on life on the stage. Thus in March 1943, *Ah! La Belle Epoque!* became a revue with flesh and feathers in two acts and twenty scenes directed at the Bobino theater by Jean Valmy, who also conducted the orchestra. Conceived according to "Radio-Paris' famous program," it offered a sequence of musical and comic attractions. It was a "triumph of laughter," boasted the advertising bills.[28] Apart from the songs, the revue offered comic turns ("numbers" and "buffooneries") pervaded by ribaldry and bawdiness: the stationmaster of Garches, the lighter of gas streetlamps, the inevitable barracks humor of soldiers. From Montparnasse, "this very '1900' amusement" then migrated to the Palace on the Right Bank, where it opened on June 18, 1943.[29] "This is a revue without stars but in which every performer does his job conscientiously to the point of making it a perfectly homogeneous show that successfully makes the audience happy and amused. One laughs wholeheartedly and applauds the many performers." The critics particularly enjoyed a sketch "imitating Maurice Chevalier and Mistinguett." The revue transferred to the Européen and then to the Bouffes-du-Nord until the end of March 1944,[30] then to the Gaîté Lyrique, where it remained on the bill until April 1944. Its "ever-young tunes" continued to exploit the good times of laughter, love, partying, and oompahs. Designing the show's poster was entrusted to Gaston Girbal, an illustrator specializing in the Parisian music hall who clearly showed its hue: a nubile young woman with an appealing smile against a sustained pink background, with just enough eroticism (open bodice, booties, an S-shaped silhouette) to beckon: "Ah! What a fine evening we are going to have!" (see fig. 5).

Lost amid these tributes, *Le Petit Parisien* was the only newspaper to offer (in August 1943, under the byline of Georges Dallain) a more critical note:

> Was this era—which oscillates around the year 1900—in fact as beautiful as it is sung? Yes, if we consider its material aspect. Life then was easy and silver was almost worth [as much as] gold. Our fathers spent it freely, so it is said. They merrily celebrated the little ladies and their frills. . . . But oh, such lost opportunities, wasted wealth, cheap sentimentalism! This is the lesson taught us by the Belle Époque, despite the subtle embellishments painted on by André Alléhaut, whose activity at Radio-Paris is well known.[31]

The statement is full of nuances, but its political meaning would not escape an alert public: Was it acceptable to celebrate (especially under the baton of an employee of a German enterprise) this "spirit of enjoyment" that had led us into the abyss? But André Alléhaut did not trouble with this subtle criticism: in the same vein, he had just composed a song titled "La Belle Époque," a tearful tune about the lost love of his twenties set to music by Max d'Yresne and published in 1944 by Marcel Labbé's record company. And this was not the only song album: already the previous year, Fortin had published *80 Chansons de la belle époque et d'aujourd'hui.*

Meanwhile, success obliged the "Belle Époque" to make its entry into the Moulin Rouge. The show that debuted in November 1943 offered a series of scenes titled "1900, the belle époque, with the Avila ballet and the Adorables. Always gaiety and good humor. Here the Belle Époque and the Vie Parisienne are relived with the dances of the day and the French cancan." Here our key term appeared on the printed program along with its German translation, *die schöne Epoche.* Thus, in less than four years, the "Belle Époque" had become the best-known motif of the capital's music halls.[32]

Should we be surprised at the emergence and rapid spread in the midst of the Occupation of an expression that bore the whole imaginary composed of *flonflons* and flightiness, insouciance, love, and Gallic bawdiness? Historians of the dark years of the Occupation have long insisted on the rapid resumption of "la vie parisienne," which was perceived as necessary by the entertainment industry and encouraged by the Germans, as well as desired by what remained of *Tout-Paris.* Rare were those who decided to desert theaters and restaurants, as did Maurice de Waleffe: "The city I loved (like Antony loved Cleopatra) died in June 1940."[33] But Maxim's and the Boeuf sur le toit were the opposite of empty, the fashion shows resumed in October 1940, and the theater experienced a period of euphoria: almost 400 plays were put on in Paris during the Occupation.[34] Music halls and revues profited even more from this frenetic context because the Germans guaranteed a faithful audience that was regularly renewed (by troop postings). Maurice Chevalier, Charles Trenet, and Tino Rossi commanded full houses. "Singing is being reborn everywhere in Paris," announced the *Jolis soirs de l'Alhambra* program in September 1943.[35] "From Montmartre to Montparnasse via the Place de la Republic and the Etoile, without forgetting Belleville, which we will cover soon, the music halls and cabarets are flowering. We are the last to complain." At the Paris Casino, Mistinguett triumphed. At the Moulin Rouge, attendance peaked in 1943, with 744,000 spectators, as opposed to barely 400,000 at the end of the 1930s.[36] The phenomenon astonished even the Germans: "In France, we note that some kinds of amusement persist, that a certain way of living still exists that has no relation with the great war," wrote a propaganda official in February 1943.[37] Yet this was their deliberate strategy, especially with respect to the radio. Although Radio-Paris had been set up for propaganda purposes, the instructions had been clear from the start: disassociate political messages from the rest of the programs, develop entertainment broadcasts with the aim of capturing audiences. *Ah! La Belle Époque!* occupied that terrain. In December 1940, a *Propaganda Abteilung* report praised the "efforts of Radio-Paris to give itself a French face."[38]

Among all these songs, favorite tunes from the start of the century were no doubt the most prized. Weren't they "very French" (but not embarrassing), these lyrics speaking of frills and furbelows and set to yesterday's tunes? The "Belle Époque" in question was quite capacious, moreover: the *Revue des trois millions*, premiering on December 3, 1942, at the Folies-Bergère, included a sequence, "Ah, la Belle Époque!" composed of two scenes set earlier in the nineteenth century: "Degas's studio," then a "*garden-party* in Compiègne" during the Second Empire.[39] But most shows made strict use of the "1900" repertoire. More threadbare than ever, they could still fill theaters and *café-concerts* at a time when stars were becoming rare. Their good humor appeared to many as an antidote to the ambient doom and gloom. "In the difficult period we are passing through, the music-hall spectacle is as necessary as the tonic taken after a strenuous day," explained a journalist in 1940, reviewing the program at the Palace. Such justifications recurred throughout the period. "It is an escape!" exclaimed theater critic Georges Preuilly. "So then let us flee for a few moments far from the infernal present."[40] Antidote and escape seemed all the more necessary because they would preserve tradition and social hierarchies, as a journalist for *L'Illustration* stated: "It is fortunate that tradition persists. Without the luxury and pleasure of some, there would be more poverty and sadness for others."[41] Some could also see this as refuge, for the purposes of revitalizing previously abused Frenchness and valorizing the country's symbolic capital. In the postwar purge, singer Charles Trenet would try to pass off "Douce France" (Sweet France) as a resistance song; Léo Marjane tried the same with "J'attendrai" (I will wait). After all, was it not an operetta in the Belle Époque style that Germaine Tillion had written while imprisoned in Ravensbrück?[42]

During the war, the city itself could seem to be plunging again into the old-fashioned atmosphere of the start of the century: automobiles and buses were soon rarer, bicycles increased, and even some horse-drawn carriages appeared, driven by cabmen in cloaks, which rendered to certain Paris streets that manure smell so appreciated by the eldest. The curfew and frequent electricity cuts plunged whole neighborhoods into darkness, so people would get out their old oil lamps, with their warmer and more enveloping light. Structurally, the city had scarcely changed, and apart from a few adjustments, it kept its turn-of-the-century appearance. Of course, some avenues had been extended in the intervening decades, and some portions of the city walls torn down, some corners of the *zone* destroyed, and some insalubrious pockets leveled, like the notorious "*îlot n° 1*" on the Beaubourg plateau. But all that had not affected the nature of the city. The only major urban renewal during the war was the destruction of the south part of the Marais, which had been condemned as insalubrious back in 1920 (*îlot n° 16*) but had been barely touched due to the thorny questions of compensation and rehousing. Profiting from the anti-Semitic persecutions that emptied the traditionally Jewish *quartier* of a large part of its inhabitants, Vichy and the Seine prefecture revived the project in 1941, in a municipal operation of a scope unseen since the urban renovation under Baron Haussmann.[43] With this exception, Paris of the Occupation remained very close to the Paris of 1900.

Mobilizing the "Belle Époque" also enabled offering German soldiers and officers the entertainment they were expecting from the capital. The music hall of 1900 corresponded perfectly to the clichés about France that circulated abroad and might therefore satisfy the voyeurism of the occupying troops as well as the soldiers on leave who made Paris their favorite destination.[44] At the music hall, it was not even necessary to understand French since the revues spoke for themselves; some venues, notably the ABC, were exclusively reserved for the Germans; the Folies-Bergère offered shows in German versions. But this kind of performance also fully accorded with the vision the Nazis had of the country. In the plan for the New European Order elaborated by Hitlerian ideologues, France was to be dedicated to agricultural production and to tourism, to luxury items, to entertainment, leisure, and love—which is exactly what the Belle Époque signified.[45] Goebbels wanted the French to produce lightweight films, empty and (if possible) stupid.[46] Remember that France of the 1900s had also been a France defeated by the Prussians in 1870, a France that had not yet won the Great War and recovered Alsace and the Moselle. Therefore it particularly suited the expectations of the Third Reich, which had insisted, as we saw, on signing the armistice in the same railway car—as if to erase twenty-two years of history.

LIBERATED PARIS, BELLE ÉPOQUE PARIS

IN THESE circumstances, we would expect that liberated France would quickly get rid of such a frame of reference that was so ostensibly linked to the complacencies of the Occupation. "The day after the Paris insurrection," wrote a journalist for *Combat* in December 1944, "Parisian shows appeared old and sunk in a past that was already distant."[1] Actually, another style would emerge; the *zazou* (hepcat) wave had been waiting in the wings and would be embodied by a very different kind of artist: Léo Ferré, Juliette Greco, the Frères Jacques, Catherine Sauvage. This very "Left Bank" style, inseparable from Saint-Germain-des-Prés, would strongly mark post-war Parisian culture. A new "nighttime tribe" flocked to the clubs and cabarets. This mixture of *philosophes*, poets, and jazz musicians—Jean-Paul Sartre, Raymond Queneau, Albert Camus, Jacques Prévert, Simon de Beauvoir, Boris Vian—seemed a thousand leagues away from the "Paris spirit" of the fashion for the Belle Époque that had prospered during the war.

Moreover, many wartime artists had to face the purge committees that got to work at the end of the summer of 1944. The one charged with the "professions of dramatic and lyric artists and of performing musicians" examined the cases of 915 artists who had continued to "celebrate Paris" during the Occupation. Several major figures (like

Charles Trenet, Suzy Solidor, Tino Rossi, and the actress Arletty)
were convicted, sometimes with prison sentences but usually only
with bans on performing for a certain length of time. All the contributors to Radio-Paris (nobody forgot it was a German station) were
also summoned to be heard. While the committee regretted that too
many artists had agreed to work for Radio-Paris, it agreed to prose-
cute only those who had made political or propagandistic statements
on the airwaves.[2] Thus Maurice Chevalier was spared, though he had
earned a lot of money from Radio-Paris, but he benefited from the
support of the Communist Party. André Alléhaut was not so lucky.
Convicted of having worked for Radio-Paris "during the entire Occupation" as producer and adaptor, he had hosted 1,260 broadcasts "for
about 50,000 Reichsmarks, or about a million francs, not to mention
the income from the revues," and he was condemned to a year's
interdiction from all professional activity, beginning on August 10,
1945. The punishment was rather severe; many other station *collabo-*
rateurs (contributors) received merely censure or shorter bans.
Alléhaut contested the sanction, but it was confirmed at the end of
November by the Conseil d'Etat.[3]

Alléhaut's self-defense merits our attention, though, since it illuminates the meaning that some people gave to the "Belle Époque"
spirit and *imaginaire*. Let's remember the torment of the demobbed
soldier in the summer of 1940 trying, like many others, to find a job.
"Pressed by the necessity of finding work, I decided, *reluctantly*, to
follow the suggestion of my former director to accept participating in
radio production at Radio-Paris, which in fact had taken over from
the Poste Parisien were I was working before the war." Once he was
hired by the station, Alléhaut asserted that he had always formally
refused to participate in political or propaganda broadcasts:

> My principal program, *Ah! La Belle Époque!*, should be enough to
> show my tendency. If for real "collaborators" the "belle époque"
> was that of the Occupation itself, for others like me, it could only be
> in the past or in the future. This was the theme that I constantly
> developed (especially in the third couplet of my song "Belle
> Époque"—attached). And by reminding my French listeners that in
> the past they had known happy days, and that these fine days would

come back again, I believe I contributed effectively to supporting their morale during this dark period when they had need of reassurance.[4]

This was the defense strategy used by all the music hall professionals who were under suspicion: they had to continue to work, plus to help the country forget its troubles by "listening to programs of a purely French spirit"—which indeed amounted to a form of resistance.[5] But that argument did not carry the day, and the commission thought that even if Alléhaut had not taken part in political programs, "there is reason to sanction such a long and important collaboration with a German radio station." In March 1947, a broadcasting memorandum still considered him undesirable on French radio. Nevertheless, we find him back on Paris-Inter in 1951 and 1952, then in the "Radio-Alger troupe" in the mid-1950s.[6]

Alléhaut was not the only one to link popular songs to the spirit of Resistance France. "This *fleur de Paris*," sang Maurice Chevalier during the first days of the Liberation, "is the old Paris that is smiling, because it is the flower of return, the return to the fine days." Composed by Maurice Vandair and Henri Bourtayre in 1944, the song became a kind of hymn to recovered freedom. Yet its enthusiasm and good humor closely resemble those songs that a few months earlier had resounded in the cabarets of occupied Paris. In fact, the spirit of the "Belle Époque" did not take long to reacclimatize to the context of the Liberation; often the return to the old days took place in song. The attachment to the "people" manifested by the Communist Party, alongside many other political actors of the Liberation, could not overlook a whole cultural imaginary that was so strongly rooted in the start of the century.[7] Of course, the music hall did suffer discredit at the end of the war, not because of its memories of the Occupation or its obsolete repertoire, but because it was being rivaled by the cinema, which was spurred by the arrival of American films that were being shown in the former *café-concert* venues. Music halls' retreat, though, was neither widespread nor absolute. Some establishments resisted, and the Moulin Rouge was sumptuously reborn in 1951. As regards the songs, they were now carried on the radio and marketed by a flourishing record industry. Even the *froufrous* did not take long to resurge. In 1946, the Catalan poet Fer-ran Canyameres, a Republican who had emigrated to France, devoted a book to his compatriot Joseph Oller, creator of the horse-race betting empire Paris Mutuel, the Moulin Rouge, and the Olympia.[8] There he celebrated "the jovial bonhomie of a slightly disheveled era," "those days that still express the unfulfilled desire for the healthy joy that filled them." For him and many others, the Moulin Rouge continued to embody "one of the universal attractions of Paris."[9] Of course the Paris of fashion and luxury could not forget the time of its past splendor. In 1946, when French designers were seeking to resume the international status that the war had taken away, the tourism commission officially advocated mobilizing the "fashion of the Belle Époque, the happy days of the end of the last century," and it vaunted using "the charming details that testify to our nostalgia for the easy life."[10]

RETURNING TO THE SCREEN

But above all the Belle Époque imaginary now migrated to the cinema, as if the theater stage had become too narrow for it. This phenomenon affected all film genres, starting with drama and "films of historical reconstruction," launching a rather long sequence of "1900" movies. Timidly inaugurated during the war (in 1943) with *Douce* by Claude Autant-Lara (amorous and social crisscrossing among masters and servants at the end of the nineteenth century), this vogue for "costume" dramas exploded after 1945 and peaked in the mid-1950s. I will return later to the nature and traits of a quasi-genre that tried to forget present pain in fantasies about the past, whose immense success is partly explained by the relative decrease in movies with contemporary settings. Most of these films reanimated the "boulevard" (and typically French) tradition that had been prominent in revues and cabarets during the war. The film by Marc Allégret called *Félicie Nanteuil*, about a music hall actress in the 1900s, had in fact been shot in 1942, then blocked by censorship due to the director's joining Free France, but it was finally released in 1945.

However, it was the documentary film (as the genre was transformed in the postwar years) that most contributed to purveying the Belle Époque imaginary. In 1946, the audience could see *Autour de 1890* (Around 1890), a short film by Maurice Théry and Pierre Bauer that dramatized the "end of the nineteenth century, an era of great creative activity but also appearing to us today as easygoing and happy." The film was sprinkled with allusions to the great political and cultural events of the day, but it closed by citing the work of Marie Curie and heralding the dangers of the atomic age. Less somber and more in tune with familiar representations, Jean Gourguet in 1947 directed another short, *La Belle Époque (sur des airs d'autrefois)* (On the tunes of yesterday) as a "cinematographic illustration of the popular refrains of the twenty-five first years of the century." The film could perpetuate the pleasant and picturesque tradition of songs from the start of the century only because everybody seemed to have forgotten the Occupation's use of them. The director even stated that the film was an "amiable and easygoing guide to songs whose words are often full of good sense and truth." In its editing, this documentary associated celebration of popular song with the early cinema, which "had just taken its first steps. . . . Thanks to this quite new invention at the time, we are now able to restore the true face to an era that is so close to us—and already somewhat legendary." The beautiful era in question seems to have blithely survived the Great War and culminated as late as 1925, testifying to the confusion that began to appear between the happy days that preceded and those that followed the Great War. "Life is beautiful, the future is full of promise, people are reconciled with each other and no longer believe in war. It may be wise to stop the memories there, set to yesterday's tunes."

Nicole Védrès's documentary film *Paris 1900*, which came out in February 1947, was quite another thing. Subtitled "An authentic and sensational document on the Belle Époque, 1900–1914," it was the first to link explicitly three competing appellations—Paris 1900, Belle Époque, 1900–1914—and to offer an ample and coherent portrait (see fig. 6). The editing is particularly audacious, even unprecedented: the film assembled 700 fragments of various kinds, taken from Pathé and Gaumont newsreels, from documentary clips, but also from fiction films, all of which it weaves into a unique story that is accompanied by continuous commentary. All the films made in 1900, director Nicole Védrès explained, "resemble each other extraordinarily—to the point that they can be assembled together."[11] It was a team effort. Védrès had begun as a journalist during the war and published a few articles in the women's press and in the *Mercure de France*. She also published two books, one on elegance and the other on the cinema,[12] which already demonstrated an original approach to montage and had attracted the attention of producer Pierre Braunberger. An assistant, Alain Resnais, then aged twenty-three and still a film school student, and a film editor (Yannick Bellon) completed the little team. Long for a documentary at seventy-nine minutes, the film portrays the period more complexly than it appears at first sight. The first hour has a light tone, carried by Claude Dauphin's "delicious" commentary that celebrates in customary fashion the insouciance of a bygone Paris. The stress is on spectacle, entertainment, and curiosities. It is a chronicle of happy hours focusing on the splendors and elegance of high society, the satisfied airs of notables enjoying themselves, and the good humor of the working classes. We also meet some celebrities of the day—scientists, novelists, stars of the theater or the *demi-monde*. The picturesque ambiance is sprinkled with the pleasant tones of gay (sometimes even jolly) music. Even political life is reduced to anecdotes, often ridiculous. But the narration abruptly changes in the last twenty minutes: the pace accelerates; the commentary becomes harsher and even brutal in describing the enduring poverty, the strikes and social conflicts, international tensions and the march to war. Here the shadow of 1947 looms over 1914.

Paris 1900 was astonishing for paradoxical reasons. First of all, it was a very original exercise in writing history through images. The cinematographic innovation was manifest: Nicole Védrès handled the images by delving into lost archives from which she drew clips and intercut sequences, contrasting and drawing parallels in a kind of montage that acts like a grammar. "We sought 1900 in that way," she stated in a television profile in 1964. "The original films were sometimes buried in a rabbit hutch, in a lilac patch. . . . It was like archeology. So we did miss some things."[13] But it does not matter that she or Resnais (in charge of collecting film strips) might have missed some pieces, because the essential thing is how they are assembled. This is why almost from the start *Paris 1900* belonged to the mythology of cinema. As soon as it came out, André Bazin, then a young film critic, made a vibrant homage: "This is pure cinema! Harrowing purity to the point of tears. I owe to Nicole Védrès's film some of the most intense emotions that I have felt in the cinema."[14] What dazzled Bazin was the film's relation with the archive, and hence with time. "Something monstrously beautiful, its appearance overthrows cinema's aesthetic norms as profoundly as the work of Marcel Proust overthrew the novel." However, unlike Proust's work that plunges into (and buries itself in) the meanderings of his personal memories, Védrès's work uses collective images, visible souvenirs, "a memory exterior to our consciousness." In the public projection of these forgotten or lost images she tries to "tame these phantoms." For Bazin this is its prodigious force: "The cinema is a machine for recovering time in order better to lose it. *Paris 1900* marks the birth of the specifically cinematographic Tragedy, that of Time." Thereafter filmmakers became fascinated with cinema archives. For example, part of Chris Marker's oeuvre is inspired by *Paris 1900*, of which a few clips appear in *Level Five* (1996). "I owe everything to Nicole Védrès," Marker wrote in a 1998 program for the French Cinémathèque.[15]

Like any tale about history, *Paris 1900* is a document "with a false bottom"; the intention is to "confront times with each other."[16] Constrained by the images that constitute it, the film is also shaped by the context in which it was made—the second postwar era—which imposed its own views. Both the film's evocation of 1900 joie de vivre as well as its abrupt acknowledgment at the end of social agitation and the conduct of Germans are incomprehensible apart from the moroseness and anxieties that beset the years 1945 and 1946. Nicole Védrès declared: "What have we done except to reconstruct, according to our own vision, a time that was dead and already solidified in its destiny?" But was that era really so solidified? The original cameramen's film stock had indeed grasped (and frozen) a whole series of representations that the film offers up to the viewer: the good old days, the joie de vivre, the frivolity, theatrical entertainment and fun fair amusements, etc. But it also tells us that the early cinema was passionate about "curiosities" and "attractions," that it often "caught on the hop" some funny detail or absurd event. Herein resides one of the limits of a film that relays images as if fascinated by their "truth," without questioning their nature or how they were put together with each other. The result is a "picturesque" effect, which in places transforms *Paris 1900* into a long gallery of clichés supported by an affable commentary.

Nicole Védrès's film was enormously successful, officially selected for the Cannes Festival in 1947, where it won the prestigious Louis Delluc Prize. The next year it was shown at the second Edinburgh Festival and won the 1948 Georges Méliès Prize. Therefore, memories of the 1900s and its imaginary, far from being dismissed after the Occupation, remained at the heart of postwar attention.

THE REVENGE OF THE AVANT-GARDES

Yet it was quite another "Belle Époque" that the Liberation and the immediate postwar period wanted to celebrate: that of painters, artists, and poets of the century's start who had been largely ignored in the 1930s and whom Vichy had deliberately stifled. Liberated Paris offered belated but fulsome recognition to these avant-gardes. Their figurehead was Picasso, who had been vilified by the Vichy regime but who in 1944 became a great figure in France restored. By appointing him head of the Conseil national des arts, the French Resistance wished to mark an absolute break with the Vichy past. Picasso had joined the Communist Party in October 1944 (sponsored by Paul Éluard and Louis Aragon), and he would also preside over the purification committee charged with sanctioning artists who had collaborated with the Occupation. The Salon of autumn 1944, dubbed the "Salon of the Liberation," held at the Grand Palais, exhibited "degenerate" works, including a large Picasso retrospective of seventy-four paintings and five recent sculptures. This was the first time that the Salon's audience could actually see Picasso's canvases, which did not fail to arouse strong reactions and debates.

The postwar era wanted to be resolutely "modern": the first major exhibition presented in Paris after the Liberation (in October 1944) was devoted to the painter Kandinsky, who would die shortly afterward.[17] Neither Picasso's nor Kandinsky's oeuvre could be considered exemplary of a "Belle Époque," which they exceeded in many respects. But the shift signaled by these exhibitions was decisive, for after the upheaval of World War Two, the "historic" avant-gardes, whose foundational works dated from 1905 to 1913, began to benefit from public and institutional recognition. This was the case with the cubists, who had begun to emerge from the shadows at the end of the 1920s thanks to critic and art historian Carl Einstein, but also with most of the artists from the start of the century, whose aesthetic "value" started to make collective sense after 1945.[18] The National Museum of Modern Art was inaugurated in June 1947, yet its return to a supposedly brilliant past that was intended to make the Occupation forgotten was not unanimously supported. Many thought that celebrating the century's start and a "School of Paris" that was now over twenty years old, whose style was "aging" and being increasingly criticized abroad, was "a great leap backward"—which moreover put France farther behind New York.[19]

This postwar revalorization not only occurred in the domain of painting but also involved the long-marginalized surrealist movement, which after the war ceased to be forgotten and discredited. With respect to literature, thanks to the generation of 1945 (especially young editors like Maurice Nadeau, Jean-Jacques Pauvert, and Eric Losfeld) the writings of André Breton, Philippe Soupault, and Paul Éluard (not to mention Raymond Queneau, Antonin Artaud, and Jacques Prévert) could now circulate freely and achieve greater recognition.[20] In addition, the publication of memoirs by actors at the forefront of the literary and artistic worlds was part of this shift. André Salmon, who had been a guest at the Bateau-Lavoir and close to Picasso, Max Jacob, and Apollinaire, began in 1945 to publish his *Souvenirs sans fin* (Endless memories). The same year also saw *L'Homme foudroyé* (The astonished man) by Blaise Cendrars, followed in 1946 by *La Main coupée* (Lice).[21] In 1948, Fernand Gregh, who along with Proust and Halévy had founded the journal *Le Banquet*, titled the first volume of his memoirs *L'Age d'or* (The golden age).[22]

Ideas that had previously been considered difficult or unacceptable suddenly became foundational, which authorized a rewriting of history in which the Belle Époque now appeared pivotal. In music, Pierre Boulez's influence promoted the whole musical inventiveness of the years 1912–1913, including Schonberg's invitation to quit the tonal system and Debussy's and Stravinsky's displacement of formal lines and rhythmic conventions.[23] A music critic who back in 1913 had described the premiere of Stravinsky's *Rite of Spring* had anticipated this chronology: "The composer has jumped the gun and this year offers us the music that we ought to be hearing around 1940."[24] At the same moment, Diaghilev's major rupture was recognized as the foundation of choreographic modernity. A few years later, in 1954, the Diaghilev Exhibition took place at the Edinburgh Festival in the Forbes House Pavilion, especially constructed for the occasion and holding 140,000 visitors.[25]

Such a gap between production and reception is not uncommon, but after the war there was a clear desire for a political break with previous cultural choices, principally those of Vichy. The postwar era invited people to consider the first years of the century, particularly the year 1913, as a matrix, a sort of crucible from which the whole creative modernity of the twentieth century would emerge, and this shift complicated and profoundly changed the reading of the "Belle Époque." Far from evoking the romance, song refrains, or stylistic frills of a pleasant and superficial age, it became instead a key to (even the womb of) aesthetic innovation. This view now predominated, and almost all the later avant-gardes laid claim to it, ranging from art brut to the Cobra movement, then Fluxus and the Situationist International. Outside the realm of culture, the Belle Époque would also appear seductive to many movements of political and social contestation that were searching for origins or historical identity; women, libertarians, and homosexuals would seek (as we shall see) their roots in the extraordinary terrain of the start of the century.

This is why the postwar time was a decisive moment, when the "Belle Époque" became a pathway to a retrospective illusion of a legitimate past proclaimed as necessary to prepare the way to an often unpredictable present. The surrealists, André Breton in the lead, were undoubtedly the most active promoters of such a strategy of justification. There, in the Paris of the Liberation, they invented a past in which the immediate pre–World War One years became the place of origin; they sought in the works of Apollinaire, Duchamp, and Picabia everything that would lead to their own emergence. Breton later commented that "1913 gradually marked the end of a remnant, the shadow that the pyramid of the nineteenth century cast over what the twentieth was starting to build."[26]

Thus the Liberation did not dismiss the "Belle Époque" despite its suspect deference to the Nazi Occupation, but rather made its history more complicated and lifted it to new prestigious heights. In truth, there was a crying need for this phenomenon. It was not only France that emerged wounded from the war, but also the French Republic, whose values had been trampled by Vichy, by the extreme Right, and by collaboration. The return to "Republican legality" that the provisional government proclaimed also assumed symbolic dimensions. In these times of revitalization, it was a particularly strategic choice to mobilize the "Belle Époque" imaginary because it was perceived as that of a past grandeur, the moment of the Republic's apogee—when it was radical, Dreyfusard, parliamentary, anticlerical—and colonialist. The triumphant Republic of 1900 could appear as a major reference point in the morose context of 1945–1948, which was compromised by economic difficulties, shaken by the power of the Communist Party and by the demands of colonized peoples. The peace and prosperity of the Belle Époque seemed reassuring as rationing persisted and a cold war loomed. Reconstruction coincided with retrospection,[27] which appeared all the more necessary for reaffirming the country's international grandeur. Despite the efforts of de Gaulle and his triumphant statements about "national recovery," France had become a secondary power that was more than ever tormented by the "specter of decline."[28] The powerful France of 1900, which had organized around itself a family of European nations, seemed to point to a way of assembling all kinds of goodwill and leaving behind the "era of doubt."[29] De Gaulle's "certain idea of France" was rooted in the first years of the century, fed by Maurice Barrès, Charles Péguy, and the philosophies of national grandeur that blossomed around 1900. Gaullist France would claim its right to play in the court of the great powers simply because it *was*

France.[30] The whole political culture of de Gaulle, born in 1890, was forged in the upheavals of the turn of the century, where all his sentiments originated:

> Nothing affected me more than the evidence of our national successes: popular enthusiasm when the Tsar of Russia passed through, a review at Longchamp, the marvel of the Exhibition, the first flights of our aviators. Nothing saddened me more profoundly than our weaknesses and mistakes, as revealed to my childhood gaze by the way people looked and by things they said: the surrender at Fashoda, the Dreyfus case, social conflicts, religious strife.[31]

Mobilizing the Belle Époque imaginary would prove just as indispensable in reaffirming the role and cultural influence of France as its actual prestige was diminishing in relation to that of the United States. During the war Vichy had arrested refugees, dumped them in internment camps, and delivered to the Nazis innumerable artists and intellectuals who had made France their second homeland, immigrants who had helped radiate other "belles époques" and now suddenly found themselves considered "undesirable foreigners," and later "individuals dangerous for national defense." Thus Vichy had brutally put an end to Paris's international cultural vocation. In 1939 more than five hundred Jewish artists from Central Europe and more than two thousand German intellectuals had been living in Paris.[32] They had come seeking (and finding) political and religious freedom as well as the creative freedom to produce art that was neither directed nor oriented by authorities. "I found in France and in Montparnasse a true paradise. Life was magnificent, carefree, and cheap, and of course we were young," remembered the sculptor Chana Orloff, who had been born in the Ukraine.[33] Many of these artists would meet each other again in one of the two hundred internment camps established by the French government during the war.[34] Many great figures of artistic Paris in the 1930s ended up as "the scum of the earth," in the expression of Arthur Koestler, who was himself imprisoned in the Vernet camp.[35] For all those who managed to flee, New York irrevocably took over as haven,[36] and the number of art galleries there went from 40 in 1941 to 150 in 1946, making the city the new capital of the art market.[37] The few American artists who still made the trip to postwar Paris war could not ignore that times had changed.[38] This was another reason to celebrate an era when Parisian avant-gardes awakened the world's aesthetic consciousness. In all respects, mobilizing the Belle Époque could signify a return to the age of cultural influence, the age of innocence, the age of France.

A LIVELY MID-CENTURY

SYMBOLICALLY OPENED by the 1947 success of the film *Paris 1900*, the time span running from just after the Second World War to the start of the 1960s incontestably marked the apogee of a Belle Époque that had become more complex, of course, but lost none of its "original" or picturesque traits.[1] It was during these years that its portrait—to which a growing number of diverse artists contributed—became enduringly fixed.

"THE MOULIN ROUGE IS REBORN"[2]

The best example of the permanence of a "spirit of 1900" concerns the return to favor of its traditional sites. Maxim's, which had suffered from its image as the favorite restaurant of Nazi officers and dignitaries during the Occupation, recovered its virginity under the leadership of Louis Vaudable, a cultured gastronome who took over the establishment in 1946 and gradually brought back *Tout-Paris*. "Maxim's rediscovers the Belle Époque," proclaimed a fashion magazine in August 1949, inaugurating a lavish period that revived the splendors of 1900. Maxim's became again the elite restaurant where crowned heads, Hollywood stars, and the world's millionaires came to dine. This was the moment chosen by Hugo, who had been Maxim's *maître d'hôtel* from 1899 to 1918, to publish his memoirs; the book contained an extraordinary gallery of portraits—kings, queens, princes, presidents of the Republic, actresses, famous courtesans—and an almost inexhaustible fund of anecdotes. Hugo even inserted his private address book, full of information and often intimate details on many of the women who dined at Maxim's. He begins his book by proclaiming that "the Belle Époque is *à la mode.*"[3]

Still more significant was the reopening in 1951 of the Moulin Rouge. Purchased by George France, the establishment at first went back to its original name, Bal du Moulin Rouge, issuing a luxurious brochure with contributions from some celebrated writers associated with Paris at the start of the century: Francis Carco, Pierre Mac Orlan, Yves Mirande, André Warnod, and others.[4] All of them lengthily evoked "la Belle Époque" and the Moulin of happy days. "It was a good time," wrote Yves Mirande, while Carco mentioned "the sweetness and drunkenness that one felt at living at that time." Most of the contributions insisted on the erotic and sensual dimensions of the place, "a pleasure factory" according to Jean Renoir, where both the old fogeys and unruly young men could come to meet the beautiful women of the day. "I quickly understood why my father and his friends spoke of the Moulin Rouge in low voices and not around their wives," remembered Yves Mirande. In fact, what people mostly came to see were naked women. "Unknown or well known, everybody came to see nudity," remarked songwriter Paul Colline. Others like Mac Orlan insisted more on the figures that congregated there, painters of course (particularly Toulouse-Lautrec) but also ordinary and forgotten people: the dancers and girls without whom nothing was possible, those who lent their flavor to "an era that was neither gentle nor tender, but instead knew how to reach the most desirable limits of social freedom."

What was at stake in reopening the Moulin, though, was not a nostalgic discourse about times past. "Today that era has disappeared. That was yesterday, and the good old days! But why can't it come back, thanks to the Moulin?" It was clearly a matter of resuscitating the spirit of Paris as the century turned. "Nothing has changed between yesterday and today at the Ball of the Moulin Rouge," boasted the program of June 1955, with loads of old images dominated by the canvases and lithographs of Toulouse-Lautrec and Jules Chéret. The new Moulin essentially combined the representations of yesterday and today in the same atmosphere of joy and eroticism. The new décor of the great dining room (by Henri Mahé) paid homage to turn-of-the-century Paris: the gaslights, the Guimard subway pinnacles, the Morris columns to which were affixed posters from 1900, everywhere the frescoes of Toulouse-Lautrec and the effigies of the great names of the Moulin at its beginnings: Bruant, La Goulue, Jane Avril, Yvette Guilbert (recall fig. 2). The new shows offered an obvious continuum—songs, burlesque tableaux, variety acts—that inevitably culminated in a cancan finale; all programs of the 1950s recall how much the La Goulue quadrille was identified with the establishment. "The French cancan was born at the Moulin Rouge . . . and this is where it is happening every evening," we read in the January 1954 program.[5] "Nothing has changed between yesterday and today at the Ball of the Moulin Rouge" (June 1955); "The French cancan is the smile of the Belle Époque, the soul of the Moulin Rouge," an immortal and intoxicating ballet that on the dance floor ensures the link with the spirit of 1900.

This renaissance was an immense success, triggering a veritable frenzy for the "Moulin Rouge" in the 1950s, when it became one of the main symbols of a rediscovered national pride. The newspapers were unanimous: "As during the Belle Époque, joie de vivre spreads under the wings of the Moulin Rouge."[6] Its tour de force, many press critics thought, was to have been able to conserve the décor and splendor of yesterday, the panels that Toulouse-Lautrec had painted for La Goulue's dive, the high reliefs of colored plaster, the posters from the days of the Chat Noir—in short, an atmosphere where "everything recalls the Belle Époque."[7] "If Lautrec came back tomorrow, he would not feel out of place in his new venue," wrote a reporter (recall fig. 1).[8] Tableaux and ballets did attempt to introduce a dose of "modernism"—especially through booking current stars like the Belgian dancer Annie Cordy—while remaining faithful "to tradition" and the "extraordinary ambiance of the Belle Époque."[9]

And its fame outstripped the world of the music hall. In 1949, the Society for the History and Archeology of Old Montmartre had the Moulin Rouge site registered on the Ministry of Fine Arts' list of "natural and legendary" monuments. The same year, producer Gilles Margaritis launched on Radiodiffusion-Télévision Française (RTF) a television show broadcast every other Wednesday evening titled *Music Hall Parade*. In addition, books about the cabaret world offered detailed portraits of the main songwriters of Montmartre;[10] a first historiography of the music hall also appeared in their wake. Journalists and chroniclers, but also former figures in that milieu (artists and producers) published illustrated books—twenty-some in French in the 1950s—that were half nostalgic, half historical, but above all trying to place this genre within the country's cultural patrimony,[11] assisted by a vinyl record industry in full flight. As confirmed by the immense success of Edith Piaf, who partly revived the "realistic" tradition, many compilations covered the great songs of 1900: "Reviens" (Come back), "Fascination," "La Valse brune" (The brown waltz), "Frou-Frou." In 1954, *Tino Rossi Sings the Belle Époque* was followed by Mathé Altéry's *Treize mélodies de la Belle Époque* (1957). Dozens of famous orchestras, like those of Philippe-Gérard, Jacques Metehen, and Franck Aussman, recorded song samplers. The phrase "Belle Époque" always figured in the album title.

This great vogue for the Moulin Rouge also passed through the cinema and television, which at the time were the most effective vectors of legitimation. In 1952, the American director John Huston adapted a romanticized biography published the year before by Pierre la Mure,[12] shooting a *Moulin Rouge* that was almost totally devoted to the figure of Toulouse-Lautrec. One year later, Gilles Margaritis presented on television a long *Toulouse-Lautrec au Moulin Rouge*, a reconstruction of the painter's life, with scenes shot amid the establishment's new décor. Jean Renoir's *French Cancan* reached the screen in 1955, though it had other intentions, including the director's desire to come back to French subjects after a long stay abroad (see fig. 7). "*French Cancan* corresponded to my major desire to make a film in a very French spirit that would be an easy and agreeable bridge between myself and the French audience," he explained a year later.[13] Other such films followed, like *Une nuit au Moulin Rouge* by Jean-Claude Roy in 1957, a rather light musical comedy propelled by Francis Lopez's score, and *Can-Can* by Walter Lang in 1960, a Montmartrean-American fantasy in which Frank Sinatra, Shirley MacLaine, and Maurice Chevalier revisit the history of the Bal du Paradis to twenties music by Cole Porter. The Moulin Rouge, like Paris itself, was transfigured, a sign of the growing prestige of both.

A WAVE OF MEMOIRS

Figures from 1900 publishing autobiographies were not a novelty, and we saw that some appeared just after the Great War and the first nostalgic wave was perceptible in the 1930s, but after 1945 the flood-gates opened. From then until 1960, more than twenty-five accounts issued from the pens of writers or celebrities who had "experienced 1900." These thousands of nostalgic pages erected a major portion of the new Belle Époque imaginary and fixed how it was represented. The ages of the authors explain this profusion (having known the period presupposed being born in the decade of the 1890s or earlier), but we also have to consider editorial and commissioning strategies. Most publishers wanted to profit from this successful trend.

The authors were mostly famous figures (the time had not yet come for the memoirs of anonymous people) who possessed wide enough cultural or social notoriety. Among them were the Belle Époque's principal "icons": André de Fouquières, Cléo de Mérode, André War-nod, Maurice Chevalier, Maurice Donnay, Roland Dorgelès, André Billy, Francis Carco. Almost all were personalities of the "*vie parisienne*"—artists, writers, journalists, socialites, aristocrats, or simply livers of the "high life." This over-representation of Paris, the salons, and its cultural milieux was a major trait that lastingly marked the era's imaginary and strengthened the impression of a period dominated by the easy life, entertainment, and the arts. Rare were books that mentioned public events, whose echoes resounded only faintly. Reading these thousands of pages, life at the time seems to have been split between two social universes: on one side, Bohe-mia and the literary and artistic youth of Montmartre and the Latin Quarter, and on the other the *Tout-Paris* of entertainment and high society. These two societies were sometimes linked within the demi-monde. From the mix, a fabulous tableau emerges that turns the start of the century into a beacon in the nation's cultural life—and is marked by a few singular characteristics.

The first emanates from the former literary and artistic youthful generation and expresses a bitter nostalgia engendered by the transformations in Paris. This motif had been incubating since 1930 but was exacerbated after the war. The disappearance of Montmartre was especially deplored. "The Late Montmartre!" Léon-Paul Fargue had noted in 1939, but now everybody observed that "this villagelike and rustic Paris, where one goes about on foot among gardens and orchards, wastelands and rubble" had totally vanished.[14] Along with it were effaced the few emblematic sites that had been celebrated in stories about past glories. First came the Bateau-Lavoir (the "floating wash house"), the enclave of artists and writers on the Rue Ravignan where Apollinaire, Picasso, Van Dongen, Max Jacob, and many others lived, and where the Rousseau Banquet took place in 1908. Today, Warnod mourned, it is "just a ruin, a phantom ship."[15] Then there was the Lapin Agile, the "village inn" according to André Salmon, hosted in its glory days by Frédéric Gérard and his donkey, Lolo, a place you could meet ("without getting involved with")[16] thugs and whores. And then the narrow streets, dead ends, boutiques, and brothels, not to mention Mimi Pinson's house at 12 Rue Cortot, where Dufy and Utrillo (the son of Suzanne Valadon) lived. That quartier no longer existed, every author groaned. Long preserved by its situation on a steep hill (carriages objected to climbing it because of the risk of killing their horses),[17] it had been disfigured by the "taxis-autos" that each day unloaded floods of tourists. It had become a Montmartre of nightclubs, a World's Fair attraction, a sort of Mont Saint-Michel for provincials coming up to the capital.[18] The streets, the buildings, the "old clubs are still in the same place—the Abbaye, the Zellis, Lajunie, the Capitole with Weilluc's frescoes, the Royal, the Pigalle, the Dead Rat, the Monico, El Garron—but it is the audience that has changed."[19] This terrible nostalgia could not even be comforted by the fading with time or actual disappearance of beloved places, but had to confront deterioration and the irreversibility of time.

Less prized than Montmartre, the Latin Quarter was valued for its literary sociability, for its cafés that had welcomed art periodical teams and hosted writers' banquets: Café Vachette, where Jean Moréas reigned; the Lorraine Tavern; the Closerie des Lilas, frequented by Jarry and the editorial committee of the *Mercure de France*. One went to cafés to meet a personage passing through town, to gather with friends, to place an article or a drawing. Le Festin d'Esope (Aesop's Feast), founded by Apollinaire and Salmon, held its meetings in a *brasserie* on Rue Christine, then at 244 Rue Saint-Jacques, at Salmon's home. *La Plume* held a weekly soirée in the vault of the Soleil d'Or: "That vault? It was the unfinished basement of a bistro on the Boulevard Saint-Michel, at the corner of the quay of the same name."[20]

So this was the Left Bank of poets, the one preferred by André Billy (who did not like Montmartre). But the two locations were linked because in fact the city extended from "Montmartre to the Latin Quarter," as Francis Carco perceived as he crisscrossed Paris. "A habit since my first Parisian winter, I have never stopped walking back and forth between the Latin Quarter (or Montparnasse) and the Butte," remembered André Salmon. "Before being offered to travelers, the north-south subway line was in my shoes."[21] One traversed the city from the Lapin to the Closerie, sometimes from the Bastille to Belleville. All these autobiographers were pedestrians of Paris, like Léon-Paul Fargue, who especially appreciated nighttime promenades. All of them were *"flâneurs* of both banks," to use the title of Apollinaire's volume that appeared in the year of his death (1918). Taking this route, one made stops along the boulevard, which "at the time, no longer had its past grandeur, of course, but was still *the* Boulevard, and not the gaudy caravan that it has become."[22] You could still find a few good establishments, like the Napolitain on the boulevard des Capucines that was frequented by Catulle Mendès, Jean Moréas, André Salmon, and André Billy. The newspaper offices were located there, and many journalists stopped by to submit copy. Roland Dorgelès was for a while a columnist at the *Journal*; Warnod had each day edited the arts and letters mail at *Comoedia* and knew all the nooks.

But the buried city was often merely a pretext: actually, people were seeking lost friendships and love affairs, the familiar figures that peopled their youth. "I started *Bouquet de Bohème*," explained Dorgelès, "in order to find what had become (apart from the war bloodbath) of the eighty guys—painters, writers, actors, designers or daubers—I was speaking about."[23] Nostalgic promenades in a vanished city were quickly transformed into a search for phantoms. Warnod depicts in *Ceux de la Butte* the motley population of Montmartre that he encountered upon his arrival so many years before. There is no end to the portraits of artists, poets, writers, the companions of his youth: Juan Gris, Van Dongen, Picasso, Jacques Vaillant, André Salmon, Max Jacob, Mac Orlan, Braque, Derain, Vlaminck, Matisse. Such galleries did render homage to the departed, of course, but they also lent grandeur to those who could boast such friendships. Some memories even nourished rancor and incited the narrator to reject the present time. Journalism had changed too. "We have become employees and functionaries," André Billy complained. "Journalism has been debased in the reader's mind, has lost its prestige."[24] Behind the worship of vanished friends and a vanished era, there sometimes appeared bitterness, an incomprehension of the present, the sour reaction of someone who has grown old. "It's so fine to be pure, candid, almost virginal, a virgin of letters, with all which that includes, and especially what it used to include, which at that time embraced enthusiasm and generosity," wrote André Salmon.[25]

Indeed, lost youth—hence nonchalance, lightness, love, and the sweetness of life—shines through each page. "We were all very young at the time depicted in this book," wrote Max Aghion, who before the war edited the arts section of *Petit Parisien*.[26] André Warnod had arrived in Montmartre in 1902, at age seventeen, with the firm intention of becoming a painter.[27] "I miss my lost youth," André de Fouquières frankly admitted.[28] Everybody recalled that time with all the more regret because it seemed to have vanished forever. Dorgelès, who "thought only about love and girls," evokes his flirtations and affairs, and the bachelor pad he rented to receive a married woman. Oh, to have fun, as only twenty-somethings can have fun! And along comes the oft-retailed story of a little-known futurist painting—*Et le soleil s'endormit sur l'Adriatique* (Sun setting over the Adriatic)—by a so-called Italian painter named Joachim-Raphael Boronali, exhibited at the Salon des Indépendants, but which was actually produced by Père Frédé's donkey's tail, to which somebody had attached a brush! Just like their amorous conquests, this hoax sent these aging artists back to the lost Paris of their youth, which miraculously dons the panoply of nonchalance, joie de vivre, and creative energy.

Meanwhile, aristocrats and socialites also fed this wave of autobiography, but they gave Paris only a cursory look. They acknowledged a loss that was much more serious: a whole class, a whole society, "a world" that had been excluded from the nation and was on its way to being drowned. They thought they had to save its memory. A key figure in these aristocratic circles, close to the Duke d'Orléans (the pretender to the throne) and the principal hosts of 1900 social gatherings, André de Fouquières was the person who best expressed the feeling of shipwreck and the urgency of finding a lifeline. He blamed the Republic, which had excluded from the nation both the Church and the Aristocracy; the Great War had done the rest. At its close, he explained, good society "had sunk, body and soul."[29] Now the tracks of its "erased footsteps," in the words of the other "prince of 1900" (Robert de Montesquiou),[30] had to be followed in order to restore meaning and dignity to such forgotten words as "prestige, élite, tradition, courtesy."[31] In his view, the rise of salons that so marked the start of the century compensated for the lack of prestige of a country degraded by a vulgar regime. But yet the current wave trying to resuscitate the golden age of the 1900s was content, according to de Fouquières, to give "the major credit to the artists—actresses and actors especially—to sporting stars, *dames galantes*, politicians. But in fact high society had played a considerable role—which seems to be forgotten—and I am going to sketch a few aspects of that life."[32]

Thus Montesquiou devotes his own memoirs to recording the high points of the Belle Époque salons. An unprecedented map of Paris emerges that leaves aside the boulevards and fashionable places to explore the palatial residences: the homes of Madame de Loynes, the Duchess d'Uzès, the Vicountess of Trédern, the Countess Fitz-James, and the dozen other *grandes salonnières* who were the cynosures of high society at the time. A very different gallery of portraits emerges, competing with that of Bohemia, where the leading figures have titles: the Prince de Sagan, Prince de Polignac, the Countess de Luynes, Countess Greffulhe, Marquise Casati, and of course Boni de Castellane. Serving up anecdotes about "a society concerned to maintain itself at the summits of its ancestral traditions,"[33] de Fouquières also recalls his close relations with Belle Époque modernity as he covers art and literature, but also automobiles and aeronautics.

Other memoirs were less partisan but still expressed the same desire to safeguard a threatened world. Pauline de Broglie, Countess de Pange, whose memoirs appeared slightly later, made herself the chronicler for the young of what "la Belle Époque" had been.[34] Her more personal story, *Comment j'ai vu 1900* (see fig. 8), recounts a way of life marked by rituals—entry into society, marriage, family, and social events. She insists on the importance of lineages, of heritage and the values transmitted from generation to generation.[35] But the cult of ancestors in her case assumes a particular aspect. A descendant of Madame de Staël, Pauline de Pange had devoted much of her life to promoting the political and literary oeuvre of her illustrious great-grandmother.[36] Nevertheless, just like those of other memoir writers of the time, her story celebrates a singular period. The weight of conventions and traditions could not preclude the search for novelty: the spread of sea bathing, the discovery of the bicycle (riding which was practiced only within the chateau's park but still constituted a major freedom), the importance of modern art—painting, art objects, furniture, interior decoration—which connects the countess's tale to all those communing in a celebration of happiness and cultural innovation.

Sometimes an author was trying to defend the honor of a reputation or a whole class. Much of Cléo de Mérode's memoir (*The Dance of My Life*) aimed to justify her name—she was born Cléopâtre Diane de Mérode and came from the Austrian branch of a family of the old Belgian nobility—and of course her virtue. As one of the grand figures of the 1900 *demi-monde*, the eighty-year-old lady recounts the "dance of her life" in 1955, intending to challenge "the fable" of her intimate liaison with King Léopold of Belgium and her "false reputation as a royal favorite," which was undoubtedly one of the most persistent rumors of the period.[37] Now everybody in society (or from well-born milieux) keenly defends the honor of the beautiful and wise Cléo, shamefully associated at the time with the world of courtesans, whereas, as André de Fouquières notes ironically, "she never set foot in Maxim's, never was the subject of scandalous gossip, and never belonged to the world of pleasure."[38] Despite the scandalous nude sculpture done of her and the malicious rumors about her love life, "the charming but peaceful Cléo de Mérode" was merely a victim of her beauty and her talent, as Maurice de Waleffe explains, while claiming he helped her write her memoir.[39]

But memoirs of the *grand monde* of the 1900s were not confined to such self-defenses or to illustrating a class under threat, but also recounted the "happy, brilliant, and elegant hours of French life," principally "high-society doings."[40] Like the memoir of Maurice de Waleffe, director of *Paris-Midi*, titled *Quand Paris était un paradis*, most also included "men of letters and women of the theater";[41] the cultural life of these "heroic" times occupied an important place in their stories. For example, the main interest of Georges de Lauris's *Souvenirs d'une belle époque* is that he knew Proust and Reynaldo Hahn and attended the Ballets Russes.[42] Whether at the theater, in a society gathering, or at some aristocratic salon, readers could vicariously run across Paul Bourget and Marcel Prévost, Maeterlinck and Georgette Leblanc, Boldini and Capiello, Feydeau, D'Annunzio, and Tristan Bernard. They could also encounter more popular figures like Max Linder, Saint-Granier, Abel Faivre, and even the lovely Otéro. The theater was dominated by playwrights Edmond Rostand and Sacha Guitry, but also by actresses like Réjane and Sarah Bernhardt. Theater remained the queen of entertainment, and the fervor of audiences often blurred lines of class and social distinction. In fact, a more mixed social fraction rushed to opening nights and chic dinners. "This *boulevardier* Paris, despite the first Universal Expositions, remained an exclusive world, where everybody knew everybody else by sight," explained de Waleffe.[43] This happy little world, gripped by the "fever to shine that the resplendent 1900 Exposition had lit at all levels of society,"[44] fed on anecdotes about fashionable authors, on witticisms and flashes of humor. *Trente ans de dîners en ville* (Thirty years of chic dinners) by Gabriel-Louis Pringué has little value except for the indiscretions he reports.[45] The publication in 1951 of Maurice Donnay's diary—*J'ai connu 1900*[46]—divulges the real motives behind elections to the Académie Française, testifying to the enduring taste for this type of social nicety. Even when recounting the worst insinuations, the tone always remains very seemly. Sexuality may seep through every page, but it is draped in allusion or double entendre. The same is true of reminiscences about the world of gallantry and courtesans. As we have seen, Cléo de Mérode denied that she had ever been part of it, mentioning in a very modest fashion the *coup de foudre* (love at first sight) she felt for her "fiancé." Even among the actual courtesans like Liane de Pougy, the story remains quite sober: she stresses her marriage to Prince Ghika, which after 1910 opened the doors of proper society to her. Only designer Paul Poiret unreservedly mentions his hotel rendezvous with his mistress, an American singer. And the lesbianism in the memoirs of Natalie Clifford Barney involves only a very singular case on the margins of society, despite her long relationship with the Duchess de Clermont-Tonnerre.

Narratives from both Bohemia and high society do converge, however, on one decisive point: they all celebrate a happy and incomparable era—an era almost incapable of being equaled. "God, but Paris seemed happy to be alive!" wrote Maurice Chevalier.[47] Together, these two quite distinct worlds required the representation of an era based on pleasure and insouciance as its horizon, and on art and culture as its very principle. Life at the time appeared full of celebrities or young people with promising talent who aspired only to realize that talent. Everywhere appeared theaters, cafés, entertainment, encounters—sometimes there were also duels that were rarely tragic. Most of all, life was full of brilliant people, who knew how to entertain friends with savory anecdotes and witticisms that continued to make people laugh long afterward. "Ah, the beautiful and astounding years!" de Fouquières exclaimed.[48] Reading these pages so full of energy, life, and panache, how could anyone doubt that Paris had been a "paradise"? It had been the good old days full of contentment and joyous living—the *belle époque*. "People call it 'La Belle Époque,'" marveled Cléo de Mérode. "Ah yes, it was a *belle époque*! An extraordinary epoch! Has one ever lived through such a powerful germination of ideas, such effervescence of creation, as at the end of the nineteenth century? Not only was science making some discovery every day and progress advancing swiftly in all directions, but there was in thought and in art a rise in generous impulses, a mixing together of currents, to which nobody could remain indifferent."[49] On top of this intensity in artistic and cultural life lay what Stefan Zweig called the "Golden Age of Security."[50] For 1950s men and women who had lived through the horror of two world wars and who were witnessing an accumulation of postwar threats, that was a notable blessing. Cléo de Mérode went on: "We were not living in perpetual uncertainty; the immediate horizon was not portending storms; we did not feel the weight on our shoulders of dangers that were impossible to predict. We could make plans, smile at tomorrow. We could let ourselves *live*."[51]

Above all, everyone asserts that this beautiful life, far from being reserved only to the social élites, was in fact widely shared. Each citizen partook of his or her own pleasures, which according to tastes might be more or less "distinguished," but peace, prosperity, and good humor also reigned among the popular classes. "The good life existed in Paris in the years preceding the 1914 war!" André Warnod summed up. "A desire for amusement animated all classes of society. Popular festivals like the Carnival or Mid-Lent brought all of Belleville and Ménilmontant down to celebrate on the Boulevard."[52] And if life was more difficult for some, the "general impression was of abundance and gaiety."[53] The good time, the *belle époque*—this is the message emanating from all these reminiscences in which the writer traces (sometimes rather vaguely) what had been the "*belle époque* of his (or her) life."

"PERIOD" CINEMA

Meanwhile, this unparalleled era that was supposedly the apogee of French culture and lifestyle was being disseminated in an unprecedented media wave. Cinema had long been the great popular medium, but now had also become the principal purveyor of social imaginaries. It seized upon the Belle Époque (making it almost a genre unto itself) and quickly earned the favor of an immense audience. The phenomenon was so massive that it intrigued both film professionals and observers. Even abroad there was astonishment: What was the meaning of this *Nostalgia per la Belle Époque?*" wondered an Italian critic in a special magazine issue on the subject.[54]

Others compared it to the vogue for the "Viennese film," particularly the Sissi cycle being made at the same time and starring Romi Schneider.

But the Belle Époque film was a distinctly French genre whose popularity had begun a little earlier, at the end of the war, as we saw, with the success of Nicole Védrès's film *Paris 1900*. From 1945 to the end of the 1950s, more than sixty French films in the "1900 spirit" came to the screens. This is an impressive number, given the average annual film production of one hundred. Therefore about 5 percent of national production was devoted to the "Belle Époque"! Some of these films were made by prestigious or solidly established directors (Jean Renoir, Max Ophuls, René Clair, Claude Autant-Lara, Henri Diamant-Berger, Sacha Guitry), while others were the work of younger *auteurs* who were asserting themselves as the talents of tomorrow (Jacques Becker, André Cayatte, Henri-Georges Clouzot, Jacqueline Audry, Georges Franju), and still others were made by more commercial filmmakers with wide audience appeal (Marcel Aboulker, Gilles Granger, Carlo Rim, André Berthomieu, Augusto Genina).[55] The whole spectrum of French cinema seemed devoted to this new genre.

These films were not all alike, of course, and were made with very different intentions. But all of them offered the audience a reconstruction "in costume" that depicted a "historic" era that is clearly identifiable. Set designs were reliably full of bourgeois interiors in heavy tones and with inimitable wallpaper, decorated with gewgaws, doilies, carafes, and squat armchairs; the sets were stuffed with 1900 artifacts: newspapers, posters, almanacs, theater programs. And the costumes were carefully accurate. Reviews were unanimous in praising meticulous efforts at reconstruction: "Jacqueline Audry has done careful work, choosing all the details able to re-create the Belle Époque atmosphere," explained a journalist reviewing *Minne l'ingénue libertine*.[56] "To furnish the Bonnadieu house," in Carlo Rim's film of the same name in 1951, whose plot unfolds in a corset-making workshop, "they went to antique dealers and the flea markets, and they even borrowed from private collections."[57]

While the décor was impeccable, many of these films merely adapted (and rather loosely at that) the great repertoire of 1900 boulevard drama and vaudeville. Playwrights Feydeau and Courteline got the lion's share of this treatment (*Monsieur chasse, La Dame de chez Maxim's, Un fil à la patte, Le Dindon, Occupe-toi d'Amélie, MM. les rond-de-cuir, La Paix chez soi,* etc.), but filmmakers also drew on Meilhac and Halévy, Flers and Cavaillet, and even Berton and Simon, the creators of *Zaza.* The immense stock of stories and novels from the turn of the century was also put to use: Maupassant, Colette, Mirbeau, Mary, Leroux, and Leblanc were all very much in fashion (the adventures of Arsène Lupin were constantly remade) and purveyed the typically French spirit of boulevard theater. These films also repeatedly met salvoes of abuse from cinephile milieux. "Nonexistent scenarios, traveling salesmen jokes, unbearable singers and comic actors, the rapid half-undressing of a starlet or an obscure star: these are the usual ingredients (we are not saying 'spices') for a film genre that maintains the tradition of healthy French gaiety," wrote a journalist in *Positif.*[58] "The era of 1900—its languorous waltzes, its carriages, its odor of manure, its elegant women strangled by their corsets and sipping adulterous port behind their veils has never ceased to fascinate the studio bosses," noted a more indulgent critic at the *Express* in 1954.[59] But this profusion of films also had its defenders, who liked their "popular" nature, thought them "well mannered," and relished their "atmosphere of Belle Époque, 1914."[60]

Their scenarios and plots were obviously quite conventional. All (or almost) were set in Paris, of course; the countryside is absent, apart from a few scenes of picnicking or bucolic retreat. But the provinces appear only incidentally, except for the Normandy town of Renoir's *Diary of a Chambermaid* or the garrison town where René Clair's *Les Grandes manoeuvres* takes place (but the heroine is a Parisienne and a divorcée, whose arrival unleashes the plot). And while the action sometimes begins in the provinces, as in *Miquette et sa mère,* the protagonists quickly "come up" to the capital, where social advancement is possible. Therefore the city is almost always Paris. The New York venture in Richard Pottier's film *La Belle Otéro* merely extended Otéro's Parisian triumph. And the Vienna used by Max Ophuls in *La Ronde* and by Pierre Gaspard-Huit in *Christine* was just the "other capital" of the Belle Époque. Moreover, one could almost believe Vienna was Paris: "Insignificant and profound, this eternal story that takes place in Vienna in 1900 might have occurred, with almost the same décor and language, in Paris in 1900."[61]

Paris rules at the heart of all these films, and a Paris that seems immutable. "Here is Paris at the start of the century, our own of course. Despite appearances, nothing has changed," begins *Scènes de ménage* by André Berthomieu. Just as with stories set in Montmartre, this still-rural city has human dimensions and has managed to conserve its gardens and its *guinguettes* (open-air bars for dancing) on the banks of the Marne River with their tables under the arbors. In this respect, the opening shots of *Casque d'or* (Golden helmet) by Becker are exemplary; although a Parisian film, it starts with a boating party along the Marne. "Montmartre is a true village. Waking up in the morning, you would think you were in the country," declares the hero of *Maxime* by Henri Verneuil. Parisian life revolves essentially around theaters, chic restaurants like Maxim's, and popular festivals and dances. It exudes nonchalance, lightness, and leisure, explains the voice-over accompanying the archive images that open *Scènes de ménage*: "1910. Belle Époque, as we like to say today, with its popular entertainments, its mid-Lent parade, its sumptuous and droll floats, and its blooming Queen of queens. All the symbols of the Republic's carefree life."

Of course in this ideal city we find good society and the customary frivolity of worldly idlers. Film critic Jacques Sadoul summarizes the framework of *Madame de . . .* by Max Ophuls: "It is the 'Belle Époque' of salons, of society gatherings where the most beautiful women of Paris shine. There wit and beauty reign. We are dealing with extremely elegant characters whose rhythm of life seems set to waltz time."[62] Here the expression "Belle Époque" encapsulates all three: a place, a time, a society. This is a Paris abounding in kings (*Zaza*), princes (*French Cancan*), barons (*Minne*), princesses (*Elena*), counts (*L'Ecole des cocottes*), viscounts (*C'est la vie parisienne*), and marquis (*Miquette et sa mère*). In comparison, the working classes do not count for much. Moreover, they are not *really* workers, except for servants, obviously; this sociology embraces a few carriage drivers, laundresses, soldiers, and officials. The better-off within these milieux belong to the delinquent margins (*Casque d'or*), especially the prostitutes and courtesans of the *demi-monde,* which serves as an interface with the *monde,* the true one. These women bring an orgy of jewels, umbrellas, muffs, long-sleeved gloves, and cigarette holders to the joyous world of parties and late-night suppers. Characters based on historical persons remain absent, and only Émile Zola, Marie Curie, Georges Méliès, and Albert Schweitzer make appearances on the screen. "Historical" plots or perspectives are very rare, apart from vague mentions of international tensions and machinations. Some *auteurs* like Guitry briefly mention the Dreyfus affair; Renoir makes use of the Boulanger episode in *Elena,* but he spices it up with a love story that tends to warp it. Nor is religion present, except for the life of Sainte Thérèse in *Procès au Vatican*; nor does the colonial empire appear, except in *Albert Schweitzer* and a quick mention of Algeria in *Zaza.* In the late 1950s, when France was being swept out of Indochina and getting embroiled in the war in Algeria and in an illusory French Union, such ellipses were meaningful. Don't bother seeking in the "Belle Époque" for memories of a more "heroic" colonial past. The aim seems to be to get rid of any sensitive issue that might lend itself to a political reading in order to sustain an entertaining *mise-en-scène* focused on popular, artistic, and social nonchalance. "It is merely *boulevard*, nothing but what is charming, lightweight, frivolous, and old-fashioned," sniffed a critic in the satiric *Le Canard enchaîné* in May 1955. Its artificial ambiance derives from paper lanterns on the boulevards, hansom cabs and horse-drawn carriages heading for the Bois de Boulogne, and popular songs. Georges-Eugène Van Parys, a veteran of light songs and film music, composed "Ballad of the Butte" for *French Cancan* and "Ballad of Infidels" for *La Maison Bonnadieu*. The recently reopened Moulin Rouge remained the best symbol of this imaginary, replete with both a flashy lifestyle and an old-fashioned elegance, where a stately uniform was sufficient to turn the heads of young girls wanting to find a husband. The wit of audeville and gallantry fed the retrospective illusion.[63] France in the war crisis of 1955 revitalized itself as best it could from this abundance of past pleasures, which nothing indicated could possibly return.

Hence the virulent criticism coming from political, intellectual, or cinephile milieux—the effervescence of "young Turks" associated with the Nouvelle Vague (New Wave)—against these "worn-out movies" as merely facile and commercial productions. "Why, we repeat, does the French cinema stray into a past that does not even have the merit of being old and that offers only a few frills and quite conventional songs?" wondered one critic.[64] Jean-Louis Bory was more severe: "We will never get free of it. But out of indigestion, new filmmakers will manage to take this exasperating and pleasant era, this fin-de-siècle that was hastily imagined and remembered (badly) as frivolous, and turn it into something ponderous."[65] Nor were the Communist militants more indulgent: "Perhaps this interests only dowagers of the old nobility who have remained sentimental. That it could captivate a metalworker from Billancourt or a farmer from Rouergue is very improbable."[66] Only Renoir, widely considered as the *boss*,[67] could escape the most acerbic criticism, though *French Cancan* was not unanimously praised: *Positif* decided it was "a commercial film . . . entertainment without any other ambition."[68]

However, even within this "insipid" and simplistic type of production, there were certain innovations and critical perspectives. Many such films centered on female characters and their fates, which testifies to a certain sensitivity that could offer "feminist" motifs: misalliances and amorous passions that fostered social diversity; cuckolded husbands, extramarital relations, and impossible love affairs that broke certainties and norms.[69] A few lesbian scenes peppered *Olivia*, whose action takes place in a girls' boarding school, and *Chéri* (from Colette's novel about an affair between a boy and an older woman) obviously had "transgressive" aspects. Among the directors there was only one female, Jacqueline Audry (close to Simone de Beauvoir through her sister, who wrote the scenario for *Olivia*), who made six films during this period in which several aspects reflect the context of women's emancipation in the 1950s, which culminated in the publication of Beauvoir's *Second Sex* in 1959.

Meanwhile, "politically engaged" *cinéaste* Jean Renoir was often criticized for having given this up in the three "Belle Époque" films he directed at the time: *Diary of a Chambermaid* in 1946, *French Cancan* in 1955, *Elena and Her Men* in 1956. They were brilliant productions, perhaps, but facile and without political impact. Yet the "Belle Époque" they dramatized was indeed full of strong tensions between a rose-colored vision (the time of pleasure, love, and joie de vivre, where divisions are euphemized and aestheticized) and a much darker version that included nationalism, anti-Semitism, and class struggle.[70] What Renoir filmed in *Diary of a Chambermaid* was the revolt of Célestine against any form of domination, both by the despised bourgeoisie and by men, as embodied in the different characters Father Lalaine, Mauger, and François. And if she does accept aid from the latter—assassin, nationalist, and anti-Semite that he is—it is in order to give more lifeblood to the Republican crowd united in the festive ambiance of a Quatorze Juillet. It would have been difficult for a director at the time to challenge more strongly the values of Vichy France. *French Cancan* offers a Belle Époque imaginary that is more conventional: Montmartre, the *café-concert*, the Gay Paree of flounces, the cultural industries (see fig. 7). But the film also pays homage to popular culture and lifestyles, to the sensual pleasures of daily life. Some critics at the time were sensitive to "this mixture of nostalgia for the past and joie de vivre that bears the stamp of Jean Renoir."[71] His attitude was more equivocal in *Elena and Her Men,* which revisited the Boulanger Affair from the angle of vaudeville, and wanted to demonstrate that a country where love plays such a great role will be immunized against dictatorship. More than offering a political message, Renoir was trying to reach beyond historical reconstruction in order to attain (via pictorial aestheticism and vaudeville outrageousness) a form of cinematographic purity. "I believe that if one day we reach a kind of *commedia dell'arte* style in the cinema, the period to choose, the only period, the period that would allow us to abandon our concern with exterior truth—the right period to choose is precisely the 1900 period. I see all films taking place in 1900 like that," Renoir explained a few years later.[72]

Among these period productions, the only truly transgressive film remains Jacques Becker's *Casque d'or*, made in 1952 (see fig. 9). The story refers to one of the most flamboyant mythologies of the Belle Époque, about bands of *apaches* (thugs) and Homeric struggles for the beautiful eyes and golden hair of a sidewalk princess (played by Simone Signoret). Everybody in France knows this story: the battle in 1902 between two gang leaders for the possession of an attractive prostitute. Duvivier had wanted to film the tale before the war, then

Clouzot and Allégret just afterward. Becker, who had been the pre-war assistant to Renoir, had shown he was sensitive to the glamorous and almost folkloric dimensions of tabloid news items. "What seduced me about *Casque d'or* was a certain pictorial aspect. I wanted to put into it the equivalent of old images in the style of the *Petit Journal illustré* of our childhood," he explained in 1952.[73] The film might seem akin to those conventional Belle Époque productions, sentimental and picturesque—for which some critics in fact reproached it. Nevertheless, the shifts made by Becker lead the film away from this expected path: the costumes of the criminals come more from the 1920s than from the crooks as depicted in the *Petit Journal* in 1902. And the portrait of Manda (played by Serge Reggiani) as a "worker" (specifically a carpenter whom we see in his workshop) also distances him from the usual representations, which stress the closed and forbidden world of the *apaches*. Becker's plot inventions—the escape and then the execution of Manda to the hallmark tune of "Le temps des cerises"—also politicize and transform the meaning of this underworld story. Even the use of black and white rather than color and the choice of a naturalistic aesthetic make the film run against the current, or at least distance it from the Belle Époque imagery the audience might expect with this story. Indeed, the film was not a box-office success when it came out. "[The film] is not reviving an era but presenting an amusing picture album," wrote a critic in *Cahiers du cinéma*.[74]

A few less well-known and atypical films do offer a distanced and more critical (even parodic) view of the 1900 vogue. The two sketches that compose Alfred Rode's *C'est la vie parisienne* (1954) expose the artifice of contrasting the morality of the start of the century with that of the 1950s, since in fact both are traversed by the same social taboos. Produced two years earlier (1952), René Clair's *Beauties of the Night* is even more explicit. A young musician, poor and unsuccessful, takes refuge in sleep, and his dreams transport him to a world where success and love await him. For it is 1900! He struts the terraces of cafés:

—You're so lucky to live in 1900. I drink to the best of epochs!
—Tell me, young man, what epoch do you mean?

—Today.

—You call 1900 the best of epochs? Crime, new taxes, talk of war, that's all there is. Terrible times.

—If you knew . . .

—The best time was when I was young—in 1830, under Louis-Philippe. What good times!

So the hero's dreams take him back to even older times, to 1830, to the Revolution, to the seventeenth century, before of course he finally understands that happiness lies in his own day and age.[75]

These few rather singular examples should not make us forget that most productions were content to distill uncritically the non-chalant and lightweight representations of a triumphant Belle Époque. Many factors explain the duration and prominence of this moment in French cinema. First, the ease of drawing on the almost inexhaustible stock of French vaudeville, a genre much in fashion: the theater was rediscovering Flers and Cavaillet, and of course Fey-deau, whom some theater directors were trying to modernize and legitimate. In 1948, the staging of *Amélie* by Jean-Louis Barrault at the Marigny Théâtre aroused the enthusiasm of Cocteau and Soupault. In March 1951, Jean Meyer put on *Le Dindon* at the Comédie-Française. Film adaptations moved in the same vaudeville direction.[76] Second, we have to consider that many directors were revisiting the time of their twenties, whether real or fantasized. Renoir had been born in 1894, Becker in 1906, Ophuls in 1902, Guitry in 1885, Clair in 1898, Rim in 1905. In the fifties older spectators could look back on their twenties too: "If you are fifty years old, go see *L'Ingénue libertine* and you will no doubt find some youthful memories," advised one critic.[77]

Filming the Belle Époque was also a way of paying homage to the infancy of the cinema, whose sixtieth birthday was celebrated in 1955. Two years earlier, Georges Franju had honored the memory of Georges Méliès (cinema's pioneer was played by his actual son) and there were frequent winks at early cinema, like *Couple idéal* (Bernard Roland and Raymond Rouleau, 1946), a pastiche about the nonstop and frantic adventure of making serials in the immediate prewar years.

Finally, these films, like all other representations of the beginning of the century, owe much to the difficult context of the fifties. The Belle Époque continued to play the role of historical antidote, as it had been doing for more than twenty years. Reviving this "brilliant" past, with its years of happiness and national grandeur, might well bring comfort in the troubled present. Moreover, the idea of "Thirty Glorious Years" of prosperity that was applied uncritically to the years following World War Two masked the scope of the difficulties that the nation was facing at the time:[78] social unrest and the permanent poverty denounced by Abbé Pierre in 1954 when he founded the Emmäus charity, the government's instability and France's withdrawal from the international scene, the anxiety aroused by the Cold War, and especially the colonial war that had resumed in Algeria. Therefore producers and audiences alike could bet without much risk on films that played the card of a consensual and superficial past. The master of ceremonies of Max Ophuls's *La Ronde* (1950) laconically introduces the setting: "It's 1900. Let's change costume. [*He puts on an opera cloak and top hat*] We're in the past. I adore the past. It is so much more peaceful than the present. And so much more certain than the future." A critic for the *Express* expressed this idea even more explicitly after viewing *Les Aventures d'Arsène Lupin* by Jacques Becker: "The sweetness of living in the 1910s . . . in a universe sheltered from wars and revolutions, that is sunny, cozy, gallant, where all the women are beautiful and where the bad boys are recruited from good families."[79] Nobody expressed this better than Sacha Guitry (simultaneously sentencious, irritating, and familiar) narrating *If Paris Were Told to Us*: "There, we lived twenty radiant years. The Entente Cordiale and the Franco-Russian alliance brought great calm to France. The Universal Exposition of 1900 seemed almost a consequence. France seemed to be saying to the whole world, 'Come look at me when I'm happy.'"

The idea seemed so patent that it was expressed not just in French cinema; a similar message came from the film Mecca of Hollywood. One had perceived its premises in Georges Cukor's *Zaza* (1938)[80] and in Mervyn Leroy's *Madame Curie* (1943), but the fifties enjoyed a prodigious wave of Belle Époque films produced in the U.S.A.[81] From *An American in Paris* (Vincente Minnelli, 1951) to *Irma la Douce* (Billy

Wilder, 1963), a good fifteen films took Paris as their setting. And many of them were very successful, like *Moulin Rouge*, *Sabrina*, *Lust for Life*, *Funny Face*, *Gigi*, and *Can-Can*. Not all these films took place in the Belle Époque strictly speaking, and some situated the action in the present, but they all ostensibly played with the great motifs of Paris 1900, whether in terms of locations—Montmartre, the Eiffel Tower, the Moulin Rouge, and the quays of the Seine, blithely mixing natural locations with studio sequences—or else traits that were meant to characterize Parisian life—lightness, good humor, the music hall, love. Even when the plot is set at the start of the nine-teenth century, as in *Scandal in Paris* (Sirk, 1946), which adapted the criminal-turned-police story of Vidocq, the film appropriates certain Belle Époque references like the figure of the Parisienne and cabaret scenes. Seen from Hollywood, Paris seems forever anchored in 1900. The characters might be Americans and the plot situated in 1950, but the Belle Époque always resurges. Some films are indeed authentic reconstructions, like *Moulin Rouge*, *Lust for Life* (Kirk Douglas as Vincent van Gogh), or *Gigi*, adapted from Colette's novel. But what matters are the effects of such hybrid productions. *Can-Can* by Walter Lang, mentioned above and taken from a successful Broadway musi-cal comedy (892 performances from 1953 to 1955), follows the story of the girl Pistache, a cabaret performer, with music supplied by Cole Porter and starring roles given to Shirley MacLaine and Frank Sina-tra. Nevertheless, we are in Paris, authenticated by the presence in the cast of French actors like Maurice Chevalier, Louis Jourdan, Dalio. These musical films, ambitious and expensive to make, were long considered as a manifestation of American imperialism, the fruit of its cultural hold over a postwar and weakened France. While such films were obviously peddling conventional and stereotyped motifs, they were also paying homage to France as the homeland of cinema and were celebrating its culture.[82] In fact, these productions were adapting French novels, tracing the lives of great French paint-ers, employing actors like Leslie Caron and Maurice Chevalier, and shooting many Paris locations with French crews. Their use of Tech-nicolor, like Renoir's in *French Cancan*, could be seen as extending the palette of the impressionists. Their perspective is not that of cul-tural predators but rather a tribute paid by Hollywood to a cultural tradition born in Paris that has now, they believe, been taken over by the United States. And thus, these films contributed powerfully to diffusing the Belle Époque imaginary.

HISTORY TAKES ON THE SUBJECT

If the 1950s contributed so much to the emergence of the Belle Époque imaginary, this was because diverse forms of expression were converging. Historians too participated in this construction; their principal contribution belongs to what is generally called picturesque or anecdotal history, a *"petite histoire"* that the English language prefers to call "popular" because it appeals to a general audience and helps build a vast shared knowledge. The result of work by a multitude of writers, journalists, and politicians, this kind of history prospered outside the academy while managing to grab the attention of the publishing world. Its books, like historical novels (a genre with which it shares many traits), were often best-sellers. It knew how to make things simple while still being "well written"; how to combine what is expected with new revelations; how to mix knowledge and escapism, education and entertainment. But this flourishing genre of popular history, produced with diverse intentions but always governed by the desire to please, also made the "Belle Époque" one of its money spinners.

Historical syntheses and huge frescos characterize this postwar historiography. The works of Jacques Chastenet offer a good example. Diplomat and journalist and codirector of *Le Temps* from 1931 to 1942, as a historian this son of a senator acceded to the Academy of Moral and Political Sciences in 1947, and then in 1956 to the French Academy. Already the author of many books of history, mainly biographies (William Pitt, Wellington, Godoy, Poincaré) and syntheses of British history, Chastenet already (like others) had his eye on the Belle Époque lode. So in 1949 Fayard (a publisher well versed in this type of book aimed at a conservative and erudite readership) issued *La France de M. Fallières: Une époque pathétique.*[83] The book was classically designed, one of those "standard-compartment displays" dominated by political and diplomatic facts—in fact, the kind of book severely condemned by the *Annales* school led by Marc Bloch and Lucien Fevbre. The goal was also to offer a reference book at a time when scholarly historiography was publishing very little on recent history. Chastenet devotes a few thematic chapters to social groups, to cultural and scientific life. All in all, his overview is classic and honest. But the significant fact is that two years later, the same publisher published a lighter version with the catchier title *La Belle Époque: La Société sous M. Fallières.*[84] The text was identical, the author had changed nothing, but the editor had slashed a dozen chapters and added illustrations, and Fayard could publish the result in a series aimed at a wider public: "Illustrated History of . . ." In the new edition, any traditional "historical" content had disappeared; political life, diplomacy, the rural world, and intellectual and scientific life—all had been whisked away. What remained was the "Belle Époque" as it was perceived in 1951, which is to say, Parisian society seen through the prism of both its elites and its working classes. Now the book opened with the "Monde et demi-monde," clearly announcing its flavor, and then oscillated between the Paris outcast *zone* and the "high life," whose rituals and codes continued to be precisely detailed. Then there were sections devoted to entertainment, music, and sport, as well as a final chapter centered on the atmosphere of pleasure, happiness, and behavioral freedom that prosperity had engendered. This example is interesting not because it reflects a common practice of editorial recycling, but rather because history is being tailored in order to frame, at the beginning of the 1950s, evidence of a resurgence of a "Belle Époque."

And we can see why that period might be propitious for this type of book. The same year (1951) saw the publication of *Paris 1900* by Robert Burnand, former student at the National School of Maps (and other ancient documents) and "man of letters," editor of the Goncourts' diaries, and author of a very eclectic book composed of biographical sketches and "daily lives." His *1900* is a sort of almanac complemented by geography (thematic routes and promenades through the city).[85] Many analogous books appeared in this decade, all modeled on Jacques Castelnau's *Belle Époque* (which won the Académie Française prize in 1962)— too many to mention.[86] But the work that stands out from this ensemble is the great enterprise of Gilbert

Guilleminault. A famous journalist, editor-in-chief of *Paris-Presse*, then of *L'Aurore,* he had been engaged for ten years in producing a vast and celebrated popular anthology to be called *The True Novel of the Third Republic.*[87] Mobilizing a team of forty-some writers, novelists, journalists, and "historians" of very contrasting political sensibilities, the first volume juxtaposed essays that each tried to make the era "resonate." This would be the "history of our fathers and grandfathers" as reconstructed in their ordinary activities, with careful concern for dramatic effects. The texts produced by the journalists (the three-part series was previewed in *Paris-Presse*) drew most of their information from attentive scouring of the principal daily newspapers of the day. *Prélude à la Belle Époque (1889–1900)* was published in 1956, followed a year later by *La Belle Époque (1900–1908),* then by *Avant 14, fin de la Belle Époque (1908–1914).* The themes were unexceptional: major events, curiosities, and spicy tidbits of the period (the fire at the Bazaar de la Charité, the *Casque d'or* story, the theft of the *Mona Lisa,* the Steinheil and Caillaux trials); controversies, attacks, and political scandals; picturesque and telling events in cultural life (birth of the cinema, the Tour de France, the Universal Exposition, the première of *Cyrano de Bergerac* and of the Ballets Russes, etc.). Edited in a lively and heartfelt way, interleaved with illustrations and picturesque dialogues, it formed a sort of popular encyclopedia of the Belle Époque as reflected in the ordinary press of the time. There was a strong affinity with analogous films and memoirs, to which the three volumes were a sort of journalistic appendix.

The same years saw the emergence of a "scholarly" historiography of the period. We know that professional historians have long hesitated to deal with matters that are too contemporaneous, due to various lacks—of perspective and critical distance, of access to the archives—and of course due to the impossibility of an exhaustive study. The main figures of the "methodical" generation of the end of the nineteenth century (like Gabriel Monod and Ernest Lavisse) had clearly refused to grant recent periods "the dignity of history," which actually left the whole discipline of history in the hands of the medievalists. History as the science of the past simply could not be contemporary. One of the principal effects of these reservations was to leave recent eras either to the Free School of Political Science (founded in 1872 by Emile Boutmy and governed by Albert Sorel, chair of diplomatic history) or else to "amateurs" who often came from the aristocracy and promoted a fundamentally anti-Republican history.[88] This evident danger led the government gradually to advocate the teaching of more contemporary history. The first textbooks, which were devoted to the French Revolution and its aftermath, merely exacerbated the methodological positivism and retained a factual and political approach, which angered the nascent field of the social sciences. For example, this was true of *Manuel historique de politique étrangère* (History of foreign policy, 1892) by Emile Bourgeois. The creation in 1915 of the Modern History Society would improve things, as would the birth of *Annales* in 1929: the famous journal created by Marc Bloch and Lucien Febvre was unhesitatingly open to the contemporary period, but for lack of real specialists, it entrusted such matters to sociologists, economists, and ethnographers. So the impression remained that academics were not very interested in the 1900s, which left the field open to many monarchist and amateur historians (Jacques Banville),[89] to legal scholars or political scientists who were often connected to the Free School of Political Science (André Siegfried, Auguste Soulier),[90] or else to essayists and political observers (Robert de Jouvenel, Daniel Halévy, Alexandre Zévaès).[91]

However, a few books had opened the way. Two events—the Dreyfus affair and the causes of World War One—had indeed been subjects for "hot" history, a book on the former written by Joseph Reinach in 1901 and one on the latter by Emile Bourgeois in 1922, then one by Pierre Renouvin in 1925.[92] In 1921 also appeared the volume devoted to the Third Republic in Ernest Lavisse's monumental *Contemporary History of France*. Written by Charles Seignobos,[93] it derived more from teaching than from fresh research and stayed with general considerations and sequences of events.[94] The evolution accelerated at the end of the twenties thanks to new academic series like "Peoples & Civilizations" (Alcan, 1928) and "Clio: Introduction to Historical Studies" (Presses Universitaires de France), which both offered expert overviews and syntheses.[95] From this watershed moment also date the basic controversies, such as how to determine "the deep causes and underlying forces" of diplomatic issues (Jules Isaac).[96]

But it was not until after World War Two that a straightforward history of the start of the century became available. In 1955 appeared the famous political chronicles of Georges Bonnefous and Jacques Gouault's study of the republicanization of France, and volume 6 of the *History of International Relations* (edited by Pierre Renouvin) that was devoted to the years 1871 to 1914.[97] Now the movement was launched: at last there was a scholarly historiography of the 1900s, but it remained exclusively diplomatic and political, and it was devoted to the triumphant Republic. The division of labor became rather clear: to the amateurs the popular history that enumerated the pleasures and glories of cultural and social life, to Sorbonne professors how a régime functioned and specific political moments. Meanwhile, the "Belle Époque" was timidly invited into secondary education. The curriculum of 1938 had introduced the study of the years 1848 to 1920 into the final year of secondary study. Starting with the Liberation, junior classes in the *lycées* could devote a few sessions to the rise of "scientific and industrial civilization" and to what the Third Republic had accomplished. In the final year, students could now study "France from 1871 to 1914" with respect to both its "economic and social transformations" and "movements in ideas, sciences, and arts." Also in these same years began the sketches (by André Billy) of a vibrant literary history of the 1900s that was open to the realities and to the true authors of that era.[98]

THE TRAITS OF AN ERA

In all respects, therefore, the fifteen years following the end of World War Two were the key moment when the "Belle Époque" imaginary grew and flowered. On top of the already dated celebrations in its music hall songs (a still-thriving genre) came the continual and burgeoning flow of remembrances, memoirs, picture albums, political and scholarly books, and especially the films, which acted as the most powerful vector of this retrospective wave. It was also the time of the first exhibitions, like the one that opened in October 1957 at the Musée des Beaux-Arts de Bordeaux, *1900: La Belle Époque à Bordeaux*. Organized around a bequest from the caricaturist Sem, it exhibited posters, sketches, and costume mannequins in an ambiance of gentle nostalgic euphoria. "Back then, existence appeared opulent. A swarm of pretty women fluttered around golden and careless youths, which indeed seemed one exterior marker of wealth."[99] In Paris, Picasso, promoted as the great heir of the 1900 avant-gardes, basked in widespread recognition. The Museum of Decorative Arts in 1955 organized a retrospective of his work—*Peintures, 1900–1955*—while Clouzot's camera tried to grasp (in *cinema vérité* mode) the "mystery" of how Picasso created a painting. The resulting film (*The Mystery of Picasso*) won the special jury prize at the 1956 Cannes Festival. There were also remakes of the great popular cycles of the 1900s (Arsène Lupin, Rouletabille, Chéri-Bibi), now presented as modern fables. "We might say our era is feeling the anguish of old age returning to its past," wrote Cocteau in *Le Figaro littéraire*.[100]

As Alfred Sauvy tartly remarked somewhat later, the middle of the century literally invented the Belle Époque: "After the Second War there was created from nothing the reactionary and idiotic myth of the 'Belle Époque.' Young French people were invited to believe that this was a long time of partying around the Place Pigalle."[101] But many observers had already noted evidence of this collective creation, like Gérard Baüer in 1950:[102] "We recently discovered this obvious truth, and now fashion has run away with '1900.'" "Press and radio, theater, film, and cabaret care only about '1900,'" commented André de Fouquières.[103] In 1955, *Le Crapouillot* took advantage of this revival by publishing a volume redundantly titled: "The Belle Époque: Panorama and Rehabilitation of the 1900s."[104] The table of contents was copious but unoriginal: one entered "High Society," then circulated among the "Who's Who of Arts and Letters," then entered the enchanted universe of social events. Everything denoted a society of leisure, superficial lifestyles, a joyous and opulent Europe that amused itself in "the drama of adultery."

Henceforth there could be no doubt that the "Belle Époque" really did exist. Its principal characteristics were now fixed at the origin of a historical and social imaginary that would endure. Some traits did evolve from a culture of defeat and were specific to the Cold War years, while other traits had been fashioned at the end of the 1920s and especially in the decade of the 1930s, and finally other characteristics would arrive later to modify the portrait—but the overall physiognomy was now frozen in time and widely shared in contemporary societies. So let us try to fill in what was briefly sketched at the beginning of this book.

The time boundaries of the period were now clear to everybody: the "Belle Époque" referred to the fifteen years that preceded the Great War, i.e., 1900 to 1914. Although it had not previously been the case, people now agreed unanimously that the year "1900 was the start of a century, of a new era."[105] And August 1, 1914, a Saturday, obviously marked the end of a world. Some writers quibbled, of course: Stefan Zweig wanted to differentiate between the "ten first years" of the period, which were indeed light and nonchalant, and the four last ones, which "carried in the clouds." But he was a historian looking backward. "In Paris, one could not see the war coming," asserted Maurice de Waleffe. "Nobody saw it, nobody thought about it. The country was not in danger and so everybody continued to attend to his pleasures or personal duties."[106] Others would differentiate between "the blessed era when M. Emile Loubet reigned at the Elysée [from 1889 to 1906]," and the (more turbulent) "France of President Fallières [1906–1913],"[107] but again, this is a matter of authorial subtleties. The Belle Époque began with the Exhibition and ended with military mobilization; it was the dawn of the twentieth century and it both contained its promises and heralded its nightmare.

Within this firmly defined time span there were spatial boundaries. First, the expression concerned France alone: there was no "Belle Époque" outside the Hexagon, and foreign versions came along later. Second, it concerned only Paris, inasmuch as the period was "symbolically perceived as essentially Parisian."[108] Not content with its having been the capital of the nineteenth century, all claimed Paris at the start of the following one to be "the liveliest city in the world," the city of eternal youth. As Stefan Zweig wrote in *The World Was Yesterday*: "Nowhere else do those with awakened minds experience such identity between their youth and the atmosphere as they do in this city." The whole city was beautiful, without exception, even if one favored one part or another according to one's occupation or social network. Montmartre and the Latin Quarter. The lovely mansions of the 16th or 8th *arrondissements* that extended toward the Bois de Boulogne. The boulevards "were still one of the most agreeable places in the world, one of the rare places on earth where pleasure is concentrated."[109] The ramparts of the old *fortifs* where kids kissed and where you went to picnic on the banks of the Marne. This peerless city was connected to many outlying dependencies where you went in the summer—the resorts of Deauville, Trouville, Royan, Biarritz—or in winter to the Riviera, or simply to Vichy to take the waters and recharge your batteries. As Paul Poiret, one of the grand figures of the period, recalls: "Having a fine house in Paris did not matter in summer because I had to hit the road to my clients and be ready to serve them in all their favorite vacation places."[110]

There, in this "larger Paris," the Belle Époque was especially a time of peace and security, as ensured by the Republic, its army, its international power, and its colonial empire. It was also a time of prosperity, guaranteed by a strong currency, a conquering science, and a solid economy. This is why the general atmosphere was the "sweetness of life," frivolity, insouciance given the prospect of a rosy future. "Optimism and trustfulness had animated us young people since the turn of the century," Stefan Zweig continued.[111] The result of all that was intense intellectual and artistic creativity, an extraordinary aspiration to culture and to aesthetic innovation, which made Paris the uncontested laboratory of modern art. From this ambiance also flowed an unrestrained passion for entertainment that pushed the French out to the theater, the *café-concert*, the cinematograph, and popular dance halls. The Belle Époque exhausted itself in entertainment, lost itself in oompahs, cotillons, and applause; it was party time.

Above all, it seemed that the French people of that time demonstrated two essential characteristics. First, laughter, good humor, health, and honest gaiety. "Being amused is a phrase whose meaning has considerably weakened this past half-century," deplored Hugo, the *maître d'hôtel* at Maxim's.[112] In 1900, people knew how to have a good time. Of course, the manner in which they did so differed according to social class. Socialites had a taste for witticisms;

everyone relished repeating the *bons mots* attributed to some wit or another. "It seems their sole goal in life was to get together to make jokes," wrote Francis de Miomandre about the élites of this "happy era."[113] One could fill whole books with the jokes, non sequiturs, pranks, anecdotes, and "*à peu près*" (comic approximations) that were pronounced in the period. Paul Morand had jeered at this, seeing the pun as one of the plagues of this imbecilic age. But laughter is democratic, and people joked in the working class just as much: they laughed, guffawed, slapped their thighs. But the jokes were just as truculent—and often bawdier. Both the buxom chanteuse Dufay, who broke nuts between her breasts, and the famous stage farter, Joseph Pujol, triggered general hilarity and scandalized the moralists. But this did not matter because France loved to laugh, and anything could satisfy its appetite for joviality.

The other trait concerns the freedom of manners and sexuality, which seems one of the nation's most widely shared characteristics. The "Belle Époque" opened under the auspices of the Parisienne figure who welcomed visitors to the Exposition, and throughout its existence it celebrated "Her Majesty the Skirt."[114] Woman was queen in those days, it was said, as witnessed by the theater and the fact that "the man of 1900 appears only as a lover. . . . Our fathers were not champions or winners, but philanderers and seducers."[115] Courtesans and mistresses were only the most visible portion of an erotic supply that involved the whole society: "Women dreamed of love, men thought of pleasure."[116] Zweig maintained that "you went about with, chatted with, and slept with the man or woman you pleased." In the 1950s, ironically on the eve of the sexual revolution, people went into ecstasy over corsets, bustles, petticoats, booties. "Women then had big rumps and full bodices," noted a journalist at the *Canard Enchaîné*.[117] The troubling and mysterious beauty of Cléo de Mérode, considered at the time the most photographed woman in the world,[118] was forever seductive. In September 1949, *Das Magazin* had a hit with the series "The Pin-up Girls of 1900."[119] Twelve years later, Armand Lanoux's *Amours 1900* offered similar titillation: a period that opened with a "fatal tryst" (the death in 1899 of President Félix Faure in the company of his mistress) and that ended with the vengeance of an outraged wife (the assassination of Gaston Calmette by Henriette

Caillaux in 1914) must have been wholly given over to the "Myth of the Infamous Woman."[120]

Obviously, this particular Belle Époque was that of the upper classes, those at the head of the "grand society parade," who exhibited themselves in the theater loges, in the Opéra foyer, in the salons, the splendid restaurants, the races, the balls, the Bois. "Idleness, openly acknowledged, allowed men to devote countless moments to the women they adulated." Of course the toffs were the most prominent, but their wealth, their glory, also reassured "the little folk, who knew that at any feast there are crumbs, and these crumbs would be for them."[121] So one was not going to miss having fun "on Saturday night, after the weekly grind!"[122] Good humor, contented living, and dirty jokes were all supposedly part of "Parisian workers'" lives. The democratic spirit of the 1950s insisted on this shared joie de vivre, which it was hoped would be rediscovered as soon as the economy recovered. This collective enthusiasm of the fifties was incarnated in the *café-concert* and popular magazines, and mainly in the 14 Juillet, the national festival of the Republic so often depicted in films of the day. "Confetti battles occurred on that day, and automobile traffic ceased. On the Quatorze, you danced continuously for two nights and one day in small balls set up in the street; the Longchamp military review attracted an immense crowd to the Bois de Boulogne. In the spring on the day of the Flower Festival, there paraded down the Avenue des Acacias a long cortège of vehicles decorated with flowers and with occupants in fancy dress pelting each other with roses, carnations, peonies."[123] And the Expo! "Was the triumphal 1900 Exposition, with its fifty million visitors from all social groups, not the zenith of the Third Republic?"[124] Truly, no matter where in society you placed yourself, "that time was honored, incontestably. Ah, the good times that were had in the 'belle époque'!"[125]

Tuesday, April 12, 2016, 7:15 p.m.

It is now more than a month that I have been working on writing this book in the magnificent research library of St. Andrews University in Scotland— Martyrs Kirk. The ribbed vaults and stained-glass windows of this deconsecrated church are propitious for thinking and writing. Occasionally I wonder what became of all the men and women of the 1900s, those whose faces, desires, and dreams have always been important to me. But maybe their actual lives dissipate in this piling up of images and stories that were supposed to pay them homage. In other words, doesn't the "Belle Époque" lose its body and soul in this maelstrom of representations?

But my uncertainty never lasts long. I remain more than ever persuaded that my approach is well founded. Understanding by what paths the apprehension of time is constructed, tracking the materials that fashion the imaginaries of yesterday and the contexts that give them life, does not mean giving up on the pact of truth upon which history is built. Quite the contrary. More than the past, which is dead and buried, time is the living subject of this discipline, and it is in the play and dialogue of temporalities that the relationship "to our dear departed" is woven. Truly, is there any other choice? No doubt fiction can nourish our fine and noble ambitions, but at the price of retrospective illusions that relate to other functions. What remains to us is the dryness and coldness of lost papers, of yellowing photographs and forgotten books.

And how could we not see that this permanent reinvention of past times also carries within itself—despite the forgetfulness, misunderstandings, and artifices that it secretes—all the evidence we need? That in the profuse exhibition of all these documents, at the intersection of thousands of pages, letters, images, and objects coming from the "Belle Époque," there lies something of the truth of the 1900s.

PART THREE

THE ORDEAL OF THE *"FIN DE SIÈCLE"*

HISTORY CONTINUES—which is perhaps the only certainty it offers us. Powerfully assembled in the 1930s, the portrait of the "Belle Époque" changed in the 1950s, as we saw in Part Two, and would be again transformed in the following decades. At first it tended to be effaced, as if the nation were trying to recover from a case of indigestion caused by overindulgence in images and certainties that appeared outmoded and old-fashioned, particularly from the perspective of the full-blooded modernity that seemed to mark the 1960s and 1970s. And when the Belle Époque did resurge, it assumed a quite different face, much more troubled, now featuring its underside, the shadowy zones, a peek behind the scenes of a period that now appeared less carefree and rosy. Transgressions and "perversions"—social, sexual, political—seemed to become its dominant traits. But what is "belle" has resources and can assert hidden qualities: from the Parisian triumphalism it had for so long incarnated, the Belle Époque turned provincial, rural, peasant; it played an intense part in the vogue for heritage that marked the end of the twentieth century.

"Culture," above all, fastened itself to its every step as the expression "Belle Époque" became internationalized, which in turn inflected its representations. Of course, many of the old traits persisted, and that permanence expressed part of the "truth" that lay within this social imaginary—or at least those traits demonstrated the vigor of the reconstructions taking place. But those reconstructions tended to lose their shining naïveté. The connotations became more complicated, tougher, and more fragmented. The Belle Époque became open to counterimages, especially in contemporary social historiography, which stressed tensions, conflicts, and the inequalities that wove through an era that historians now questioned whether it had been truly so happy. Then, as the last witnesses of the era died, other figures and other memories came forth to recount quite other stories.

THE "BELLE ÉPOQUE" ISN'T WHAT IT USED TO BE

SOUND AND IMAGES

The 1960s were "cinematographic"—and profoundly musical. In songs and often in movies, youth of the sixties reinvented their world. Remember the decisive roles of image and sound in the construction of the Belle Époque imaginary? We will take them as guides to the new inflections of the concept. Of course no change is absolute, nor abrupt. Very traditional films and songs were still issued and would be for a long time. But a clear change in tone was perceptible in the sixties and seventies.

Let's turn first to the cinema. *Jules et Jim* by François Truffaut, which came to the screens in January 1962, was incontestably a "Belle Époque" film. The action starts in Paris in 1912 (the novel by Henri-Pierre Roché on which it was based began two years earlier, in 1910), and the director took care to sprinkle the film with many temporal markers: the costumes, of course, but also newspapers, posters that discreetly quote art nouveau, and canvases by Picasso appear furtively, plus French boxing and the vaudevillian atmosphere of the opening scenes. Yet Truffaut was deliberately deconstructing the setting. We know that the filmmaker, like other *auteurs* of the Nouvelle Vague, had constantly criticized films of "a certain tendency of

French cinema," which had multiplied since the Liberation.[1] Close to André Bazin and *Cahiers du cinéma*, to which he contributed many articles, Truffaut had only contempt for that "French quality" that had been so well represented by films about the Belle Époque. I am not arguing that *Jules et Jim* was intended to attack a genre and an imaginary that so many feature films had been popularizing. But that was indeed its effect. Once the director had put décor in place, everything he did ran against it: the characters, the plot, the narration. Nothing was conventional, neither the friendship between a young Frenchman and a young German in a patriotic era of strong antagonism between these two nations, nor the boldness and sexual freedom of Catherine (Jeanne Moreau), nor the strange *ménage-à-trois* that gives no place to adultery. The time frame of the film does not conform to type, either, since it skips over the years of World War One in order to make a seamless link between prewar and postwar. And the story ends later, somewhere in the mid-1930s, at a time when memorializing the "1900 era" had already begun. Even if this was not Truffaut's intention, we may consider that *Jules et Jim* symbolically closed the subgenre of "Belle Époque" cinema by dynamiting it from within.

The break is even more evident because other directors rushed into the breach. Taken in hand by Nouvelle Vague figures, "1900 cinema" changed in tone. *The Thief of Paris*, directed by Louis Malle in 1967, comparably disrespects conventional representations; the "romantic adventure" aspect and the star cast (Jean-Paul Belmondo) were just window dressing. An adaptation of a novel by Georges Darien, one of the darkest and most transgressive writers of the 1900s, the film amounts to a violent and acerbic critique of a social world that seems to have no exit. The sinister rapacity of bourgeois society is matched by the nihilistic universe of disillusioned thieves, or as Darien put it, "Ignominy on one side and infamy on the other; everything fits and everything blends together."[2] What kind of "Belle Époque" is this? The following year, 1968, the young Philippe Fourastié, aged twenty-eight and former assistant to directors Schoendoerffer, Godard, and Rivette, made *La Bande à Bonnot* about a group of anarchist bandits that operated in 1911–1912. Contrary to the films of the 1950s, here the period reconstruction is minimal. The director's concern is manifestly elsewhere: to analyze the motivations and gestures of political violence when it is committed in the name of revolutionary values. In an interview, Fourastié described Bonnot and his accomplices as "precursors" of far-left terrorist organizations. "They were just ordinary men," added Jacques Brel, who played one of them, insisting on the courage of the anarchists. The film's analysis remains rather cursory, but one is struck by the way it acknowledges the political context in which it was made. Che Guevara had been killed the preceding year, and location shooting was interrupted by the events of May '68.[3] The inspiration for, and the dynamic the film gave to, the "tragic bandits" of anarchy may have been the acts of direct-action terrorism organized in Germany by the "Baader-Meinhof gang" before spreading to Italy, Spain, and France. Here Bonnot becomes a "bandit 1900 style, but also a protester like in May '68."[4] Incontestably, a radically different Belle Époque emerges from this film.

Obviously not all the films set around 1900 followed this path. Daniel Moosman's adaptation in 1970 of Darien's novel *Biribi*, a violent denunciation of military repression in North African penal colonies,[5] was a fiasco. But nobody wanted the comic and triumphant Belle Époque style that had emerged in the 1950s, either, and it gradually disappeared from the screen. Afterward, the 1900s remained a "historical" framework that was occasionally chosen for cinematographic and many television productions, but their representations became complicated and diversified, causing the fragmentation of a previously homogeneous imaginary. The cinema was soon featuring large frescoes or historical epics in which 1900 was merely a starting point—or an episode, as in *1900* by Bernardo Bertolucci, made in 1976. The desire for historical "truth" was now strongly accentuated, as was attention to social and political realities. Bertrand Tavernier's reconstitution of the crimes and trial of Vacher in *The Judge and the Assassin* (1976) was answered by Alain Corneau's big-budget drama set in the Sahara before World War One, *Fort Saganne* (1984).

The same concern for diversity and accurate reconstruction dominated the production of films made for television. Apart from Guy de Maupassant, whose novels and short stories had been frequently adapted, "historical" television in the 1960s forsook the start of the century and plunged into older periods.[6] Only the series *En votre âme et conscience* (In good conscience), with the format of restaging famous criminal trials, was tempted by some "fine crimes" of the 1900s. As in the cinema, the Belle Époque did make a notable return to television after 1970, principally thanks to *Arsène Lupin* by Jacques Nahum (1971–1974) and *Brigades du Tigre* by Claude Desailly, a series that began in 1974. Both of them "mythic" TV series, they chose two different kinds of representation: the former conformed to what remained of the French "spirit" and panache of the Belle Époque, while the latter was more "historical" and concerned to set its plots in well-researched political and social contexts.

A rather similar phenomenon of reorienting what had become threadbare took place in musical production. In its lightweight dimensions, the *café-concert* songs in "1900 style" were rapidly discredited; like the accordion at the *musette*, their style seemed outmoded. Maurice Chevalier and Charles Trenet were abandoned by new audiences; all that seemed obsolete and sounded *ringard* (square). The remaining music hall venues had lost their luster. In the winter of 1965–1966, the Municipal Theater in Reims mounted a show called *La Belle Époque* containing "songs, monologues, poems" that clashed with the contemporary musical landscape. Everywhere in retreat, the 1900 style was still invoked out of curiosity or nostalgia, as in the television appearances of Gaston Ouvrard, a comic performer born in 1890 (and himself the son of Eloi Ouvrard, a pioneer of this kind of musical comedy). Likewise, the tradition of revues and the French cancan barely survived. The Moulin Rouge and the Folies-Bergère remained "Parisian" attractions, but they had lost their living force. Starting in the early 1960s the "cabaret-dinner show" formula spread, attracting a provincial or touristic clientele with "all-inclusive" tickets covering the show and a glass of champagne. In 1963, the Club du Vieux-Colombier was taken over by Fernand Dailly, who renamed it La Belle Époque and tried to revive it, but without much success. The Moulin Rouge show seemed frozen in time. Its grand revues—*Frou-Frou* (1963–1965), *Frisson* (1965–1967), *Fascination* (1967–1970), and *Fantastic* (1970–1973)—appeared faded and outmoded spectacles, a sort of "poor man's opera" that survived only thanks to tourist rituals that continued to make the Moulin Rouge a key to visiting Paris, alongside dinner at the Eiffel Tower. Here, as in the few establishments that still offered such entertainment (like the Lido, the Folies-Bergère, and the Paradis Latin that opened in 1977), the French cancan and the "1900" spirit remained standard—but nobody's heart was in it anymore. Music hall was now called "cabaret" and tried to modernize its shows, but without managing to avoid inevitable obsolescence and the consequent loss of interest. On the stage, the Belle Époque was merely a marginal and congealed motif, a dead memory.

The song version of the 1900 *imaginaire* resisted better, thanks to its "realist" aspect and notably the immense success of Edith Piaf. Born in 1915, the *môme* (kid) continued to ensure a sort of generational link with the start of the century. She covered Aristide Bruant's "Les Mômes de la Butte" and "Nini peau de chien," but she also managed to modernize them. Her death in October 1963 left the stage rather empty. There were heirs like Cora Vaucaire, whom Fréhel had nominated to succeed her, and Michèle Bernard and Marcel Mouloudji, but the genre could barely be renewed: relying on cover versions and with few new songs, it gradually declined.

Yet, another tradition from the 1900s did resurface: political songs (largely forgotten until then) about the rebels of the Paris streets, the victims of the 1870 Commune, the *insurgés*, militants, and guys "who turned out badly." Some themes linked this tradition to the realist song: fatalism, "worker-ism," and those who transited the social scene via prison, penal colony, and hard labor. But the strongest ties were to the anarchism associated with protest singers like Montéhus, Gaston Couté, and Charles d'Avray. This heritage had been forgotten, but its spirit began to be rediscovered in the mid-1950s. Well served by his tragic air and his red shirt, Léo Ferré helped reactivate the protest and antimilitarist song, which he blended with poetry of the "Paris-*Canaille*" (riffraff).[7] But just as in the case of Georges Brassens, contemporaries would compare him to Bruant. Similarly, in 1961 the daily newspaper *Libération* compared Ferré to Bruant because like him "Ferré managed to win over all the fat cats that he had insulted to the point of getting himself warmly applauded by them."[8] Boris Vian too reanimated some of this spirit of contestation, especially in the dozen songs he composed in 1954—including "La Complainte de Bonnot," "La Java des chaussettes à clous," and "Les Joyeux Bouchers

de la Villette"—for *La Bande à Bonnot* by Henri-François Rey, a burlesque comedy performed at the Théâtre du Quartier Latin. The play
was a fiasco and it was only later, thanks to the records produced by
Jacques Canetti, that Vian's songs became successful.

The protest song was a 1960s phenomenon. After having devoted
a show to Louis Aragon, the singer Marc Ogeret in 1968 recorded
Autour de la Commune (1848–1880), then the album *Chansons contre
(1880–1914)*, which adapted, with Belle Époque iconography, texts by
Montéhus, MacNab, Charles d'Avray, and Léo Taxil, as well as Bruant.
Curiously, although in real life Bruant had been a militant nationalist and anti-Semite, his work continued to be associated (thanks to
his populism) with songs of "struggle" tinged with anarchism. But
most of Ogeret's repertoire insisted on an anarchist and revolutionary heritage. Others followed, carried along by the spirit of protest
and rediscovery of anarchist and antimilitarist traditions that char-
acterized the post-'68 context. Mouloudji, known until then for a
more classically realist repertoire, in 1970 recorded Commune songs
and "union ballads." More political and attuned to memorializing,
Guy Debord composed in 1974 "La Java des bons enfants," which he
attributed sarcastically to Raymond Callemin, the most erudite of
Bonnot's companions. The song was a pastiche, but it subtly played
with the cultural codes of subversion; one line went: "they thought it
was the [masked] Fantômas, but it was the class struggle."

Therefore, starting in the 1960s, memories and uses of the Belle
Époque were deeply transformed. Had too much been made of it?
Ten years before, a *Canard Enchaîné* journalist thought so: "This
overabundance of 1900 retrospectives . . . will make us take a dislike
to this era."[9] Yet there was a clear subsiding of this social imaginary
after 1960. The times they were "a-changing," marked by the death of
the last great icons of the turn of the century. "It is a whole era that is
disappearing," wrote a journalist when Cléo de Mérode died in October 1966.[10] But not everything faded away at the same rate. The ascendancy of painters, poets, and the avant-gardes from the start of the
century tended in fact to be accentuated, with an increasing rhythm
of monographs, biographies, and exhibitions devoted to them. New
sectors of artistic creation won revived attention, like art nouveau,
which for many years had barely been appreciated (and sometimes

even vilified). "For the past ten years we have witnessed new interest in Art Nouveau," wrote Maurice Rheims in 1964, mentioning Gallé, Toulet, Guimard; he was worried about increasing demolition, particularly of restaurants. "It is time to take care of '1900.' "[11]

Also newly appreciated were fashion and *haute couture*. In November 1961 the city of Paris opened at its Costume Museum an ambitious exhibition devoted to *Fashions of the Belle Époque: 1890–1910 and Portraits*. The curator presented more than 300 objects (costumes, accessories, paintings, fashion magazines), as well as many mannequins clad in outfits designed by Paul Poiret and Jeanne Lanvin. And in fact the train of anecdotal books never really stopped, with memoirs of bohemians (like Jean Mollet, who had been Apollinaire's secretary and took part in all the prewar literary enterprises)[12] and anthologies devoted to *Tout-Paris* celebrities and their witticisms. In 1964, the humorist Hervé Lauwick, a friend to Maurice Donnay and Sacha Guitry, published an imagined conversation with his grandparents and dedicated it to the *Secret Life of the Belle Époque*.[13] In 1966 and 1967, successful book series like *Grand Enigmas of the Belle Époque* continued to appear.[14] Yet, as cineastes and interpreters were starting to tell us, something in the grand parade of 1900 had broken down. "Personally, I think that this Belle Époque as it is recounted was a boring and sometimes even tragic period," wrote the American poet and art critic John Ashbery in 1964. "The ball at the Moulin Rouge was a mediocre show and . . . drinking champagne at Maxim's at 3:00 a.m. from Cléo de Mérode's slipper was nothing like the ultimate sensual experience."[15]

MURDERING THE BELLE ÉPOQUE?

My book has stressed Paris as key to the construction of the Belle Époque imaginary. The city—its avenues, buildings, kiosks, and theaters—literally shaped the souvenir album of 1900, which derived from a mournful view of what the city had lost. "We will never get rid of nostalgia for Paris,"[16] Warnod had written in 1955. But something happened in the mid-1960s: the city changed enormously as it reached the centennial of Hausmann's urban renewal, a time span in

which 1900 stood at the exact midpoint. Until then, much urban renovation had remained cosmetic; only a few forward-looking projects
involved structural changes, such as the widening of the Avenue de
l'Opéra in 1955, which required cutting down its trees. But in the following years, urban renewal changed everything.[17] In March 1956, the
ban on building higher than 31 meters (100 feet) was rescinded; there
was a new "governing scheme" for a taller and more modern Paris.
Many people found the city dirty and unsuitable for automobile traffic. There were dreams of a remodeled, even futurist Paris, like the
one that was the setting for Jacques Tati's *Playtime* (filmed between
1964 and 1967). The actual results were less extravagant, but there was
indeed a radical molting. In 1959, the Council of State made the deci-
sion to shift to Rungis in the suburbs the traditional "belly of Paris."
Les Halles, the emblematic site where the Parisians of 1900 ended
their nighttime "tours," was doomed to disappear. The transfer took
place in 1969, and the old Baltard pavilions were destroyed or relo-
cated in 1971; the new shopping center, called Forum des Halles,
appeared shortly thereafter. Other symbols of old Paris disappeared:
everywhere, paving stones gave way to asphalt; gone were the last
remnants of the city's fortifications, which had been vanishing since
the 1920s, as well as the Wine Hall. Twenty-some of the Guimard-
designed aedicula and pinnacles of the metro stations were replaced
in the 1960s.[18]

On top of that, modern infrastructure appeared on the Paris sky-
line. Inscribed in the 1959 governing urban plan for Paris, the Boulevard *périphérique* (ring road) emerged in segments along the stretches
of what was still the peripheral *zone*. Decreed in 1958, the first towers
of the La Défense business district sprang up in the mid-1960s. Other
high-rises soon appeared in the center of Paris: in Montparnasse, on
the Jussieu campus of the university, in the Place des Fêtes. Envis-
aged many years before, grand projects to "reconquer" the city really
got under way in 1964–1965 and proceeded briskly. In 1966 began the
expressway on the Right Bank that enabled cars to traverse the whole
city quickly. Renovation of the Italie neighborhood and rearrange-
ment of Porte Maillot were planned the same year. The new Montparnasse station was built in 1969, which removed the last uncertainty about whether the tower would be erected, and it was

FIGURE 1 Aristide Bruant painted by Toulouse-Lautrec. Cover of Russell Ash, *Toulouse-Lautrec: The Complete Posters* ([London]: Pavilion, [1991])

FIGURE 2 Publicity poster for the Moulin Rouge and dancers of the French cancan, illustrated by Jules Chéret (1836–1932), 1890

Bridgeman Images

FIGURE 3 *The Girl from Maxim's* stage show, adapted by Julius Cahn from George Feydeau's play, made into French (*La Dame de chez Maxim* [1932]) and English films by Alexander Korda (1934)

FIGURE 4 *Le Paradis perdu* (Paradise lost), shot by Abel Gance in 1939
and released in 1940

FIGURE 5 *Ah! La Belle Epoque!* Palace revue adapted from
André Alléhaut's program on Radio-Paris

FIGURE 6 Poster for documentary *Paris 1900*, directed by
Nicole Védrès, 1948

Bridgeman Images

FIGURE 7 Poster for the film *French Cancan* (1955), about the early days of the Moulin Rouge, directed by Jean Renoir and starring Jean Gabin

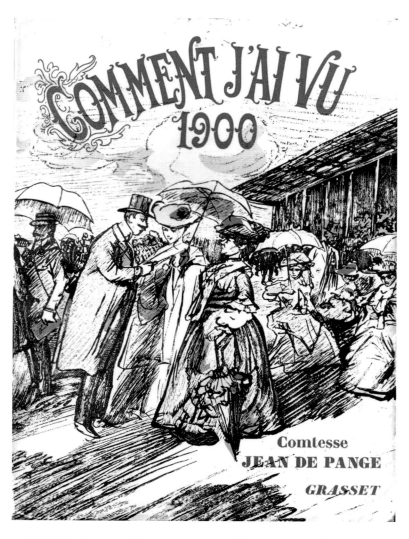

FIGURE 8 *Comment j'ai vu 1900*, cover of Comtesse Jean de Pange's memoir (Paris: Grasset, 1962)

FIGURE 9 Movie poster for *Casque d'Or* [Golden Helmet] (1952), directed by Jacques Becker and starring Simone Signoret and Serge Reggiani

Bridgeman Images

FIGURE 10 "Impératrices, artistes et cocottes sur la Riviera à la Belle Epoque," conference poster, Médiathèque de Monaco, 2019

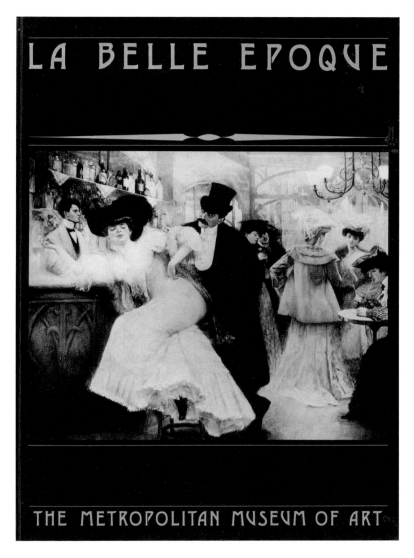

FIGURE 11 *La Belle Epoque*, front cover of exhibition catalogue, The Metropolitan Museum of Art, December 6, 1982–September 4, 1983. Galland, French, *The Bar at Maxim's* (detail). Watercolor, 15 3/4 x 18 1/8 in.

FIGURE 12 Cover of Esther Crain, *The Gilded Age in New York,*
1870–1910 (New York: Black Dog & Leventhal Publishers, 2016)

completed a few years later. The new layout of the Quai de Grenelle began in 1967 and its first low-rises appeared in 1970. Work was begun on the future Centre Pompidou and the Beaubourg, which was inaugurated in 1977.

That Paris changes is its right. But neither the skyscrapers at La Défense nor the Seine riverfront nor the expressways along its banks paid the least homage to Paris of the Belle Époque. In 1969, René Clair, who had long cherished the idea of filming a *Fantômas* and even drafted an adaptation, finally gave up the plan. "To reconstitute the Paris of Fantômas would be as expensive as to reconstruct the Paris of Louis XIV," he wrote to the author of the series, Marcel Allain.[19] Of course, many vestiges of Paris 1900 remained: the top of Montmartre, the sites of the Exhibitions of 1889 and 1900 (the Eiffel Tower, both the Grand and Petit Palais, the Gare d'Orsay, and the Alexandre III bridge). More vestiges were scattered across the city: Guimard's metro aedicula, the Théâtre des Champs-Elysées, the Samaritaine department store, and dozens of hotels, restaurants, "art nouveau" buildings, or simply edifices constructed at the start of the century. Significantly, these were the places that had always attracted tourists. But the break was profound: a cycle was being completed, in which the year 1900 was the symbol and the heart, as Paris entered a different phase of its history. For Louis Chevalier, then teaching the history of Paris at the Collège de France, it was a matter of assassination, and he described its premeditation in an angry book: "A landscape disappeared body and soul" between 1960 and 1968, and along with it a society that for better or worse was the heir of Paris at the beginning of the century.[20]

The capital city was not the only thing changing; great transformations were taking place in the whole country's structure and identity. A "modern" France emerged that decided to turn the page on the past, maybe with a few nostalgic regrets. The context was one of strong economic growth and a modernization of the nation's economic fabric. Sociologist Henri Mendras published *La Fin des paysans* (The vanishing peasant) in 1967; he saw this as a decisive mutation and the start of a "second French revolution."[21] Urbanization accelerated, carrying along with it social shifts as the managerial and middle classes came to the fore. Likewise, contemporary upheavals in traditional and religious values were noted by the Vatican II Council that ended in 1965. Political transformations were just as decisive. Starting in 1962, a France without its former colonies had to rediscover a path to international power. The Republic was now firm in its fifth incarnation and increasingly Gaullist; it had no need of this *imaginary de référence* that 1900 had been. While it had seemed useful in 1944, in 1950, and in 1955, it was no longer relevant, especially after the institutional reform in the autumn of 1962. The connotations of the old parliamentary régime and its imperial dimension were even embarrassing these days. This "modern" France, freed of its museum-city and its colonial burden, turned its back resolutely on nostalgia for a fuddy-duddy past. "Dear old France!" declared a tongue-in-cheek President Pompidou during a press conference in November 1972. "Good cuisine! The Folies-Bergère! Gay Paris! Fashion and good exports . . . like Cognac, Champagne, and even Bordeaux and Bourgogne [wines]. . . . It's all over. France has begun an industrial revolution."[22]

COUNTERCURRENTS

But the "Belle Époque" was sturdy. It bent but did not break, changing its face in order to adapt to contemporary uses. Previously aristocratic and worldly, it now made itself more popular, more antiestablishment, and even revolutionary. Forgotten figures and hidden memories were dredged up. "The Belle Époque has one face that sings and another face that weeps," Hubert Juin astutely noticed.[23] It was the crying face that now took over. The set and its decor were turned upside down, and it was now peopled with the poor, women, strikers, convicts, "deviants." The meaning ascribed to these years changed drastically; the background became red, black, and feminist.

This shift owes much to ideological movements that brought to the fore ideas impregnated with critical theory and with political and social radicalism. Marxism, anarchism, Third Worldism, and feminism converged, not without ambiguities and contradictions, but with a jubilant spirit of ideological profusion[24] that could reinterpret the turn from the nineteenth to the twentieth century. History teaching in universities was overhauled and now paid great attention to these years, which contributed to that shift in interpretation. Dropping the story of the Republic's triumph, historians became more socially conscious and tried to discern the composition, behavior, and rivalries among the major collective actors of the Belle Époque. High society élites and salons were not completely abandoned, but the center of gravity shifted to the working classes. The history of "social movements"—social unrest, strikes, repression, unionism, and various sects of French socialism—was covered between 1965 and 1975 by a number of doctoral theses as well as first-rate books by prominent figures in French historiography.[25] The "beauty" and carefree spirit of the turn of the century lost much of their sparkle. For example, when an important exhibition at the National Archives was devoted to the Belle Époque in 1972, fashion, ostentation, and technological innovation continued to be featured, although the opening section focused on the *classes populaires*, the world and language of work, and political and social tensions. A map detailing the sociology and demographics of deaths from tuberculosis in 1901 bore the following commentary: "On the contrary, for the great mass of Frenchmen, this period was difficult and harsh; the workers organized themselves."[26]

Of course, the general audience was not reading history dissertations, but such ideas circulated and gradually affected popular history too. The traditional image of a carefree and happy era was altering. This was particularly visible in school textbooks. With 1957's new curricula (referred to as "Braudel") that encouraged a more global and "civilizational" history, schools partly dropped the traditional view. But those that did address the period were much more critical. In 1961, a textbook covering the birth of the modern world mentioned only briefly "what has been called the Belle Époque" in connection with élites and artistic creation. Instead it offered an anguished view of the prewar years: "a political life dominated by social problems: the agrarian issue, the workers issue, the civil service issue . . . aggravation of the foreign affairs issue."[27] Textbooks in the 1970s tried to include advances in historiography. "The Belle Époque still hides many marginalities and inequalities," one of them stated in 1978.[28]

A different meaning began to be attached to the period. It was described as a cauldron in which new forces and multiple identities simmered. Certain of the new identities were like toddlers trying to overcome the constraints that had hobbled them, but many were bearers of the turbulence and contestations to come. The idea of a matrix remained, but one that was much more complex and pertained not just to cultural creation but also to individuals, their urges, and the social worlds to which they aspired.[29] All these displacements bore traces of "1968": the focus on the excluded, the defeated, and those marginalized by history; the rediscovery of anarchism and other alternative political projects, which kicked off the identity claims of "minorities"—social, sexual, ethnic—that were searching history for forms of legitimation. Another influence was the work of Michel Foucault, whose major books appeared between 1961 (*Madness and Civilization*) and the second half of the 1970s (*Discipline and Punish, The History of Sexuality*).

The effects of this shift were dual. First, it helped plumb the reverse side of a society that had seemed so peaceful, balanced, and satisfied, that had applauded the revues of the Quatorze Juillet and the refrains at the *café-concerts*, in order to expose the flaws, neuroses, and fantasies that haunted it. A whole continent of transgression gradually emerged for analysis: alcoholism, madness, suicide, crime, prostitution, degeneration, and perversions of all kinds. These underground aspects offered keys to thinking otherwise of the aesthetic creation of the 1900s, which of course was when psychoanalysis had been invented. The second consequence was the advent of new figures and new social actors (the weak, the dominated, the marginal) that "Belle Époque" history had previously ignored. First came forth working-class militants, revolutionaries, and antimilitarists. The historian of the anarchist movement, Jean Maitron, launched in 1960 the journal *The Social Movement,* and four years later the immense enterprise of his *Biographical Dictionary of the Workers' Movement* tried to restore dignity to the anonymous agitators of social struggle.[30] Attention was also paid to colonized peoples, for whom the "Belle Époque" remained dramatically associated with the apogee of French domination. Empire had been little mentioned (due to the lingering colonial wars between 1945 and 1962), but now it resurfaced—stressing the forms of exploitation and the resistance of the exploited and their expressions of anticolonialism.[31] On the margins of the universities, writers like Daniel Guérin combined engagement in favor of homosexual rights and/or against colonialism to produce notable books in the 1960s,[32] a trend encouraged by new publishing houses like Maspero (founded 1959) and Editions Champ libre (founded 1969).

People now realized that the France of 1900 had been full of poor peasants, domestic servants, prostitutes, prisoners, criminals, and the insane. Encouraged by Louis Aragon, the poet and novelist Georges-Emmanuel Clancier finished *Le Pain noir* (The black bread) in 1961, a social saga tracing from 1870 to the First World War the story of a poor country family. It won a literary prize and was adapted into a TV serial by Serge Moati that was broadcast from 1974 to 1976. Even art history started to render justice to those previously forgotten in official celebrations. In 1966, Jean-Paul Crespelle dedicated a book to these "little masters of the Belle Époque" who had been disdained by the innovators' pantheon.[33] The Paul Ricard Foundation organized a "Belle Époque" exhibition (September 1971) devoted to the "real aesthetics" of the period, to the cohort of "mediocrities"— official painters, illustrators, pretentious artists, or artisans of the decorative arts—whom Jean Cassou had long been recommending should be studied.[34] This was also the case with graphic designers and illustrators of the satirical press, principally among anarchist-leaning papers like *L'Assiette au beurre*.[35] The many exhibitions of illustrations and press layout, which had previously favored classical and "cultural" work (Charles Huard, Forain, Caran d'Ache, Toulouse-Lautrec), were now open to fresh and more transgressive artists like Jossot and Grandjouan.[36]

The view of women at the turn of the century was also transformed. The "Belle Époque" had so long appeared as the sanctuary of the "eternal woman," the wife or mistress who in a patriarchal society could rule underhandedly, then as the favorite terrain of the "New Woman" who initiated progress toward professional and social emancipation,[37] but now it was being promoted as the home of wholehearted feminism. On the model of the postwar avant-gardes who had sought their legitimacy in a heroic past, the feminists of the 1960s (and still more the "third wave" later on) drew on resources from the start of the century, in which they detected an effervescent matrix. Women's writing (both its figures and its forms) became the subject of new studies, from which emerged a nebula of writers who had been previously ignored: Gabriel Reval, Daniel Lesueur, Marcelle Tynaire, Jeanne Marni, Colette Yver.[38] Jean Rabaut's *Féministes de la Belle Époque* appeared in 1985, aiming at a general audience but trying to explode the myth of Belle Époque femininity. Here the upheaval in perspectives was radical. One could rediscover the thinking and activity of forgotten militants like Hubertine Auclert, Madeleine Pelletier, and Marguerite Durand, founder in 1897 of the daily *La Fronde*. The first biography of Hubertine Auclert, a pacifist and anticolonial woman who was hostile to marriage, was published in 1987,[39] showing her as the exact antithesis of the fantasy "woman of 1900" figure. A woman whom moderate feminists between the wars had rejected due to her radicalism and her vision "nonconforming to the nature of things"[40] was now hailed as a precursor as her speeches and writings were reissued. The same was true of Madeleine Pelletier, first female doctor to choose to specialize in "alienism," also a suffragette and militant neo-Malthusian. Linking sexuality, clothing, and emancipation, she had defended the necessary masculinization of women. As a psychiatrist, though, Pelletier had "troubles in judgment" and ended her days at an insane asylum in 1939.[41] Finally, stressing figures of the 1900s Sapphic culture—Colette, Natalie Barney, Liane de Pougy, Renée Vivien[42]—helped legitimize the lesbian identities that were being asserted at the time.

A more transgressive, scandalous, and "perverse" kind of literature also resurged, having been forgotten or relegated to the margins of what was "readable." In this case the phenomenon was less marked than elsewhere, because the existence and rehabilitation of "accursed poets" had been a literary tradition ever since Verlaine's day. André Breton, for example, edited in 1955 a new edition of *Le Voleur* with a preface titled: "Darien the Damned." The same year, Pierre La Bracherie in *Le Crapouillot* worried about the effacement of a body of literature that he wanted to restore. "Someday it will be desirable to have specialized teams excavate the sub-basements of

1900 in order to discover forgotten and disdained figures,"[43] listing Darien, Willy, Alfred Capus, Pierre Véber, Lucien Muhlfeld, and Maurice Beaubourg (who had already won in 1924 the prize of the unsung). The "countercurrent" sensibility that dominated these years of protest pushed toward exploring a new literary nebula that lay far from the sententious cluster of "thesis" novels from the previous era, and which might become the matrix of "modern" literary transgression.[44] Those in favor this time had wielded irony, provocation, or incendiary laughter, whereas those who lost themselves in ether, alcohol, or pornography; those who had been partial to anarchy, antimilitarism, or revolution; those who sought social or sexual transgression or who undermined certainties—in short, all those writers who had been *personae non grata* in 1900 literature—were gradually redeemed.

Early literary criticism was coming from the United States because in both history and literature, foreign specialists on France often turned to innovative topics in order to be recognized. Kenneth Cornell's thesis on the symbolist movement dated from 1951 and Roger Shattuck's famous *The Banquet Years* from 1958.[45] French scholarship increased throughout the 1960s with theses, articles, critical anthologies, and thematic analyses,[46] and this trend continued into the 1970s.[47] In 1964, André Billy had founded the Flammarion paperback collection "1900 vécu," but it ceased with the editor's death in 1971.[48] Biographies were devoted to rediscovered authors, most of them arising from editorial commissions, principally from Belgian critic Hubert Juin. "Interest was lively in the 1900 era, but then that was a fashion, a caprice, and improvisation," he wrote in 1972 in the introduction to his *Écrivains de l'Avant-Siècle*.[49] "We should be getting serious monographs and detailed studies! This is the means to restore to us, beyond its myths, this fascinating Belle Époque." Actual texts mattered more than academic studies of them. Juin's collection "Fin-de-siècle" (1977 to 1986) was decisive in this respect. In 1979 there already existed six collections of "decadent" writers.[50] Others emerged later, such as the collection "Around 1900" founded by Christian Pirot in 1984, and the "Bibliothèque Décadente" launched by Jean de Palacio at Séguier. From Feydeau to Jean Lorrain, from Paul Bourget to Charles-Louis Philippe, Belle Époque literature got a facelift.

As we see, the reinvention was rather radical and affected the whole understanding of the period. Even the political and social régime now appeared much less solid than it had before, shot through with tensions and terrible contradictions. The radical Republic, triumphant yesterday, was exhibiting its weaknesses. "The now-banal theme of the republican consensus, of a quasi-unanimous adherence to the republican model, was a nice legend; in fact until its final days, the Republic had ferocious enemies," noted René Rémond. Today historiography rightly insists on the fragility of the régime at the start of the century, which might also explain its saber-rattling and demonstrations of force. Illuminating social struggles (working classes, poverty, disease, insecurity) provided indispensable correctives. The mature landscape became more detailed, but when the pendulum had swung, it may have gone too far. For example, it became more difficult to understand why so many people could guffaw at *café-concerts* and also rush to military parades and maneuvers to "appreciate and compliment the French army." No doubt it was a matter of fine-tuning the balance. Nevertheless, the expression "Belle Époque" continued to prosper, even if it was now playing against type, insisting ironically and tendentiously on all that lay behind the set decoration.

ALL OF FRANCE IN THE BELLE ÉPOQUE

JUST AS decisive, a second shift in the final quarter of the twentieth century modified the period's principal uses and significance. There was a noticeable return at the end of the 1970s to the Belle Époque, but with another new face resulting from the immense heritage and commemorative wave that overcame the nation. The past, and especially the recent past, became "vintage," offering values of reassurance and refuge. The "retro" was in fashion and stimulated increasing consumption of cultural nostalgia that celebrated landscapes, the daily life of old France, and the artifacts it had produced. People started to buy what yesterday had been stuffed into attics and basements: faded clothing and lingerie, old posters and postcards, old dishes, and advertising tins.[1] In its wake the cultural decentralization sought by Culture Minister André Malraux finally became rooted across the country, constantly valorizing a patrimony that was both near at hand and increasingly "carried along by emotion."[2] In 1977 several new departments of the Cultural Affairs ministry were created.[3] The trend was in favor of history of the countryside, particularly detailed examination of local situations—yesterday's places, people, and gestures. Each locale wanted "its own history and so once 'forgotten holes' became potentially full of radiant meaning."[4] There was no need to have experienced what was being reclaimed, since nostalgia was also attached to a world that had not been known personally. Melancholy could be historical. This process privileged a few key and very stereotyped eras, among which the "Belle Époque" quickly came to the fore because it was neither too close nor too distant and because items from one's grandparents' times could be found in the attics of family homes and in secondhand shops that "bore the memory of a rural and preindustrial world."[5]

The context largely explains this investment in the past. In many respects the future had again become uncertain. Collective life was marked by economic crisis, social insecurity, and disturbing aspects of progress: pollution, nuclear weapons, an unhinged climate, and industrial contamination. The crisis in representation and the crumbling of the great ideological narratives were blurring the political horizon and discouraging any kind of commitment. Private life itself was overcome with the sexual anxiety that AIDS had unleashed. To everyone faced with a threatening world—or worse, an "empty" society—the past appeared as a reassuring repository of values, which invited individual and collective withdrawal into local identities. The moment belonged to desire, to the "exasperation of rootedness."[6]

The result was a growing need for history and for *"lieux de mémoire"* (places of memory). People wanted to know, valorize, and rehabilitate Old France. *Le patrimoine* had once been legal and financial, but now became cultural—even today's imperative. In 1978, a *Délégation du patrimoine* was created inside the Culture Ministry to encourage and endow initiatives. The year 1980 was declared the "Year of Heritage." Philippe Lecat, Minister of Culture from 1978 to 1981, wanted to involve the French people in holding national wealth "in common," wealth that had to be conserved, enriched, and transmitted. The focus was on "masterpieces" that were in danger, like manor houses and churches, but also farms, chapels, and homes. Books and films made for television featured local *terroirs*; novelists like Claude Vincenot and Claude praised the good old days and their "quality of life," as did rural rusticators. We learned in 1982 that the rural exodus had ended in France; the neologism *rurbain* appeared in 1989.[7] The desire grew to conserve the traces of a recent but vanished past and to rediscover common roots. The parish church of

Sermages, made famous by François Mitterrand's campaign poster in 1981, became the symbol of this "tranquil force," the France of *terroirs*. Retired people took up genealogy, and everybody tried to resuscitate the events and life stages that marked the personal histories of those close to them. Quickly the Great War became the heart of this "memorial activism," in which the genealogical fervor led to ransacking attics, which converged with both local initiatives and a militant ethos.[8] Nobody had forgotten that the *poilus* (World War One infantrymen), like their officers and their families waiting at home, all belonged to France of the "Belle Époque."

"MY VILLAGE DURING THE BELLE ÉPOQUE"

Starting in the mid-1970s a new type of pictorial book appeared. Dropping the subjects of socialite luxury and the artistic high life in the Belle Époque, as well as abandoning the saga of workers' struggles, these publications amounted to a myriad of microstories about "my town," "my region," even "my village" during the Belle Époque. Some such ventures had come out in the 1960s,[9] but it became a widespread phenomenon after 1975. Few regions or localities could escape having their own "Belle Époque" portrait, a genre of which one Brussels publisher (Willy De Hertogh, head of Sodim) made himself a specialist. From 1974 to 1977, Sodim published more than eighty of these books, sometimes devoted to regions (Brittany, Normandy, Champagne, Flanders, Bourbonnais), or more commonly to cities (Nantes, Bordeaux, Reims, Soissons, Marseille, Angoulême, etc.), and occasionally even to very small towns (Rambouillet, Le Tréport, Crépy-en-Valois, Brunoy)—all "in the Belle Époque." Since the niche product was booming, De Hertogh soon added thematic volumes to his list—aeronautics, the post office, woman in the Belle Époque—or picture albums dedicated to occupations—policing, milling, shoemaking. And Sodim was not the only publishing house to exploit this lode. In France, many regional and local publishers hopped onto the bandwagon. In Brest, Editions de la Cité launched a series called "Bretagne of the Belle Époque." Municipal and departmental archives and museums recuperated some of this manna, which also stimulated "countryside" publishing. An example was Orep, a small publisher in Normandy that began in 1987 to promote that region: "We proclaim the region and its history, its rich past, and its living patrimony," explained its director, Annie Fettu. Its collection "Belle Époque— memorable images" included numerous monographs devoted to particular cantons and to local trades around 1900.[10]

This total of about two hundred titles, of which some were self-published by their authors, composes a rather surprising map of France during the Belle Époque. Did singular landscapes, monuments, or picturesque trades justify a book's being devoted to a locality "around 1900"? In fact, no, this profusion is not explained by possible "curiosities" but resulted almost exclusively from the nature of these artifacts.

In fact all of these books were picture albums of postcards, combined with an often cursory commentary that was always pleasant and nostalgic. We know about the fascination at the start of the twentieth century for the "letter-card," an innovation from Austria to which the Exhibitions of 1889 and 1900 had given an extraordinary impetus. Many French printers were already devoted to the postcard format, like ELD (Ernest-Louis Le Deley) and Société Lévy et Neurdein in Paris, one in Nancy, one in Saint-Brieuc, and the Labouche Brothers in Toulouse. National production went from eight million cards per year in 1899 to 123 million per year in 1910.[11] At the time, more than 30,000 workers were employed in this sector, and about 50 journals or clubs were created to appeal to postcard collectors.[12] Paris was at the heart of many of these series. The principal ones (published by Tout Paris, Gondry, ND, LL, FF, CM) produced more than 10,000 views of the capital, to which should be added those focused on small streets, jobs, or specialized subjects.[13] No locality escaped the vigilant eyes of hundreds of traveling photographers who were roaming the country. Everybody—regardless of age, class, or gender—wrote postcards. "This is the necessary complement to railroads, bicycles, and automobiles," declared a journalist at *Figaro illustré* on October 1904, one of the new means of "dashing around existence."[14] This gigantic output covered everything: "views," "types," personalities, small trades, scenes of ordinary life, dramatic events. In this mix, pornography could bump into political demonstrations and workers' strikes; spectacular accidents could rub shoulders with "curiosities" and fantasies of daily life; crimes, floods, and baptismal flights had their place alongside pig roasts and dogsled races. The whole Belle Époque strutted its stuff in postcards.

Thus hundreds of millions of snaps produced at the start of the twentieth century were ready to constitute the material for this grass-roots "patrimonialization." In Albi, for example, Grand Sud Editions was founded by the grandson of a publisher of postcards.[15] The emergence of this type of anthology precisely corresponds to the moment when the market for old postcards took off. The first price guide came out in 1975, followed by many others that pinpointed rarities and oriented enthusiasts' collecting.[16] The first official exhibition was organized by Sylvie Forestier at the Museum of Popular Arts and Traditions in 1978,[17] when almost 50 specialized magazines and 400 associations could be counted.[18] A study a few years later under the aegis of the Society for French Ethnography showed that the nation boasted 10,000 members in postcard collectors' circles, 15,000 buyers of the postcard price guide, and almost a million amateurs.[19] All were "trying to resuscitate the past—the near past about which they had heard the previous generation speak." In fact, this fascination for postcards rhymed with the Belle Époque, as the first book devoted to it underscored: *1889–1914: 25 Years of Events Through Postcards.*[20] The organization of collections promoted by the Naudin collectors, at first thematic and then by commune and "sites concerned," lay behind the publication of all Belle Époque monographs.

To these should be added dozens of retro-photographic books functioning as so many benevolent, pleasant, and illustrated chronicles of the period: *Peasant France in 1900, Vanished France, Daily Life of the French Before 1914.*[21] Unsurprisingly, they all stressed anecdotes and curiosities of a "quirky France," doting on *faits divers* (bizarre news items), the comic, the ludicrous. They delighted in rural carnival parades, the Bal des Quat'zarts in the Latin Quarter, spectacular accidents (like the well-known scene of an out-of-control locomotive crashing through the facade of the Montparnasse train station in December 1895 or the collapse of a bridge near Angers in 1907, where 6,000 curious people had come to have their photograph taken at the site). Suicides and crimes of passion, duels and the exploits of *apaches*, the professional "fartist" Pujol, and the mayor's banquet all lent their crazy or bizarre images to an inexhaustible photographic bank. "The quirkiness of the subject lies more in the fact of appearing in a postcard than in the subject itself," commented one editor.[22] All of them activated nostalgia for a vanished world that had been obliterated by urban settings and modern living that were both deplored. "Whereas thirty-five years ago we had fields and prairies, now nothing grows but concrete; village homes are torn down to be replaced by 'quality' buildings with 'unobstructed views' of . . . in fact the apartment opposite, and sometimes there is even a private garden (the peak of a developer's munificence) just big enough to hold a rolling trash can and two pots of geraniums!" wrote the author of a book on the now-suburbanized village of Brie-Comte-Robert.[23]

The result was a picture album that ran through all the imaginable curiosities of an old-fashioned and antiquated era, the world "of yesterday" that was still a little like ours, on which we cast a retrospective and emotional glance. From 1890 to 1914, Martial Aubrespy, a local attorney in the Hérault, had taken more than 600 photographs of his family, village folk, and all the events that occurred nearby: hunts, festivals, grape harvests, marriages. Many other photographers imitated him. These images were simple and modest, but they were also *true*. "An image of the poor that is not a poor image," wrote a journalist for the Belgian daily *Le Soir*.[24] Objects, views, and also silhouettes and faces are all touching and moving—but also vaguely ridiculous. A passerby, a pretty girl, a waiter serving coffee, a bonnet maker, and children look into the lens. This might be your grandfather, or your great-grandmother. Somebody who perhaps would die in the war. A whole folklore emanates from the shot, a cultural anthropology of primal value that also demonstrates an aesthetic close to the "poetics of the diverse" that Victor Segalen describes in his *Essay on Exoticism*: notes that are brief, fleeting, "Other."[25] These curiosities speak to us of a vanished world, but one also familiar because it managed to invent objects with which we are still familiar: electricity, the telephone, the automobile, the airplane, the phonograph, advertising, the cinema, the comic strip. This past invented a modernity that is a little out of date but nevertheless warm and touching. Because it is simultaneously so close and so distant, this past arouses backward glances that are empathic and nostalgic. This is how we pay homage to the sources of our own time.

But the most decisive effect was geographical: the "Belle Époque," which until then had been exclusively Parisian and class-conscious (devoted to celebrating the high life, dinners at Maxim's, the great courtesans of the day), was suddenly discovered to be provincial, peasantlike, artisanal. Attention shifted from the glamour of *la vie parisienne* and leisure pursuits in outposts like the Riviera (see fig. 10) toward the most minor *"terroirs"* in a space that suddenly swelled to the dimensions of France as a whole; the focus turned to the working and daily lives of the most humble inhabitants of the nation. What emerged was a different Belle Époque, perhaps more "true" but certainly rural and populated by the anonymous, full of the smells and sounds of daily life. The history it told remained just as much a "summary sketch." It still barely explained anything and was always content to accumulate, to hoard,[26] but it was henceforth open to the whole country. It was now democratized.

IF THE BELLE ÉPOQUE WERE TOLD TO ME . . .

At the end of the twentieth century, the craving for 1900 could not be satisfied by postcard anthologies alone. People wanted the picturesque, but they also wanted what was true, had been experienced, and was emotionally vivifying, something that spoke to us of people's real lives. Launched in 1978, the series called "Si 1900 m'était conté" (If 1900 were told to me) tried to respond to these needs. Published by Editions France-Empire, a mass-market publisher that since its creation in 1945 had specialized in historical witness accounts and was directed by journalist Claude Pasteur (who had written popular biographies), the series had a solid publishing base and would issue twenty-nine volumes from 1978 to 1988. The goal was to offer readers a series of authentic accounts emanating from men and women of the 1900s who emerged from all social milieux. "Each of these books wants to reflect aspects of some specific social class, occupation, region, and well-defined place," explained Claude Pasteur in the catalogue description. And this is how the series started out, with personal stories that tried to be "both the document *and* the novel of a life," rich in anecdotes and the flavor of what had been "experienced." The local anchoring determined how the story was told: the use of local dialect, anecdotes, and folktales accentuated the regional past or yesterday's ways of life, in the tradition of the social gatherings that had taken place around 1900. Adding documents— letters, photographs, personal papers—further highlighted this dimension. But gradually the goal changed, maybe because the initial vein had been exhausted, and so the series evolved toward fictional or more literary texts written by authors from the commercial pole. It also published reprints and moved away from the focus on 1900, which may explain its termination a few years later. But its existence chimed with the new representations of the Belle Époque, forsaking Paris to cover all of France, giving speech to the anonymous and celebrating local situations, regional traditions, and artisanal trades.

Its relative failure also showed that celebrity autobiographies and potential memoirs were becoming rare. By 1980, the last living wit- nesses of the Belle Époque were about a hundred years old, and most of the great names and prestigious figures had already been covered. The novelist Maurice Genevoix, who died that year at age ninety, did leave an autobiography—*Trente mille jours* (Thirty thousand days)— but it gave little space to the prewar years. Rare were the lucky edi- tors who could lay hands on an unpublished major text like the memoirs of the famous courtesan Liane de Pougy, published by Plon only in 1977.[27] But what *did* come into print perhaps corresponded better to the expectations of the time: anonymous people speaking of a difficult or different life—a Flemish squire who offered family memories, a union worker who told about militancy, a film camera- man, an unknown student at the elite teachers' college, and espe- cially simple folk like Marlène, a Breton peasant whose life inaugu- rated the "Brittany in the Belle Époque" series.[28] A hybrid sort of text like *Mémé Santerre: une vie* by Serge Grafteaux (1977) enjoyed consid- erable success. Others went unnoticed; perhaps their sociology and stories strayed too far from expected representations. "Although this was the Belle Époque, there was a spirit of segregation between peo- ple of the city and those of the countryside," Marcel Voisin, a former neo-Malthusian, wrote ironically.[29]

Readers now had to look elsewhere for something to satisfy their demand for finding their roots back in 1900. Certain towns were lucky enough to have a "historiographer." In Marseille, there was former journalist Jean Contrucci, veteran reporter at the *Provençal* and also *Le Monde*'s correspondent in Marseille. With his historical crime novels and his recent *Marseille de la Belle Époque,* Contrucci published in five volumes *It Happened in Marseille,* intended—like the postcard albums—to acknowledge places, identify personalities, and offer "a bouquet of chronicles to be listened to like a slow waltz, while breathing the perfume of yesterday's flowers."[30] Other initiatives moved in a similar direction, like *Editions 1900,* which reissued "minor masters" and period "documents" from that decade: dictionaries, almanacs, the Vilmorin gardening manual, the catalogue of the Saint-Etienne factory for weapons and cycles, etc.

The sequence of picturesque and anecdotal history books did not slow down. Arthur Conte published in 1975 *Le Premier Janvier 1900,* which inaugurated an eponymous series, in addition to such tomes as *Histoire anecdotique de la Belle Époque* and *Histoires vraies du vingtième siècle.*[31] Preparing such books posed no problem for the authors: the corpus of events or anecdotes was easily available from the mass of similar books published in earlier decades; they could rely also on an immense and accessible iconography, rich and always pleasant: starting with postcards, of course, but also posters, amusing and suggestive advertising—for Bibendum, Cadum Baby, Pink Pills, Globéol, Kub broth, Job cigarette papers—plus fashion and ladies' magazine illustrations, and an almost infinite ocean of illustrated supplements to Belle Époque newspapers.[32] We may add the continuous flow of biographies, always on the same subjects, of celebrities in the world of arts and letters, and especially in the *demi-monde* (Jane Avril, La Belle Otero, Marguerite Steinheil, and Mata Hari).[33]

The Belle Époque at the end of the twentieth century appeared to be a paradise for the popularization industry. In France and abroad, there was no end to the theme of Paris 1900, Paris Art Nouveau, and Paris on the Eve. The formula was advantageous: mentioning the "Miraculous Years" was always pleasant, especially when this could be associated with a place everybody knew, like Paris, "homeland for all of us," and could mobilize names, images, and references that belonged to the world's cultural heritage: Proust, Guimard, Debussy, art nouveau, Toulouse-Lautrec, Picasso, Sarah Bernhardt, Diaghilev, etc.[34] Could anyone not admit that such richly illustrated coffee-table books were educational? And that your guests would be pleased to take a look at them? A common narrative artifice was to use some "historic" depth as ballast. Alongside the intense moments of happiness and artistic flourishing, it sufficed to mention the accumulation of threats and dangers on the horizon, perils that contemporaries could not see but the modern reader could fully appreciate. "Dancing on a volcano" was the relevant phrase. In its extreme form, the "volcano" could even be transformed into the "cauldron of the apocalypse"![35] With respect to World War One, this reached the height of teleology—a sort of dual teleology since the "Belle Époque," a retrospective expression we know was forged much later, was being associated with prescience of a war that had not yet occurred. A book by American Mary McAuliffe exemplifies this type of coffee-table book. Starting with its title, *Dawn of the Belle Époque: The Paris of Monet, Zola, Bernhardt, Eiffel, Debussy, Clemenceau, and Their Friends* (2011) enumerated the gallery of famous people whose life and work were being honored. She followed up in 2014 with *Twilight of the Belle Époque: The Paris of Picasso, Stravinsky, Proust, Renault, Marie Curie, Gertrude Stein, and Their Friends Through the Great War.*[36] The principle was the same: short chapters composing a sort of almanac centered on key personalities and notable events of cultural (and occasionally political) life. The figures were famous and the illustrations—photographs of Paris, portraits, reproductions of artworks—were gorgeous. We perceive the interest for publishers as well as for readers: a cultured, pleasant, and "quality" voyage in a universe that was already partly known, which could only increase the attraction.

On top of these serious books came in the same years a lighter and sometimes even obscene variant, anthologies of pornographic postcards, which had great international success. I have already noted the erotic and sexual content of the Belle Époque imaginary. Back in 1964, Patrick Waldberg had pointed to the modern "suaveness," the knowing scenes of undress, the fetishism of laced corsets, furs, ankle boots.[37] We know from *Claudine* by Willy to *Pierrette* by

Antonin Reschal that the period had been obsessed by mistresses. The rediscovery of thousands of forbidden cards abruptly reinvigorated this imaginary. These collections were known to specialists, but now publishers' marketing put them at the disposal of a wide audience that suddenly discovered that their grandparents were more licentious than it previously believed. The weekly titillation in yesterday's *Folichonneries*[38] was now exhibited in contemporary bookstore displays.

Here again, a strange mixture of distance and proximity may explain the success: these women, these men, these couples who were surprised in "scabrous" positions do indeed oddly resemble us; their bodies, their genitals, might be ours. But something separates us from them, which relates not merely to the "old auntie" décor, the black-and-white or sepia tone of the photographs. The women are certainly beautiful, but do they arouse my desire? A strange distance has slipped between them and me, between them and us, which also explains why they seem less shocking than they really are. Philippe Sollers was one of the first writers to celebrate (in 1987) these *Licentious Photos of the Belle Époque*.[39] "Whence comes this magnetic attraction of this time between two centuries, before everything accelerated into destruction? Treasures of a lost time. The curtain rises."

These treasures nourished a veritable genre that spread across France and abroad at the end of the twentieth century. People spoke of the golden age of erotic photography;[40] like the clothing and the furniture, it now possessed the quality of being *vintage*.[41] Similar books were distributed in Europe and the United States,[42] yet curiously, it was considered a French specialty. England, Germany, Austria-Hungary, the United States, and Mexico produced thousands of these cards,[43] but the French ones seemed to have a particular charm and savor, to the point that the term "French postcards" came to designate these erotic images in English. Why France? Undoubtedly due to the effective breadth of the national market for obscenity, if we may believe the police seizures of it, which rose at the start of the century to several hundred thousand items (including at least seventy films[44]). But we must acknowledge the strength of the imaginary that made Gay Paree of 1900 the capital of love, pleasure, and licentiousness.

A VERY BROAD "BELLE ÉPOQUE"

AT THE end of the century, a third and final shift affected the Belle Époque social imaginary: it was inordinately stretched, extended, dilated. Turning away from Paris and even from France, the term "Belle Epoque" was exported and came to be used in a growing number of languages to signify phenomena that were often far removed from the original. In general, the term remained focused on the turn from the nineteenth to the twentieth century and still evoked forms of social and cultural life, but now "Belle Époque" seemed more and more to escape the history of France alone. It also tended to escape history altogether and become a sort of cultural label with a rather broad significance. The commercial motive, partly decontextualized, soon was to satisfy the passion for the "retro" and then for the "vintage" that gripped many societies.

APPROPRIATED BY THE WORLD

The Belle Époque was born in France and for a long time had not sought to leave it. The natural dazzle of Paris 1900 sufficed to ensure its international influence. To be fair, Belgium was bound to be included, and there the phrase was used analogously. The time boundaries somewhat differed, with Belgium's starting a little earlier (around 1885, date of the acquisition of the Congo by King Leopold II), as demonstrated by the "Belle Époque" rooms at the Belvue Museum in Brussels.[1] But the representations were indeed the same, centering on cultural euphoria and high society life. What would Cléo de Mérode's fate have been without the white beard and tall stature of her consort, the King of the Belgians? In 1949, the novelist Paul Prist remembered the happy time when Brussels artists and poets gathered at the Roi Gambrinus, at Hulstkamp, at Ravenstein, at the Caves de Maastricht.[2] In parts of Belgium, the formula did suffer from its Frenchness, which was repugnant to the Flemish, but it was much used by the French-speaking Walloons. The exhibition of posters (*Affiches de la Belle Époque*) organized in 1961 at the château de Fraiture-en-Condroz, near Liège, drew equally on French and Belgian artists.[3] And even that separation was overcome: two Flemish academics recently decided to use the expression (the time period enlarged to 1925) in writing a transnational history of Belgium.[4]

These two words, *Belle* and *Époque*, have the advantage that they are easily understood in many other languages. Therefore they were often used as a catchphrase for France at the end of the nineteenth century. In English, which has its own terms to describe the period ("Late Victorianism" and then the "Edwardian Age" in England, the "Gilded Age" and the "Progressive Era" in the United States), *the* Belle Époque was exclusively French. This was also long the case in German: it is under this title that Hermann Schreiber described in 1967 Paris at the turn of the century; Shattuck's *The Banquet Years* was translated into German as *Die Belle Epoque*, even though he did not use the expression in English.[5] Moreover, the "Belle Époque" had competition from "fin de siècle," a prized expression in English-speaking countries, and which was used both for the 1890s and for the start of the twentieth century, as explained by the editors of a *Fin-de-Siècle Reader.*[6] The British author Raymond Rudorff maintains (perhaps hastily) that subsequent generations called "Belle Époque" what contemporaries had called "fin de siècle."[7] Some British scholars ventured further, contrasting "Belle Époque" (as a French and nationalist phrase that glosses over social realities) with "fin de siècle" (which by contrast stresses a chaotic period of anxiety, repression, sexual antagonism, and class tensions).[8] Finally, even discussing a "belle époque" in Munich, Prague, or even Vienna[9] could even smack of French cultural imperialism—though publishers' marketing choices sometimes got the better of writers' intentions. By the last third of the twentieth century, however, other languages (and hence other national histories) were gradually adopting the expression, whose use expanded to describe a widely shared moment, a sort of cultural state of Europe, not just of France.

Italy was the pioneer in appropriating the expression, and it conserved the French spelling. In 1954, almost fifteen years after France, the writer Angiolo Biancotti published under this title a critical anthology of Italian poets of the start of the century who were all looking for their lost youth.[10] Three years later, in 1957, Giuseppe Chiassi's diary (which opened in the years preceding the Great War) was published under the eloquent title *The Rome of My Twenties: Our "Belle Époque."*[11] This same notion of the "Belle Époque" was used in film critic Francesco Dorigo's 1960 study of the films devoted to 1900.[12] In 1961, Manlio Miserocchi called the artist Pierro Romanelli "a personage of the Belle Époque."[13] For the Italians, by now it was clear that the expression was no longer reserved for France. Tom Antongini, who was the friend, secretary, and biographer of the poet d'Annunzio, delivered in 1965 (at the age of almost ninety, having been born in 1877) a series of souvenir portraits. Apart from d'Annunzio, we find Clemenceau, Giovanni Papini, Valery Larbaud, Eleonora Duse, Oscar Wilde, Peppino Garibaldi, Felice Cavallotti, Cécile Sorel, Marco Praga, Francis de Miomandre—and La Belle Otéro. His book was of course titled *La Belle Époque.*[14]

Soon every Italian city had its own "Belle Époque" portrait: Trieste, Verona, Rome (there are dozens of *Roma nella Belle Époque*), Bari, Capri, Milan, and Riccione, the green pearl of the Adriatic.[15] But Naples took the prize as the most "Belle Époque" Italian city thanks to its turn-of-the-century newspaper *Il Mattino*, its department store Mele, its café Gambrinus, and especially its Salon Margherita, the first "singing café" in Italy (opened in November 1890), a twin of the Moulin Rouge where all the stars of the day appeared, including Lina Cavalieri, Mata Hari, and even the chaste Cléo de Mérode.[16]

Italian historiography seized upon the expression as a natural temporal marker, speaking of Belle Époque theater, arts, criminality, bicycles, anarchists, etc.[17] The two words were found everywhere in the 1980s, with no reference to France and no editor wanting to translate it into Italian. While the end point was fixed at 1915 (the date of Italy's entry into the war), the earlier time boundary was more fluid, sometimes the 1880s, or 1870s, or simply "the decade preceding the Great War."[18] Historical overviews and textbooks used it as a chronological marker with transparent meaning: "L'Italia della 'Belle Époque,'" "dall'invasione napoleonica alla Belle Époque," "dalla belle époque al fascismo."[19] The permanence of the French form could be considered imperialist, though, so writers would explain the crucial role of Paris in the culture of the time: "Italy of the *bella epoca* or of the *Belle Époque*, referring to the life and customs of Paris, which was then the heart of the European 'new wave,' which lasted from the dawn of the twentieth century to the war of 1914."[20]

This gave birth to a final usage, later found in other languages like English and German,[21] but which the Italians were the first to employ: the "Belle Époque" as a singular chapter in the history of Europe as a whole. As Francesco Dorigo explained, the expression was full of nostalgia for a great "cultural moment in the great European capitals."[22] "Belle Époque: two words, but an expression that endures to designate, in all languages, that more or less happy era at the turn of the nineteenth to the twentieth centuries, especially in Europe," explained Franco Fava.[23] At the end of the 1970s, Italian writers offered vast frescoes of this slice of history when Paris, Vienna, and Milan rubbed shoulders, when d'Annunzio met Wilde and Nietzsche, when the Brooklyn Bridge, the Eiffel Tower, Boldini, and the French cancan ran in concert with each other. For example, journalist Giovanni Castelani's *La Belle Époque* offered a "chronicle of manners, scandals, and the most significant events of Europe of the Belle Époque (1871–1915)."[24] More ambitious was *La Belle Époque* (1977), edited by the art historian Eleonora Bairati. Subtitled "the deceptive euphoria of fifteen years of European history," the book was translated into English and French.[25] Richly illustrated, it offered a wide panorama of the cultural life of the start of the century, while of course stressing the important Italian contribution—by Boldini, Capiello, Chirico, Saviano, d'Annunzio, Marinetti Boccioni, and the Futurists—to the glad era. Italy had made the "Belle Époque" into a moment of "world culture."

Also very early on (1967), Brazil appropriated the expression to apply to its own history, starting with its former capital, Rio de Janeiro, mainly because of the similarities between the transformations of Rio and Baron Haussmann's urban project.[26] Fernando Pereira Passos, the mayor of Rio at the time, sojourned in Paris (from 1857 to 1860, then again in 1880 and 1881) and with the help of engineers (often trained in French schools), he undertook between 1902 and 1906 to rearrange the city. The worksites resembled each other: leveling, digging, or enlarging avenues lined with prestigious buildings (the municipal theater, the Palácio Monroe) with aligned facades, creating large squares, planting green spaces and parks such as the hanging garden of Valongo. Associated with the sanitary reforms undertaken in the same years by the hygienist Oswaldo Cruz, a veritable "tropical Paris" emerged on the Brazilian coast, not without the gradual relegation—*favelizaçao*—of the working class being chased out of the city center by this "embellishment." But the ambition of the authorities was to "civilize" the *carioca* way of life, in full agreement with élites who were passionate about "modernism" and French culture. The good society of Rio had experienced this start of the century in a very Parisian atmosphere: theaters, salons, the press, and literature flaunted their fascination with a city that for Brazilian élites was also a major tourist destination.[27] The photographs of Rio taken by Augusto Malta starting in 1903 transport us to a sort of "universal" Belle Époque, and we find the same illusion of absolute "modernity" in many films from the young Brazilian cinema.[28] The arrival of electricity, of "merchandise emblematic of the Belle Époque," and then the national exhibition of 1908 added still more to this identification.[29]

Carried along by this usage, the expression "Belle Époque"—still in its French form—spread rapidly in Brazilian history writing. From Rio, it moved to Sao Paulo, which in 1974 got its own belle époque,[30] then to other cities in the country: Fortaleza[31] and Porto Alegre,[32] even to Manaus and Amazonian towns, where the term "Belle

Époque" evoked the golden age of the rubber industry and the consequent social and cultural euphoria.[33] By the end of the 1980s, the
expression had become "natural": as in France and in Italy, it was
used to characterize the turn of the century, to suggest a period of
growth, democratization, and a positivist spirit. "Rio in the Belle
Époque" and "Brazil of the Belle Époque" became current phrases in
works of social, cultural, or literary history.[34] An important personality like the chronicler João do Rio, whose articles in the *Gazeta de
Notícias* had described the social life at the start of the twentieth century, became in everybody's eyes an eminent "Belle Époque" figure.
The expression was transformed into a simple temporal marker,[35]
though the start and end points of the era were not really fixed;
as in works in other languages, they continued to fluctuate enormously. It was sometimes a very short sequence—1913–1917 for one
musicologist[36]—but most often dates were pinned to consequential
moments, for example, starting in 1889 because of the proclamation
of the Brazilian Republic and ending with the revolution of 1930 that
overthrew President Washington Luis.[37] But others thought its heart
lay in the 1920s[38] or identified it with the era of Getulio Vargas,[39] who
governed Brazil from 1930 to 1954. It was even used to describe the
time when filmmaker Lima Barreto made *Os cangaceiros,* which won
the 1953 prize at the Cannes Festival![40] As in France, there was a marketing formula that consisted of calling a book "The Belle Époque of
[whatever]."[41] In truth, these temporal variations did not matter
much, except to show how much the expression "Belle Époque" was
unquestioningly able to prevail in other languages as a synonym,
both scholarly and popular, for the cultural and social modernity of
the twentieth century.

This took place throughout Latin America, but Mexico is a special
case. The city was also marked early on by the cultural influence of
the model of Paris, its press, and its literature. *The "Belle Époque" in
México* (published in 1971 by Juan Somolinos) demonstrates this
ascendancy. Paris was the "metropolis of pleasure" and artistic creation, and a model for Mexico City, which the revolution of 1910 had
transformed into a modern city where fashion, the graphic arts,
architecture, and especially art nouveau flourished, expressed in
many buildings of the Colonia Juarez.[42] Nevertheless, the phrase had

a hard time taking root in a country where endogenous notions like *porfiriato* (the period of modernization linked to the presidency of Porfirio Diaz from 1876 to 1910) and then *revolución* were strong competitors. Ultimately, this left the "Mexican Belle Époque" to describe only its "art nouveau" of the early twentieth century.[43]

Everywhere else in South America the impetus came from Rio. The strong identity of the city and the rise of Brazilian power in the last quarter of the twentieth century contributed to spreading the expression among its Hispanic neighbors. In 1974, the Paraguayan writer Jose Maria Rivarola Matto used it in a series of articles published in *La Tribuna* of Asunción to depict the years preceding the Chaco War (1932–1935).[44] Montevideo, in love with "Parisian chic," also used the term in reference to its prosperous 1900s, marked by the rise of entertainment shows, worldly leisure activities, and an economy of consumption.[45] In Lima, the expression was linked to the figure of Pedro Valdelomar, a writer and poet who was considered to be the father of the Peruvian avant-gardes at the start of the twentieth century.[46] Starting in 1980, all the great cities of South America had used it at least once in writing their history: Caracas, Buenos Aires, Bogota, Santiago de Chile, Valparaiso.[47] It was used elsewhere less frequently and less naturally than in Brazil, of course, but it did demonstrate the evident "globalization" of the Belle Époque. On the other hand, it was abandoned in Portugal and used only belatedly and differently in Spain, as in Fernando Trueba's 1992 film, *Belle Époque*, which described the Spanish society of 1931, the good old days of the second republic.[48]

Since then, the expression has constantly spread to other languages. It is now used in German to evoke Munich or Zurich society, but also in Polish and in Greek.[49] Certain forms of its internationalization arise from less erudite intentions. Thus in the 1990s, Egypt discovered its own "Belle Époque" (here too in French), which had not existed before.[50] Here, the "good old days" were a golden age with rather vague boundaries, sometimes associated with the reign of King Farouk (1936–1952) and sometimes with that of King Fouad (1918–1936) or with the Khedive era—in any case, before Nasser became president. It was the "glamorous Egypt of pashas and monarchs," of grand hotels and cruises on the Nile. While this patrimonial invention did lead to some efforts at restoration or architectural preservation, it expressed strong nostalgia for colonialism and obeyed primarily political and mercantile imperatives. "Belle Époque" became a sort of talisman, a magic formula referring to a vague (almost mythic) era of happiness and shared fulfillment. We would need to survey other languages and other cultures—in Africa, Asia, or the Middle East—to detect similar uses that might make "Belle Époque" a tool of postcolonial rhetoric.

The year 1900 had incontestably marked the apogee of European imperialism. Does celebrating it amount to implicitly accepting its colonial dimension? The Belle Époque social imaginary, as we have said, had very little to do with anything overseas, probably due to the context in which it emerged in a decade marked by colonial wars and the policies of "cooperation" that followed them. Europe was the focus, a Europe enlarged to those cities of Latin America that were still so close, a Europe that was triumphing by itself and for itself. This Europe had dominated its colonies—that cannot be denied—and drew profit from them, but now it did not wish to express or even acknowledge that. It tried to make itself cozy in a quasi-supernatural state of cultural creationism. And the Belle Époque—the expression as well as the imaginary—had come to signify the "European miracle" that was born in France.

This internationalization of the Belle Époque was boosted by numerous exhibitions that circulated throughout the world. We have to be careful, of course: not all the retrospectives of Toulouse-Lautrec, Picasso, or Diaghilev were (or are) necessarily "Belle Époque" exhibitions. Even if there are many overlaps and although these manifestations sometimes pose the question of the "Frenchness" of the Belle Époque, we may distinguish between shows actually devoted to 1900s Paris or France or celebrate a particular French artist of that time, and those devoted more generally to European art of the years from 1880 to 1914.

The international career of the period actually began with *The Belle Époque, 1890–1914*, a prestigious international exhibition organized in 1981 at the Metropolitan Museum of Art in New York (see fig. 11). The event could not have been more important: the Met is one of the greatest museums in the world, and the curator of the exhibition,

Diana Vreeland, was at the time one of the most famous fashion journalists of the twentieth century. Very Francophile (she was born in
Paris in 1903 into Anglo-American high society), she became in 1936
editor-in-chief of *Harper's Bazaar,* then in 1962 editor of *Vogue.*[51] Con-
sultant at the Met since 1972, Vreeland had already organized a series
of spectacular exhibitions there (*The World of Balenciaga* in 1973, *Hollywood Design* in 1974, *The Glory of Russian Costumes* in 1976, *Vanity
Fair* in 1977) that gave the Costume Institute an international stature.
The Belle Époque was the apex of this trajectory.

The exhibition was wholly devoted to the luxury of Parisian high
society at a time when "women believed in the sumptuousness of
their ecstatic beauty." Eight gallery rooms reconstructed the key sites
of Parisian life (Maxim's, the Bois de Boulogne, the Heure bleue,
etc.). More than fifty mannequins were displayed in them, wearing
prestigious costumes: robes that had belonged to Queen Alexandra,
to the wife of Edward VII, to Sarah Bernhardt, to Eleonora Duse,
and to Countess Greffulhe. The exhibition almost perfectly corresponded to its élite audience. The New York upper crust attended the
inaugural dinner at $500 a plate, then the ball afterward. Pierre Car-
din, one of the event's sponsors, spent $500,000 just on the recon-
struction of the interior of Maxim's restaurant, fountain included.
All the clichéd images were assembled to idealize the Paris of the
Belle Époque, "the City of Light, the flickering shadow of chestnut
trees along the boulevards . . . the charming terraces and restaurants around the Bois de Boulogne—that 'woods' where at teatime
children dressed in velvet and mauve lace are taken, and where rich
messieurs in the evening attract the famous *demi-mondaines, belles
cocottes,* and *grandes dames,* in the splendor of their perfumed furs,
long gloves, and gigantic hats."[52] The catalogue contains a posthumous text by Philippe Jullian, grandson of the historian Camille Jullian and a great collector.[53] More nuanced, he tried to relativize the
splendor of the era, to distinguish the 1900s from the fin de siècle
that preceded it, and to describe their respective tenors. But the great
luxuriousness of the exhibit struck people's minds more than did
Jullian's commentary in the catalogue. Above all, it helped popularize the "Belle Époque" in the United States, making the notion a sort
of aesthetic and social label with international prestige.[54]

Other major exhibitions followed, like *Paris Belle Époque: 1880–1914*, organized in 1994 at the Villa Hügel in Essen, paying homage to the "capital of the nineteenth century," its theaters, its *cafés-concerts*, and its avant-gardes.[55] Or the more recent *Paris en scène, 1889–1914*, organized in 2013 at the Civilizations Museum of Québec, which tried to reconstruct faithfully the capital's urban identity, the boulevards with their sounds and movements, outside cafes and advertising posters, and the whole of boulevard sociability, its invitation to the spectacle of the city itself. This was an enchanted Paris, a city in a state of cultural grace being offered to delight the whole world.

Many other exhibitions were devoted to artists, French or foreign, whose destiny was tied to Paris of the Belle Époque. The list would be interminable, and Toulouse-Lautrec would emerge the great winner, since his work (despite his early death in 1901) seemed to embody the period (see again fig. 1).[56] Undoubtedly the Belle Époque was most internationalized in this domain of the arts, specifically painting. Wasn't Paris, its epicenter, populated by artists who had come from all over the continent? By laying claim to the Belle Époque, Europe was merely claiming its due, a brand name, an appellation with rather fluid contours—Paris, Europe, 1900—but one that guaranteed high cultural quality. In 1964 the Singer Museum in Laren (Netherlands) organized an exhibition on painting in the "Belle Époque" that presented many canvases by European artists in the years 1880–1914, both Dutch (Jan Hendriks, Jan Sluijtrs, Max Slevogt) and French (Vuillard, Pissarro). Obviously, the expression—universally comprehensible—now designated a moment in the European aesthetic and its pictorial art.[57] The show could equally well have been called *Europa 1900*, as was the Kursaal's in Ostend during the summer of 1967.[58] But "Belle Époque" sounded more chic, evoking Paris, Marcel Proust, and a whole universe of more muted distinction. The exhibition *La Belle Époque* organized in 1970 at the Library of Congress in Washington, D.C., presented a collection of Belgian drawings and posters;[59] *Belle Époque Posters* in 1979 at the Vleeshuis Museum in Antwerp offered a collection of Belgian, English, and American works.[60] And the same melange was true in London, New York, Barcelona, Brussels, etc.[61]

Though the links with Paris were never broken, the expression had now won its independence. In a Brussels exhibition devoted to "visionary works from before 1914,"[62] the curator reflected on the meaning of this widening to the scale of Europe: "Was the Belle Époque the arrival of an uncertain future or else the prelude to the ineluctable catastrophe of World War One?" Behind the use of the expression "Belle Époque," the gathering of forty-some artists coming from six European nations was meant to question the "plastic signature of an era wallowing in the uncertainties . . . of a world in revolution that we are trying to understand *a posteriori* as the visionary images of a somber future."

In short, the notion had been totally transformed over twenty years. Sometimes it even lost all reference to Paris and to the history of France. Here is how an Australian historian recently defined it: "The European period known as the Belle Époque was a time of intense and dynamic modernization that affected social and political organization, artistic and literary life, as well as the scientific movement."[63] Some writers even turn it into the matrix of an unprecedented process of cultural globalization . . . until war put a stop to it. In this crisscrossing of influences and lineages, France is usually top of the heap because it is transformed into an active social and cultural laboratory. But France might also be seen as losing, being just the frame within which palpitated the whole world's heart. "The dashing Edward VII was the true father of the Belle Époque," explained an American preface writer.[64] As so often, the truth was somewhere in between the preeminence and insignificance of Paris. When James Gordon Bennett Jr., the eccentric son of the founder of the *New York Herald,* settled in 1887 along the Avenue de l'Opéra to found the *Paris Herald,* his intention was to publish a paper that would be read by the crowned heads of the Old Continent and by millionaires and *nouveaux riches,* which was why he could not bypass Paris. He is said to have opined that "a dog crushed on the Rue du Louvre is more interesting than a devastating flood in China."[65] His newspaper hawked a purely Parisian "Belle Époque" more than it did an international imaginary. This explains why even today the *Herald*'s memorable pages are reprinted.

EVERYTHING IS CULTURAL IN
THE ERA OF THE VINTAGE

THE BELLE époque occurring at our own turn of the century—
from the twentieth to the twenty-first—cultivated this paradox.
On the one hand, it is proclaimed as a unique moment of the
cultural influence of France, which today remembers less the triumph
of the radical Republic (or the vigorous social struggles) than the
1900s' extraordinary capacity for aesthetic innovation and artistic creation. In any case, that is what the cinema, literature, exhibitions (and
to a lesser extent, history) orchestrate. But on the other hand, it has
become a commercial motif, focused on exploiting a best-selling
theme. If we look more closely, the paradox is perhaps more apparent
than real, since the original Belle Époque was also a period of a mass
culture eager to blur boundaries and genres.

A VERY CULTURAL BELLE ÉPOQUE

This primacy of "culture," whose rise is one of the definitive traits of
the end of the twentieth century, found many things in the Belle
Époque to nourish every kind of expectation: a passion for entertainment spectacles, an intensity of creation, and strong avant-gardes.
Here is how an American encyclopedia summarized the Belle Époque:

The period is defined by a cultural revolution carried by a feeling of optimism and creative enthusiasm. Paris prospered as an artistic, literary, and fashion center. The artistic scene was flourishing and everybody looked vigorously for the pleasure of life. The era also witnessed the spectacular rise of cafés-concerts, music-halls, exhibitions. The restaurants and cabarets of Montmartre attracted intellectuals and avant-garde artists; music and theater adopted forms free from the classical artistic constraints and were open to all social classes.[1]

In 2012, a course on the subject for New York University students stated that "this period in the life of the Third Republic (1871–1914) is one of extraordinary artistic successes. Not only was Paris the undisputed Western capital of painting and sculpture, it was also the most important site of musical, theatrical, and also literary production."[2] We know that such interpretations are far from new, but they find increased resonance in the current context of "everything is cultural" and its ideal of democratization. There have never been so many exhibitions, and attendance has followed the frenetic pace of public presentations. Grand patrimonial retrospectives like that of *1900* that opened at the National Galleries of the Grand Palais on March 14, 2000,[3] vie with smaller exhibitions trying to rediscover less well-known artists like Augustin Grass-Mick, Jean Béraud, Charles Huard, Jacques-Emile Blanche, Jules Chéret, and Félix Vallotton. Posters, since the first great exhibition at the Strasbourg Museum in 1981,[4] have enjoyed rising fortunes, as have press illustrations and caricatures. Accompanied by their catalogues and coffee-table books, these manifestations constantly celebrate the inventiveness and creative vigor of those years.

The Internet has catapulted the spread of the images of 1900 to new heights: many sites and "Facebook communities" continuously feed to Internet surfers "photographic albums" full of reproductions of paintings, drawing, engravings. The site called "Belle Époque Europe" has more than 107,000 likes and shares hundreds of photographs and videos "lingering over the history of this fascinating period, and thereby resuscitating it." Other sites like "Belle Époque," "Retronaut," and "World of Elegance" pursue similar objectives.

Films of the silent era are restored and projected with musicians or orchestras accompanying them, while forgotten innovations such as the phono-cinema-theater productions projected during the 1900 Exposition are updated for today's taste, restored and digitized by *cinemathèques*. Moreover, never has the cinema devoted so many biographies to the great figures of the era, from *Vincent and Theo* by Robert Altman (1990) to *Renoir* by Gilles Burdos (2013), via portraits of *Van Gogh* (Maurice Pialat, 1991), *Lautrec* (Roger Planchon, 1998), *Gauguin* (Mario Andreacchio, 2003), *Modigliani* (Mick Davis, 2004), *Klimt* (Raoul Ruiz, 2006), and Marie and Pierre Curie, depicted by Claude Pinoteau in *Les Palmes de Monsieur Schutz* (1997). French television does the same by devoting ambitious telefilms to Marie Curie, Pasteur, Jean Jaurès, and Toulouse-Lautrec.[5] Lautrec! He is incontestably the champion of the era, embodying all its excesses and contradictions: grandeur and transgression, the sublime and the grotesque, art subsumed by advertising. The fate of this aristocrat who took refuge in the Moulin Rouge bore all the stigmata of his era to the point of death—alcohol, syphilis, prostitution—but also epitomized artistic genius. His aura is essential even outside France. "For the Australian audience," we read in a Melbourne catalogue, "this exhibition will serve as introduction to France of the Belle Époque, for we really could call Toulouse-Lautrec the portraitist of this era."[6]

More than ever, works by famous writers are being adapted for the screen: Proust, Alain Fournier, Pagnol, Colette, Martin du Gard.[7] In their own way, school textbooks take part in this cultural revivalism. The Belle Époque became a strong theme in high school history at the end of the 1980s; it made its official appearance in the curriculum for 2002, which invited teachers to draw up in the eleventh grade a "Tableau of France in the 'Belle Époque.' " While they obviously stressed the "progress of democracy" and the unequal division of the benefits of economic growth, a lot of space was provided for emblems of scientific and technical modernity, and for progress in leisure pursuits and cultural consumption, which both purveyed an iconography that enables featuring the posters and advertising campaigns of the day.

The culture of 1900 that thrills our own fin de siècle is not just that of artists and novelists, however. We also seek the popular gestures and activities of the Belle Époque. Places, practices, and occupations commonly associated with the start of the century have come back into favor and fashion. After decades of discredit as schmaltzy, this is the case with the *bal musette* and accordion music, as well as a certain "joie de vivre" spirit—saucy and free of hang-ups—associated with the national tradition. Particularly in the time of AIDS, people looked back eagerly at the carefree sexuality of yesterday, forgetting the deep anguish caused by syphilis and those frightful photographs of "damaged" people in medical publications of the day. Similarly, "gay and good-natured binges" or "Gallic drunkenness" was being praised as constitutive of French identity,[8] as incarnated in wine and other "hygienic beverages"—while forgotten were the ravages of absinthe, which was why it was banned in 1916. Many clubs and societies were concerned to "revitalize" lost traditions. For example, the association "Culture Guinguette" worked to encourage and perpetuate the dance cafés along the Marne River, conceived as hot spots of our cultural patrimony. The imaginary of the Belle Époque is at the heart of this revivalism; brought back are the impressionists, postcards, décor, and costumes of 1900, all "in the bygone style." Efforts were often required to rehabilitate these places, the music and the dances, and the "art of living" associated with them; financial support was urged in a 2000 report by the Mission for Ethnological Patrimony to preserve a "popular culture" that was on its way to extinction.[9]

Similarly, the neorealist song is now considered a powerful vector of French identity and has become part of the national patrimony.[10] But despite the rowdy effervescence that accompanied the Moulin Rouge's centenary in 1989,[11] that particular flame could not be rekindled. *Féérie* (Enchantment), its revue starting in 2000, tried and failed to be something other than the mechanical reiteration of a tired tradition, boasting that "The one and only *French Cancan*, the original one, is the Moulin Rouge's—forever!"[12] Nor did other venues like the Belle Époque music hall, which opened in 1979 on the Rue des Petits-Champs, or the Folies-Bergère, which slowly transformed into a venue for musical comedies, manage any better. However, "neoburlesque" dances and performances, groomed in the American style and embellished with a feminist touch that took pride in women's bodies, in *all* women's bodies, did resurface in Parisian culture. They proclaimed their Belle Époque heritage but it was mixed with other traditions such as Berlin cabaret and the striptease of the 1940s and 1950s.

In a similar way, images of popular and cheeky Paris are now prominent in the social imaginary. Once again, several eras and traditions are mixed up, but the mythology of *apache* Paris at the turn of the century—bruisers wearing bandanas and caps, with tattoos and a rolling gait—is the principal element. This remarkable revival demonstrates the sea change that has affected various forms of popular culture in the late twentieth century. Nothing had been more deprecated than the depressed world of young workers who had broken their ties with family and workshop, an urban landscape that was usually contrasted with the "good" popular culture of villages, from which the nation supposedly draws its roots. Of course, people had applauded Aristide Bruant and appreciated a few "populist" novelists and the urban poetry associated with the classic films of the 1930s and 1940s. But this remained part of a taste for the picturesque and the exotic, which did not represent the "legitimate" forms and figures of yesterday's culture. Yet "legitimate" is what these young marginals tended to become at the end of the twentieth century, particularly in a city like Paris that had lost its traditional working class and was trying to accentuate its "urban culture."

Part of this revival came from alternative milieux that had conserved something of the initial transgressive and antiestablishment values. The singer Renaud was no doubt the first, in 1975, to link the "rebel" culture of that day, incarnated by the figure of the hoodlum, back to *apache* youth. Many songs on his first record, *Amoureux de Paname*, paid homage to louts at the start of the century as Renaud sang sad melodies ("joyless java") to accordion accompaniment, even covering Bruant. Formerly uncool postures and gestures were rejuvenated, a trend adopted in the following years by a fringe of alternative youth who were brandishing street culture, *apache* "resistance," gangland songs, and taking part in what the punk band Bérurier Noir called the "folklore of the global *zone*." Another representative punk rock group, Garçons Bouchers (Butcher boys), ended all their concerts in the 1990s with a reprise of "Où sont-ils donc?" (made famous by Fréhel), which testified to the survival of working-class

Paris. The same imaginary inspires the songs of the group Parabellum, who recorded Bruant's "A Saint-Lazare" (a prison for prostitutes) that celebrates Cayenne convicts and the exploits of *"la bande"* (anarchist bandits). Such investments in history were sometimes laden with ambiguity. Far from inciting revolt, the fatalism of both realist poetry and 1900s street culture actually promoted social resignation; as we know, Bruant had professed nationalism and anti-Semitism. These aspects did not escape certain extreme right-wing movements like Project Apache, whose members made themselves the heralds of an urban and xenophobic culture (*"bien de chez nous"*), keen on apéros, accordions, and baseball caps. As so often in this kind of revival, the stakes were not won by either Left or Right, but the profits went to the trendy boutiques and catalogues that had invested in the *apache* tendency, originally concentrated in the Les Halles neighborhood, then in the Marais and at Oberkampf, before moving outward to Belleville and Ménilmontant.

FICTIONS AND INTRIGUES

This "historical framework" was also seductive to novelistic fiction. Situating your story at the turn of the century had many advantages: as we have seen, the period was both close and distant, and hence could make use of exotic elements (costumes, accessories, attitudes) that were still familiar. The disorientation these fictions produced did not preclude a tender and affectionate gaze at old-fashioned interiors, those fine brilliantined mustaches, those "collectible" automobiles. After all, "we still know" something about this period: its décor, its celebrities, and its events "speak to us," even if in an uncertain or confused way. The period is said to be erotic, sentimental, transgressive—above all else, it ends in war, which galvanizes plots, offers rupture points and easy demises. Thus popular novels and adventure stories often take this narrative path,[13] which also offers a port of entry for writers who wish to undertake one of those sagas that put a whole century into perspective: once World War One is over, the characters can pursue their journeys through the troubled times that will follow.[14] For foreign novelists, the Belle Époque also offers a fertile historical framework. Thanks to the cinema, this period in the history of France is certainly one of the best-known and most appreciated by the public, especially when associated with Paris, as almost always. Thus it bolsters the publication of appetizing historical novels: the charms of the plot are garnished with the hope of learning a little more about France and Paris at the time.[15] "Paris, 1909: a city of contrasts and ambition, of beauty and treachery," explains the publisher of the novels of Imogen Robertson, a young British author of historical thrillers.

The detective novel, whose commercial fortunes never slacken, has for the last twenty years been marked by the vogue for historical settings. By 2004, almost 1,200 "historical" titles had already been published in France.[16] Of course, these crime novels represented all periods, but the Belle Époque got the lion's share. The fact that police literature was born then might partly explain this over-representation as the paying of homage to the founding fathers. "I really love this Belle Époque ambiance because it belongs to the great serial writers I admire and envy (Ponson du Terrail, Gaston Leroux, Souvestre and Allain, Maurice Leblanc)—and because the Belle Époque in Marseille has not yet been exploited," explains novelist Jean Contrucci.[17] So "Belle Époque" crime novels are legion. The most famous series, authored by the pseudonymous Claude Izner, traces the adventures of the bookseller and amateur photographer Victor Legris. The action always takes place in Paris between the Exposition of 1899 and that of 1900, in various parts of the city, which incidentally allows it the overall title *Les Mystères parisiens* as a throwback to Eugène Sue. Each of the twelve documented volumes tries to illustrate one of the traits of the culture of this time: spiritualism, vitriol, anarchist attacks, abattoirs, the Exposition, etc. Despite success (800,000 copies sold and translations into eight languages), the authors (two sisters) did not want to prolong a cycle conceived as belonging to a precise time and imaginary: "From the beginning, we knew we would stop in 1900," one of them explained.

Fortunately, Victor Legris was not alone. Raoul Signoret, reporter and legal chronicler at the *Petit Provençal*, assisted by his uncle, superintendent Eugène Baruteau, continues to plunge into *Nouveaux mystères de Marseille*, by Jean Contrucci, of which twelve volumes have appeared since 2001. The principle suggested by editor Jean-Claude Lattès is ingenious: to reopen criminal "cold cases" from 1900. Many other crime investigators had already leaped into the breach: Raoul Thibault de Mézières, a president's assistant at the Elysée, since 2007 (under Jacques Neireynck's pen) has been delving into political intrigues occurring between 1899 and 1906. Toulouse-Lautrec himself, accompanied by Inspector Berflaut, conducts investigations (at Giverny, the Moulin Rouge, and the Bazaar de la Charité) in a series by Renée Bonneau. Meanwhile, Inspector Gaston Cervi operates on the *grands boulevards* while the young Blanche, orphaned by the Paris Commune, explores various facets of fin-de-siècle Paris crime.[18] This vein's success and longevity are far from exhausted. And we could add the frequent attempts to resuscitate the authentic heroes from the start of the century, starting with the incomparable Arsène Lupin.

The graphic novel genre has also produced a series that, just like films and detective novels, allows paying homage to the era of its birth. Jacques Tardi was the first (in 1976) to settle back there amid the retro wave, with *The Most Extraordinary Adventures of Adèle Blanc-Sec*.[19] Playing with the traditional codes of the serial, he describes a Belle Époque that is simultaneously burlesque, technological, and fantastic, in the tradition of turn-of-the-century "lost worlds," to which protagonist Adèle brings a feminist and anarchist aspect. Dozens of other graphic novelists have followed suit, for the same reasons. Moreover, the graphic dimension specific to this genre encourages frequent winks at the era's aesthetics: paintings, posters, modern style, or art nouveau decoration. Many such comics are devoted to the lives of famous painters like van Gogh, Toulouse-Lautrec, Picasso.[20] Others exploit the main historical events like the Dreyfus affair or anarchist attacks, set in journalistic or criminal milieux.[21]

SO GLAMOROUS AN ERA

The 1900s may well sink into the past, but they remain quite modern—even *excessively* modern because they could see that time and history are accelerating. Let us listen to fashion designer Christian Lacroix: "The nineteenth century gave birth to the twentieth in convulsions of progress, speed, and the 'never-seen-before': people flew, telephoned, recorded sounds, captured the images of life and projected them onto a screen; funny machines smashed Space and Time at the speed of Light. Art, Politics, Daily Life—and hence Fashion—were also caught in this syncopated rhythm."[22] This feeling of advancing in leaps and bounds explains why we continue to find the period exhilarating. Fashion occupies an important place in these reconstructions, giving them a *style,* a sense of *chic,* that always makes the era elegant and glamorous. Poiret and Doucet were the tutelary figures of that day, which also saw the beginnings of Coco Chanel. The soirées, balls, and grand *premières* that fill a Belle Époque album would hardly have much meaning without the costumes exhibited in them, as was grasped by Diana Vreeland when she organized the great exhibition at the Metropolitan Museum in New York (see fig. 11, where the painting on the catalogue cover is of patrons at Maxim's bar). The modernization that blew fresh life into those fashion years made them intoxicating. In 1982, a major American publisher issued a luxurious *Great Fashion Designs of the Belle Époque* that offered thirty "paper dolls" to be dressed to reconstruct costumes by Worth, Lanvin, Pasquier, and Poiret. While fashions were not actually limited to France or restricted to the usual time boundaries, the goal was to celebrate "the inspired and imaginative fashion of the Belle Époque."[23] Films, books, websites, and blogs devoted to the period continue to highlight its fashions. Society portraitists like Boldini, Helleu, La Gandara, and Jacques-Emile Blanche, who all tried to capture the sensuality emanating from the elegance of the time, were on the right track.[24] Much of the troubling beauty of the models lies in the draped fabric, the lightness and movement of veils, the jewels and the hats. The very flattering representations offered by the cinema to the courtesans of the Belle Époque (*Moulin Rouge, La Belle Otéro, French Cancan, Gigi*) owe much to the opulence and luxury of their costumes and *toilettes.*[25] The men are included, since that era fixed the codes of masculine elegance and modern dandyism, as incarnated by Marcel Proust and Robert de Montesquiou: "A carnation in the jacket buttonhole, a *cravat* from Jourdain & Brown, a walking cane, and English gloves."[26] These figures continue to inspire representations of contemporary dandyism, and like the Arsène Lupin figure or the Guerlain perfumery, to signify "a certain idea of France."[27]

Strengthened by these appropriations, the merchandising and tourist industries have hurried to promote such lucrative décor in the urban framework—Paris—that was its matrix. Innumerable cafés and restaurants, usually mentioned in tourist guides, now offer customers a "Parisian" ambiance that blends décors running from the end of the Second Empire to the Roaring Twenties, a range that corresponds in commercial culture to an enlarged Belle Époque. The Train Bleu at the Gare de Lyon, Maxim's, the brasseries Zimmer and Flo, Angelina, Bofinger, Allard, Poulette, Ladurée, Mollard, the Café de la Paix, Chez Julien, the Pavillon Montsouris, the Bœuf couronné, etc.—all vaunt their "historic" ambiance, their art nouveau style.[28] The 1900 style actually governs all of Paris tourism. From the Place du Tertre to the Esplanade of the Champ-de-Mars, the principal sites and monuments chime in with the turn of the century. Guidebooks signpost the Métro entrances designed by Guimard, the Wallace fountains, the Morris columns. Maxim's conserves its famous décor. In 2013 the locating of a Starbucks in Montmartre aroused the hostility of residents—until the company had the bright idea of painting it in postimpressionist colors![29] In Bercy-Village, a waffle seller has a green kiosk that is very Belle Époque. The carousels and horse rides of the "Bois 1900"—some authentic, but many imitations—sprout up everywhere that tourists are directed by guidebooks. The Flo Group, owner of a few authentic Belle Époque brasseries and a chain of inexpensive restaurants, has moved into the provinces and even set up subsidiaries abroad. The cooking of 1900, or what is presumed as such, is all the rage.[30] The candy and confection chain La Cure Gourmande, created in 1989 "in search of lost flavors," poses biscuits on lace doilies in order to "rediscover the affective emotions of the traditional ones of yesterday." Sold almost everywhere are reproductions of pictures by Renoir and Toulouse-Lautrec, postcards and dolls of 1900, featuring Parisian urchins and Menier chocolate, advertised in posters and sold in tin boxes illustrated by Mucha. The Belle Époque is a prosperous tourist industry.

And this vogue involves not just Paris. Vichy, on the pretext of having constructed (between 1901 and 1903) its Opéra, its baths and kiosks, and its arcades surrounding the park, each summer organizes exhibitions and animations in period costume. Evian has the same ambiance: the town exhibits stereoscopic glass plates conserved in its collections to celebrate "La Belle Époque on the banks of Lake Geneva." In Rochefort, the Ocean tourist office offers holidays in the "ambiance of 1900, the Belle Époque," which guarantee a "multisensory discovery" of the trades and activities of the time. Visitors are first invited to dawdle in the twenty boutiques in the "museum of yesterday's shops," then take a ferry and bridge to the "charming seaside resort of Fouras-les-Bains." At Bournat, in the heart of Périgord, lies a Belle Époque leisure park. "Living craftsmen, from cutler to blacksmith, via the potter, the saddler, the miller, the sculptor in wood, the pretty shepherdess," each summer bring to life the village as it was at the start of the twentieth century. In the school, visitors can take the tests for the certificate of study under the benevolent eye of a teacher in period costume. But the star attraction is a Ferris wheel sixty feet high, a vestige of the 1900 Exposition. In the village streets near the windmill where dogs, chickens, and pigs wander freely, you can get yourself photographed in a 1900 costume. In Belgium, "The Tourist Centre of Wool and Fashion in Verviers lets you go back in time and discover the period of the Belle Époque (1874–1914)." An exhibition (*La Belle Époque en cent coups d'oeil*) shows you costumes, accessories, furniture, and objects of everyday life, but also exhibits canvases and lithographs from private collections in the region. Live events are also offered: a writing workshop following the traces of Rimbaud and Zola, a visit to the Gileppe Dam that was inaugurated by Léopold II, and various lectures on the Belle Époque. In Blankenberge, a Flemish seaside resort on the shores of the North Sea, the Belle Époque Centrum "lets you discover the period between 1870 and 1914." Installed in one of the majestic villas built near the pier in 1894, the Centrum "will plunge you into the carefree and festive ambiance that reigned there during the belle époque." The only false note comes from Papeete, where "Yesterday's Tahiti: Crazy nights in the belle époque" brings visitors to a dance hall of the 1960s!

However, it seems more difficult to gauge the draw of the Belle Époque in the contemporary art and antiques markets. Obviously, important pieces find their places in prestigious auction catalogues like Christie's and Sotheby's, which frequently offer lots under the rubric "Belle Époque,"[31] useful for promotional purposes. The world of antique dealers is more complex. A questionnaire addressed in 2015 to 220 of them had disappointing results:[32] of course, all of them correctly identified the time period ("from the end of the nineteenth century to 1914") and they thought its originality lay in the "art nouveau" aesthetic as represented by Guimard and the famous poster designers. But no strong motif emerged. Most of the Belle Époque antiques on offer were vases, knickknacks, jewelry, and other fashion accessories like fans, furniture, and paintings, which they sold to a clientele of antique collectors.

A DECONTEXTUALIZED BELLE ÉPOQUE

Perhaps new audiences prefer the decontextualized periods that our contemporaries are fond of. Many film adaptations try to modernize the imaginary of the Belle Époque, to disfigure it with deliberate anachronisms, with quirky burlesque, or else special effects that could be called "retro-futurist." The French director André Hunebelle had opened the way with a trilogy of *Fantômas* films (1964–1967): the elusive criminal of Souvestre and Allain circa 1911 is projected forward into 1960s Paris, where he loses his terrifying power. But this type of adaptation mushroomed at the end of the twentieth century, under the effect of steampunk, as for example in Baz Luhrmann's *Moulin Rouge* (2001). Contrary to previous films that had focused on the opening of the venue in 1889, we are informed at the start that the action is situated in "Paris 1900." The hero, a young English poet, and the dancer Satine exist in an ambiance that is both burlesque and fantastic. The makeup is outrageous, the dancers' underclothes anachronistic; Lautrec is a grotesque dwarf; and the Moulin Rouge rings with disco music. This example is extreme, but focusing on effect and on "modern adaptation" has propelled many filmmakers along that path, as witnessed earlier in *Arsène Lupin* by Jean-Paul Salomé (2004),[33] *Les Brigades du Tigre* by Jérôme Cornuau (2006), and *Aventures extraordinaires d'Adèle Blanc-Sec* by Luc Besson (2010).

Other directors instead have tried to revive the derision and ironic distance that were present at the start of the century: viz. Olivier Assayas (*Irma Vep* in 1996) and Bruno Podalydès (*Le Mystère de la Chambre jaune* in 2003 and *Le Parfum de la dame en noir* in 2005).

For the same reason, 1900 is the preferred framework for most of the alternate histories, time travel, or telescoping of temporalities favored by steampunk culture. Its role here is similar to the one played by Late Victorianism in Great Britain: Jules Verne dons the costume of H. G. Wells. The retro-futurist imaginary born in postwar decades settles easily into the technicist society of 1900. In such fantasies, we may be in 1913, several years after "Napoléon IV, son of Napoléon III, has swept away the Third Republic"; or else we may be in 1899, when the energy of ether has revolutionized technology and filled society with flying machines and robots. Everywhere are dirigibles, pneumatic networks, disturbing empires under the control of megalomaniacs, criminal dioramas, and mechanical causeways that try to perform knowing collisions and temporal collusions.[34]

In comparison, role-playing games appear quite restrained. *Maléfices* chooses the Belle Époque because it is "a period strong in contradictions" between science and occultism, between positivist reason and countryside magic, and such tensions are propitious for the proposed scenarios. But the context is very precisely respected: the game is accompanied by a practical guide on "Living in 1900," which gives us all the necessary information, from mealtimes to the available railway companies, from customary clothing to the cost of a Métro ticket. *Crimes*, "a game of historic roles anchored in the heart of the Belle Époque," exploits a similar verisimilitude, that of clashing time frames, a society torn between growth and scientific optimism on one side and melancholy and decline on the other. But here the principle is even more frightening, since the players must obey the laws of degeneration that were so worrying to people at the end of the nineteenth century, and therefore they must combat the impulses that "lead them inexorably toward their own hell," madness, and death. The idea is subtle and well informed, but replicates in its very conception the whole teleology from which the Belle Époque imaginary first proceeded.[35]

EPILOGUE

Tangled Times

THE "BELLE Époque" is an imaginary, an era that has been constructed and constantly reconstructed by nostalgia. But is it therefore a falsified past, a mystification that we need to deconstruct? Historians are often unsympathetic to nostalgia, defining it as a "cultural phenomenon that tells us about the present through the falsification of the past."[1] Nevertheless, having come to the end of this journey, I think that the posthumous life of all of our stories—and not just the painful and traumatic episodes that historians favor[2]—is indispensable for comprehending the past. Of course nothing is simple about such an approach. Which "Belle Époque" have I exhumed in the preceding pages? That of 1900, which did not yet exist? That of 1930, which was called "1900"? The ones imagined in 1940, in 1950, in 1968, or even the one at the start of the twenty-first century? Do all of them speak to us of the time before we were born? Of course everything is mixed up, since none of us lives outside time, which permanently reshapes our relation to the past.

It would be wrong to think that the men and women of the 1900s are absent from this book. Of course, they are reconstructions fashioned by souvenirs, memories, or simply the flight of time. And no doubt some of their aspects are unacceptable to contemporary audiences—though nobody ever really believed in the idea of a transparent "belle époque." In fact, "there was no 'belle époque' except for a small number of privileged people," Armand Lanoux wrote in 1961—and this common-sense observation is widely shared.[3]

Instead, I am referring to those condescending views that many held—and still hold—of the people at the start of the century; their smirking gazes back at striped bathing costumes, sock suspenders, or an era with a maximum speed of thirty kilometers an hour. Those people appear like "big children," whose appearances, objects, or supposed "modernity" now seem obsolete and slightly ridiculous. Yet are they not also touching, with a sort of out-of-date freshness that is conferred by old photographs? Didn't they actually "pose" deliberately, like that woman with a haughty look, alone and erect in front of a high pedestal table? Or that prim gathering in front of the village café on a wedding day? Their thin moustaches, their long day dresses, their bicycles—all that may seem quaint, and film archives in fact accentuate that impression. For a long time, films from before 1914 (shot first hand-cranked, then at different rhythms, then at sixteen frames per second) were shown on projectors made after 1927 that rolled at twenty-four images per second. The effect was guaranteed: comically accelerated steps, gestures, and movements, which of course did not correspond either to the film's intentions or to how people initially appeared on film. Our forebears were given a pace that was never their own. Their world was turned into a pantomime circus: passersby, automobiles, and omnibuses agitate jerkily in a burlesque scene. Some writers spoke of "silent clowns," of a "round of seductive marionettes."[4] All that, of course, stopped in 1914. Suddenly the images were not funny at all, which by contrast increased the pleasant dimensions of this prewar period. For me, this snide view of the people of the Belle Époque continues to be unbearable. If this book has one ambition, it would be to plead for a humbler kind of history, a history that avoids any complacency, starting with the kind—so illusory—procured by the simple fact of "coming along afterward."

But if we stick to a simple and modest view of these thousands of archive pages and of the documents exhibited in them—the letters, drawings, images, photographs, objects—then I think they do actually express part of the "truth" about the 1900s. As worked over as this imaginary may be by nostalgia and by the contexts that have given it form, it does retain something of the imprint, the hold, that these years have over us. Words, sights, gestures, and ways of life do emerge, and along with them some fragments of experience from that dawn of a century. Images, especially, have a durable life, if we can observe them without arrogance or anachronism. From the forever submerged past, they alone can "restore" a portion to us, and for this reason the visual dimension of the history is decisive: for many people, the identity of a past time lies in effervescent images.[5] But while that identity sometimes takes liberties with the exactitude of facts—which obviously we should correct—and while it is often content to reiterate commonplaces—which obviously we should point out as such—the profusion of these picturesque, anecdotal, "popular" histories carries a form of knowledge that it would be improper to sweep away. Nostalgia is not history—it reconstructs or recollects more than it explains—but nor is it programmed falsification. It organizes memory, stimulates the imagination, and may also lift the veil here and there on forgotten figures or disdained realities. Forms of knowledge are concealed in the folds of its reconstructions.[6] Moreover, history does not belong to professional historians alone, and in any case their voices often do not carry. We have to accept (also humbly) the fact that society partly writes its own history, and that this history matters.

But the main story told in this book belongs to the eras that followed, those of tangled times. "The only past that counts is the living past, which is transformed along with us," Dorgelès wrote in his recollections of Montmartre.[7] Far from the dreams of resurrection so dear to nineteenth-century historians, we know thanks to Walter Benjamin's reflections on history how much the past does live on in the present, which in turn determines how it is used, as well as how much it is up to the future to reinvent it.[8] The history of the "Belle Époque" offers a clear demonstration of this: it truly exists only because we have needed it to. The 1930s, which gave it its first form, experienced the uncertainty of a time marked by threats of war and by a rapid deterioration in expectations of the future. Whatever the judgment one made on the "value" of 1900—whether it was chic, snobbish, dopey, or heroic—it was first of all an age of security, when one could just let oneself live. The apotheosis of the "Belle Époque" coming out of World War Two was still more transparent. After a conflict that appeared like a modern Thirty Years' War, the start of the century (pre-1914) seemed by contrast adorned in colorful silk: a time of innocence, "happy" modernity, the calm before the great massacres. Hence the focus on pleasure, laughter, and lightness, marvelously incarnated in vaudeville. Other Belles Époques would follow—rebellious, avant-gardist, fuddy-duddy, erotic, transgressive, rural, aesthetic, patrimonial. And no doubt we will see others tomorrow. Like all periods in history, the "Belle Époque" is of variable geometry; it changes its face according to the moment, how we look back, and according to our needs. Its boundary dates and its contours are uncertain and they sometimes clash. If the Paris of 1900 seems a solid anchor point, we have seen how it could migrate upstream, downstream, sideways. Often it was merely associated, among so many writers and poets, with the "time of my twenties." That particular Belle Époque has something of a cubist canvas about it, unless it remembers something from Bergson's lectures on duration or else anticipates the conceptual shake-up of space and time elaborated by Einstein, precisely between 1905 and 1912.

There remains an attachment, a particular affection, that seems to link us to the start of this century. That era still speaks to us, no doubt due to a mixture of distance and proximity that we think we perceive. The twentieth century, which believed in its historic destiny, made that its matrix. It does not matter that the paths taken since then have diverged so much, since everything that constitutes our world seems to have appeared at that time: the automobile and the cinematograph, aeronautics and electricity, the telephone, abstract art, and international congresses. Some of these innovations were clumsy or experimental, but I think that makes them touching. Through them, we constantly pay homage to the sources of our modernity. But we also remember that people then spoke in dialect and wore wooden clogs, and the Quatorze Juillet was *the* great popular festival. Those years seem to recount the story of our childhood. It is time suspended, a sort of "between two worlds, a time that is already modern but not yet contemporary."[9] With this kind of time, we can daydream of a France that is both Parisian and rural, of a modern society that is still archaic, of entertainment where we can laugh without restraint. Innovation exalts us, but we still respect customs and forms. Law and government seem to be held in common, but it is also via strikes that we build the future. With bonhomie we experience a situation that is not always rosy, but we may always hope in good faith to be able to improve it. The "Belle Époque" is our dream of a lost unity, a dream that can be brought up in moments of doubt or crisis. It has the "beauty of death," which still moves us. Like the music of Eric Satie, it expresses the "sweetness and poignant nostalgia of time escaping, of time fleeting, of time lost."[10] In the twentieth century it was one of the places where one could circumvent the present and imagine the future. But nothing guarantees that it will stay like that in the twenty-first.

Finally, beyond the 1900s that have always been dear to me, beyond the history of the twentieth century that it revisits in other ways, there is another stake in this book: it concerns the very nature of writing history, which ultimately has little to do with the past. That past is dead, vanished, disappeared, and nothing will resuscitate it. To consider it as a stock of events or actions that can be restored is an enduring illusion—but still an illusion. Obviously, their traces do remain, and it is the noblest mission of history to evaluate them. But working on historical traces always depends on a relational perspective, whose object is time. Time is the substance of history, and it is rarely linear. The "Belle Époque" that I have tracked here has nothing of a frozen time or "dead" time about it: it is a living matter that squeals, that reacts, that gets carried away or gets lost. "You have created a new time, the 'past-present,'" writes Dr. Jean Gautier, founder of the Society of Art and Archeology in the Yerres valley, in the preface to a study devoted to Brie-Comte-Robert in the Belle Époque.[11] The formula is naïve, but it does reach the heart of the issue, which is not just that the present looks back at the past. Only textbooks and high school essays care much about periodization. Between the present of the historian and his or her quest for the past, a multitude of other times interfere with the subject, various of yesterdays' presents and pasts. There—"suspended in the void between the old and new," between pasts, presents, and future— stands the Angel of History, comprised of knowledge, prescience, and nostalgia.[12] Elucidating the "names of times," as this book has tried to do with the "Belle Époque," helps us to consider the past for what it is: a reality that is mobile, changing, "historic," and worked over by the men and women who inhabited it, but also by the views, the readings, the displacements that people of later eras have subjected it to. How could this be otherwise? And considered in this way, our relation with the past—free of any triumphalism—means admitting that one always writes in this tangle of temporalities, in this rhapsodic and almost kaleidoscopic "between times" that constitutes History.

Martyrs Kirk, St Andrews, May 2016

POSTSCRIPT: THE BELLE ÉPOQUE AND THE GILDED AGE

Venita Datta

DOMINIQUE KALIFA left us on September 12, 2020—well before his time. Historians and literary scholars of the nineteenth century deeply mourn the loss of not only our cherished friend but also a brilliant and generous colleague. One of the leading practitioners of the cultural history of the long nineteenth century, Kalifa succeeded Alain Corbin in 2002 at the Sorbonne (Paris I-Panthéon), where he left a lasting mark on both his colleagues and students. More than any other historian, he made the Belle Époque come to life, examining mass culture during this period, notably the press, as well as crime stories, including the celebrated *Fantômas* series penned by Marcel Allain and Pierre Souvestre. His first book, *L'Encre et le sang* (Ink and blood) explored not only how crime stories of the Belle Époque captured the national imagination but also how their popularity was grounded in genuine anxieties about crime, the rise of the lower classes, and the changing roles of women during a time of great upheaval. Kalifa's style, both erudite and witty, always made his books lively and fun to read.

Of his numerous works, none is more insightful than *Les Bas-fonds: L'histoire d'un imaginaire*, published in English by Columbia University Press in 2019 as *Vice, Crime, and Poverty: How the Western World Invented the Underworld*. In this tour de force, Kalifa focused on the urban underworld as a social imaginary, shaped by nineteenth-century fears of the dangers of industrialization and urban life. Seamlessly weaving the examination of high and popular culture, Kalifa always remained tethered to the social, political, economic, and cultural conditions of the period in question. A hallmark of Kalifa's work is his attention to how different eras viewed historical actors or phenomena based on the needs and issues of their times. The past, as he so eloquently observed, is "a reality that is mobile, changing, 'historic,' and worked over by the men and women who inhabited it, but also by the views, the readings, the displacements that people of other eras imposed on it" (p. 182). Such an investigation of the evolving ways both historians and contemporaries view the past speaks eloquently to our current moment, as we are forced to grapple, in the United States, France, and elsewhere, with the legacy of colonization, slavery, and genocide of indigenous peoples. As Kalifa noted in his work, historical events don't change, but our perceptions of them do—even those of professional historians, who, after all, are also products of their time.

Kalifa undertakes a similar approach in *La Véritable histoire de la Belle Époque,* translated into English by Susan Emanuel as *The Belle Époque: A Cultural History.* The term "Belle Époque," which covers the years from 1900 to 1914, may not have the same resonance for foreigners as for the French, but most will certainly be familiar with the Parisian sites associated with the period. The numerous "Belle Époque" tours available to tourists in Paris feature not only the Moulin Rouge, located in Montmartre, but also Maxim's and the Folies-Bèrgere, as well as the Grand and Petit Palais, built for the 1900 Universal Exhibition. The Paris of the Belle Époque has also been immortalized in American musical comedies of the 1950s and 1960s, among them *Gigi* (1958), based on a Colette novella, and the iconic *An American in Paris* (1951), which although it is set after World War Two, features the inimitable Gene Kelly in a dream sequence in which a Toulouse-Lautrec painting comes to life.[1] Museumgoers will also be well aware of the Belle Époque, given the number of exhibitions organized by American art museums, among them "Toulouse-Lautrec and the Stars of Paris" at the Museum of Fine Arts in Boston in 2019. Not only did the curators showcase Toulouse-Lautrec's work, they also situated it firmly within the historical context of the period, providing film footage of the 1900 Exhibition and a map of Toulouse-Lautrec's Paris highlighting bohemian Montmartre, as well as music and fashion of the period.

The Belle Époque is thus not only integral to the images produced about France beyond its borders but also very much a part of French national identity, in other words, the ways the French imagine themselves and their past. Indeed, the Belle Époque constitutes what French historian Pierre Nora has dubbed a "lieu de mémoire," that is, one of the people, places, and events that have been enshrined in French national memory.[2] It is no accident that many of the entries in the renowned series of books translated into English as *Realms of Memory* include symbols of the period, from the Eiffel Tower and Montmartre to the tricolor flag and the "Marseillaise," both of which were adopted during the early years of the Third Republic (1870–1940).

Contemporaries never used the term "Belle Époque," although they did dub the period of the last two decades of the nineteenth century the "fin de siècle," a term that was then adopted by cultural historians, some of whom collapsed the two periods. While the "fin de siècle" and the "Belle Époque" both have resonance beyond France, the former term conveyed anxiety, decadence, and millenarianism,[3] while the latter was born of the nostalgia of contemporaries on the eve of World War Two, looking back at a bygone and happier past. In the American context, the expression "Gilded Age" is perhaps the one that best corresponds with these terms, although it has an exclusive American resonance that did not translate to other countries.[4] Coined in 1873 by Mark Twain and Charles Dudley Warner in their eponymous *The Gilded Age: A Story of Today*, the expression, which carried connotations of corruption and lavish spending, did not take off until the 1920s (see fig. 12).

In the aftermath of World War One, reformist American intellectuals, observing the connections between a materialist and superficial culture and the political and economic exploitation associated with urban industrial capitalism, elaborated a discourse on the Gilded Age that wove together a desire for cultural reform and social democracy. These intellectuals decried the era spanning the 1870s to

1898, which marked the entry of the United States on the world stage with the Spanish-American War,[5] as one in which the making of money had been elevated to a sacred duty, to the detriment of creativity and art. Holding up the following period, known as the Progressive Era, as a model for social and political reforms, they, in common with European critics like Max Nordau, lamented the rise of mass culture and popular entertainments. Nevertheless, they also pointed to the achievements of the age, from the inventions of Thomas Edison, Alexander Graham Bell, and George Eastman to the extraordinary literary production of Emily Dickinson, Walt Whitman, and Herman Melville. Starting in the 1950s, but especially in the 1970s and 1980s, professional historians attempted to rehabilitate the period. Describing the Gilded Age as an era of great transition and change, they also recognized in it the origins of the modern United States. Moreover, they contested the idea of a "corrupt" Gilded Age as opposed to a "fruitful" Progressive Era, arguing that the two periods needed to be examined together since the roots of the Progressive Era lay in the Gilded Age, with one prominent historian positing the idea of a "Long Progressive Era" while another opted for the term the "Long Gilded Age."[6]

The parallels between the Belle Époque and the Gilded Age are striking. Both witnessed urbanization, industrialization, and the concentration of wealth. Even more important, both periods were key for the construction of modern French and American national identities, respectively. The United States emerged from the Civil War and Reconstruction to conquer the American West, in part through the technologies of the rifle and the transcontinental railroad. It entered the Gilded Age as a great industrial power and eventually an imperial one, in the wake of the Spanish-American War.

For France, this era marked a resurgence from defeat in the Franco-Prussian War and its own civil war—the Commune—and the establishment of the secular Third Republic, whose leaders not only proclaimed France's role as world leader in art, science, and technology but also expanded its colonial possessions, making it the world's second colonial power. This period also marked the conversion of most French people to republicanism and a civic culture, exemplified by the adoption of republican symbols like the "Marseillaise" as the national hymn and July 14 as an official national holiday. Republicans also founded free, obligatory, and secular primary schools and built roads and railways linking regions of the country together, thereby contributing to the development of a national economy. These years also saw the emergence of mass culture, illustrated not only by the department store but also by the rise of the mass press and a burgeoning entertainment industry. As Kalifa notes (quoting Neutres), the Belle Époque represents the source of our modernity: "it is time suspended, a sort of 'between two worlds, a time that is already modern but not yet contemporary'" (p. 185). One could say the same of the Gilded Age; simultaneously close to us and far away, it continues to fascinate us.

The two periods have both had abundant afterlives, that is, they have been seen in different lights during subsequent periods. In recent years, the notion of a "Second Gilded Age" has emerged in the American national press, with journalists and economists making a new set of parallels between the concentration of wealth and political and economic corruption. On the other hand, the Belle Époque, translated literally as the "beautiful period" and more loosely as "the golden age," carries with it positive connotations in a way that the Gilded Age, associated with fake gold and gilt, does not.

One of Kalifa's most original arguments revolves around the Belle Époque as a touchstone for French national identity as well as a source of nostalgia. Rather than a history of the Belle Époque per se, that is, a traditional history that chronicles the political, cultural, and social highlights of the era, it provides an archeology of a historical term, known as a chrononym, that many historians take for granted. First introduced by a linguist in 1996, a chrononym is a name for a particular time period. While other historians have subsequently made occasional use of the term, Kalifa has the distinction of being the historian who has done the most both to popularize it and to oblige historians to reflect upon the way we name historical periods.[7] In this book, Kalifa seeks to understand when and why the term "Belle Époque" was born and to analyze how it was subsequently defined and redefined later. Far from being neutral, the names given to historical eras reflect the concerns of a particular period, what he calls the "historical imaginary" of a reconstructed past (p. 12). Yet the men and women of the Belle Époque are never absent from this work, and Kalifa makes an impassioned plea to respect the people of the past, to avoid looking at them with condescension by arguing for a "humbler kind of history, a history that avoids any complacency" (p. 183).

Kalifa also shifts the chronology of the Belle Époque's emergence. For years, historians have claimed with little basis that the term "Belle Époque" was born in the aftermath of World War One, created by those looking back with nostalgia to the peaceful era that preceded it. But as Kalifa illustrates, such a view is patently false. While contemporaries of the 1920s recalled with fondness the peaceful and prosperous prewar decades, they had little desire to turn back the clock. Instead, they sought to reproduce those qualities in the present, in the somewhat frenzied way that characterizes the "Roaring Twenties," or in French, *les années folles*. Perhaps, remarks Kalifa, this is the reason so many of us still confuse the Belle Époque with the 1920s. In reality, the term "Belle Époque," although it surfaced in the 1930s, was born of the experience of World War Two, specifically, the context of the Occupation. German authorities, who wished to maintain an air of normality in Paris, encouraged the vogue of the Belle Époque in music hall and cabaret shows attended by German soldiers on leave, thereby contributing to this imaginary with their clichéd views of Paris.

Dispelling the myth about the Belle Époque by uncovering the origins of the term is in and of itself a major contribution to French history and historiography. Indeed, Kalifa's book does for the Belle Époque what the work of Henry Rousso did for the memory of Vichy and the Occupation,[8] which traced the evolution of the ways future generations viewed the difficult events of the period through an examination of public debates, commemorations, and films. Like Rousso, Kalifa undertakes a study of memoirs, films, and fiction, but adds to them songs, postcards, and museum exhibitions, not the usual terrain of most historians.

Ultimately, Kalifa's book sheds light on subsequent periods of French history, including our own time. Why did the twentieth century feel the need to celebrate the first years of the century? As the author illustrates, contemporaries of successive eras after the Belle

Époque needed to connect with this formative period in modern French history to make sense of their present. In doing so, they focused on only one or two aspects of the period. By examining how different historical eras viewed the Belle Époque, Kalifa presents a rich, multilayered view of it, illuminating as well the needs of the time of those defining it. Today, the popularity of the Belle Époque is reflected in steampunk fiction and film, as well as the aforementioned tours of Paris. As I write, two recent popular French series, *The Bonfire of Destiny* and *Mystery in Paris,* based on period events, are available for streaming. The Belle Époque is thus very much a part of French national consciousness, whether or not ordinary French people can actually identify the years to which it corresponds.

Perhaps the misidentification of the Belle Époque with the 1920s is no accident since it recalls Woody Allen's 2011 film, *Midnight in Paris*, in which the main character, Gil Pender, played by Owen Wilson, longs for Paris of the 1920s, which he sees as an ideal period and place for real writers and artists. Yet, as he learns, each of us has a different golden age. For his love interest, Adriana (Marion Cotillard), the real Belle Époque is the object of her fantasizing, as she revels in her meeting with Toulouse-Lautrec and Paul Gauguin at Maxim's. For those of us who were fond of Dominique Kalifa, our "belle époque" is located in a Paris of the recent past, in which we share lively conversations with our friend in his graduate seminar at the Sorbonne, in cafés, at his home around the dinner table, and finally in his considerable oeuvre, in which the true history of the Belle Époque lives on.

NOTES

PROLOGUE

1. Robert Burnand, *Paris 1900* (Paris: Hachette, 1951), 8.
2. Pierre Dominique, "Les hommes publics," *Le Crapouillot* 29 (1955): 8.
3. Maurice Donnasy, *J'ai vécu 1900* (Paris: Fayard, 1951), 31.
4. Marie-Claire Bancquart, *Paris "Belle Époque" par ses écrivains* (Paris: Adam Biro/Paris Musées, 1997), 10.
5. Philippe Gaboriau, *Le Tour de France et le vélo: Histoire social d'une épopée contemporaine* (Paris: L'Harmattan, 1995).
6. Syllabus for a course by Thomas Ertman, New York University, 2012.
7. Maurice Chevalier, *Ma route et mes chansons* (Paris: Julliard, 1946); *The Man in the Straw Hat: My Story* (New York: Crowell, 1949).
8. André Warnod, *Ceux de la Butte* (Paris: Julliard, 1947), 63.
9. Armand Lanoux, *Amours 1900* (Paris: Hachette, 1961).
10. Diana Holmes and Carrie Tarr, *A Belle Époque? Women in French Society and Culture 1890–1914* (New York: Berghahn Books, 2006), 2.
11. This term was coined by the Swiss linguist Eva Büchi, in *Les Structures du "Franzoisches Etymologisches Worterbuch." Recherches métalexicographiques et métalexicologiques* (Tübingen: Niemeyer, 1996), 271. Paul Bacot, Laurent Douzou, and Jean-Paul Honoré defined it as "a simple or complex expression that serves to designate a portion of time that the social community apprehends and singularizes, associated with acts that are meant to give it coherence, which is accompanied by the need to name it" ("Chronoymes: La politisation du temps," *Mots: Les langages du politique* 87 [2008]: 5–12. Kalifa, ed., *Les Noms d'époques* (Paris: Gallimard, 2019).

12. Jean-Jacques Lévesque, *Les Années de la Belle Époque* (Paris: ARC édition, 1991), 6.

13. Alype-Jean Noirot, *Le Département de l'Yonne comme diocèse* (self-pub. available as Google book, 1979).

14. Eugen Weber, *France, Fin de Siècle* (Cambridge, Mass.: Harvard University Press, 1986), 2; Charles Rearick, *Paris Dreams, Paris Memories: The City and Its Mystique* (Stanford, Calif.: Stanford University Press, 2011), xi.

15. Hubert Juin, *Le Livre de Paris 1900* (Paris: Belfond, 1977), 9.

16. Lucien François, *Les Elégances de Paris* (Paris: Tourist Bureau, 1946), unpaginated.

17. Marius Dargaud, *La Belle Époque, mythes et réalités* (Alençon: Archives départementales de l'Orne, 1972), 1.

18. *Du côté de chez Jacques-Emile Blanche: Un salon a la Belle Époque* (Paris: Fondation Pierre Bergé-Yves Saint Laurent/Skira Flammarion, 2012), 19.

19. Vincent Cronin, *Paris on the Eve 1900–1914* (New York: St. Martin's Press, 1990), 17.

20. Rearick, *Paris Dreams,* 44; Jacqueline Lalouette, *La France de la Belle Époque: Dictionnaire des curiosités* (Paris: Tallandier, 2013), 7.

21. Octave Mirabeau, "Les Dialogues tristes: sur la berge," *L'Echo de Paris,* June 14, 1892, used in *La Vache tachetée* (The spotted cow) (Paris: Flammarion, 1921), 119–121.

22. Dr. Boucher, *Impressions de voyage de Marseille à Constantine* (Rouen: L. Guy, 1904), 15; Marcel Proust, *Swann's Way* [1913], trans. C. K. Scott Moncrieff (New Haven, Conn.: Yale University Press, 2013), 279.

23. Georges Feydeau and Maurice Desvallieres, *L'Age d'or,* musical comedy in three acts and nine scenes, premiered at the Variétés Theater on August 31, 1905.

24. Guillaume Apollinaire, *Calligrammes: Poems of War and Peace* (1918), trans. Ann Greer (Berkeley: University of California Press, 2004), 105.

25. *Mémoires de l'Académie des sciences, belles lettres et arts de Lyon* (1924), 3; Camille Duguest, *Femmes seules* 5 (1928): 30; Lucien Dubech, "L'imperialisme dans l'arene. A propos des Jeux olympiques," *Revue hebdomadaire* (September 1924): 295.

26. *Poésie pure* 6 (1928–1930): 312; *Les Marges, Revue de littérature et d'art* 90 (1932): 14.

27. Jean Valdois, "1900 vu par 1933," *Cinémagazine* (February 1933).

28. *La Poule*, operetta in three acts and four scenes by Henri Duvernois and André Barde, music by Henri Christiné (Paris: Dorel, 1936).

PART ONE: "THE 1900 ÉPOQUE"

1. François Hartog, *Régimes d'historicité. Présentisme et expériences du temps* (Paris: Seuil, 2003), 19.

2. Title of the first part of Paul Claudel's *Art Poétique* (Paris: Mercure de France, 1907).

DAWN OF THE CENTURY

1. Eugen Weber, *France fin-de-siècle* (Cambridge, Mass.: Harvard University Press, 1986); Christophe Charle, *Paris fin de siècle. Culture et politique* (Paris: Seuil, 1998), and "Fin-de-siècle," *Revue d'histoire du xixe siècle* 60 (2016): 103–117; Christophe Prochasson, *Paris 1900. Essai d'histoire culturelle* (Paris: Calmann-Lévy, 1999).

2. Louis Blanc, *Questions d'aujourd'hui et de demain* (Paris: Dentu 1873), 400.

3. Max Nordau, *Degeneration* [1892] (London: William Heinemann, 1989).

4. Alfred Fouillée, *L'Évolutionnisme des idées-forces* (Paris: Alcan, 1890); *La Psychologie des idées-forces* (Paris: Alcan, 1893); and *La Morale des idées-forces* (Paris: Alcan, 1908).

5. Gabriel Tarde, *Les Lois de l'imitation* (Paris: Alcan, 1890).

6. Marc Angenot, *1889: un état du discours social* (Longueil: Le Préambule, 1989), 13.

7. Angenot, *1889*; and also *Le Cru et le faisandé: sexe, discours social et littérature à la Belle Époque* (Brussels: Labor, 1986); *Ce que l'on dit des Juifs en 1889. Antisémitisme et discours social* (Saint-Denis: Presses de l'Université de Vincennes, 1989); *Topographie du socialisme français, 1889–1890* (Montréal: Discours social, 1990); *Le Café-concert, archéologie d'une industrie culturelle* (Montréal: CIADEST, 1991).

8. Prochasson, *Paris 1900*, 238–249; "Enquête sur l'enquête," *Mil neuf cent. Revue d'histoire intellectuelle* 22 (2004); Dominique Kalifa, "Enquête et culture de l'enquête au xixe siècle," *Romantisme* 149 (2010): 3–23.

9. Pierre Du Maroussem, *Les Enquêtes. Pratique et théorie* (Paris: Alcan, 1900).

10. Nordau, *Degeneration*, 6.

11. Robert Burnand, *Paris 1900* (Cambridge, Mass.: Harvard University Press, 1986), 8.

12. Gaston Jougla, "Les curiosités du calendrier de 1900," *Le Gaulois*, January 1, 1900.

13. *1900. Comment ils voyaient le nouveau siècle? Comment ils voyaient l'avenir* (Paris: Centre d'histoire sociale, 1999), http://fr.calameo.com/read/000290379a0e07ff3d5e5; Tiphaine Joyeux, "1900, une année en stuc. Impressions immédiates" (master's thesis, Université Paris 1, 2015).

14. Camille Flammarion, "En quelle année commencera le vingtième siècle?," *La Revue des revues* (October 1899).

15. "Le Dix-neuvième ou vingtième siècle?," *Le Gaulois*, January 2, 1900.

16. "La Fin du siècle," *Le Matin*, January 1, 1900. The consultation went on until January 6.

17. *Annuaire pour l'an 1900 publié par le Bureau des longitudes* (Paris: Gauthier-Villars, 1900), 5.

18. *La Croix*, January 3, 1900; J. Dhonbree, "L'an 1 du xxe siècle," *Le Figaro*, January 1, 1900.

19. Jules Claretie, *La Vie à Paris* (Paris: Charpentier et Fasquelle, 1900), 400–402.

20. The measure, to be effective, required a law that was definitively passed on March 14, 1900.

21. "Les curiosités du calendrier de 1900," *Le Gaulois*, January 1, 1900.

22. Charles Simond, *La Vie parisienne à travers le xixe siècle: Paris de 1800 à 1900, d'après des estampes et des mémoires du temps* (Paris: Plon, 1900–1901), 576.

23. Simond, *La Vie parisienne*, 576.

24. *Le Temps*, April 15, 1900.

25. Quoted by Brigitte Schoeder-Gudehus and Anne Rasmussen, *Les Fastes du progrès. Le Guide des Expositions universelles, 1851–1992* (Paris: Flammarion, 1992), 133.

26. Anne-Claude Ambroise-Rendu, "L'exposition universelle de 1900. Gloires et ambiguïtés d'une célébration du fin de siècle," *L'Affaire Dreyfus et le tournant du siècle, 1894–1910*, ed. Laurent Gervereau and Christophe Prochasson (Nanterre: BDIC, 1994), 228–233.

27. Stanislas Rzewuski, "Olympio à l'Exposition," *Gil Blas*, October 1, 1900.

28. Jules Roche, *Rapport adressé au Président de la République Sadi Carnot*, July 13, 1892, quoted by Chantal Georgel, "1895–1905. Fins de siècle en Europe," in *1900*, ed. Philippe Thiebaut (Paris: RMN, 2000), 3.

29. Prochasson, *Paris 1900*, 130.

30. René Doumic, "Le bilan d'une génération," *Revue des deux mondes*, Paris, January 15, 1900.

31. Quoted in Lucio Levi, ed., *Da un secolo all'altro. Il passato letto al presente* (Torino: Utet Librería 2000), 13.

32. Anne-Claude Ambroise-Rendu, "La perception de la puissance française en 1900: l'exemple de l'exposition universelle dans la presse," in *La Puissance française à la Belle Époque. Mythe ou réalité*, ed. P. Milza and R. Poidevin (Brussels: Complexe, 1992), 143–157.

33. Quoted by Marie-Claude Blanc-Chaleard, "L'image de la puissance française dans les manuels d'histoire et de géographie autour de 1900," in Milza and Poidevin, eds., *Puissance française*, 63.

34. Prochasson, *Paris 1900*; Pascal Ory, "Le mythe de Paris, Ville-Lumière, dans les années 1900," in Milza and Poidevin, eds., *La Puissance française*, 131.

35. "La clôture de l'Exposition," *Le Petit Parisien*, November 13 1900.

36. Gustave Rouanet, "Fin de siècle," *La Lanterne*, December 31, 1899.

37. Christophe Charle, *Discordance des temps. Une brève histoire de la modernité* (Paris: Colin, 2011), 326.

38. Charle, *Discordance des temps*, 326–327. See the list given in the introduction of *1900. Comment ils voyaient le nouveau siècle?*.

39. Hubert Juin, *Le Livre de Paris 1900* (Paris: Belfond, 1977), 54.

40. "La Fin de l'Exposition," *Le Petit Parisien*, November 14, 1900.

41. Joyeux, "1900, une année en stuc."
42. Jean Frollo, "L'Atelier familial," *Le Petit Parisien*, November 10, 1900.
43. "Fin de rêve," *Le Figaro*, November 13, 1900.

TIME IN FLIGHT

1. Emilio Gentile, *L'Apocalypse de la modernité: La Grande Guerre et l'homme nouveau*, trans Stéphanie Lanfranchi (Paris: Editions Aubier, 2011).
2. Virginia Woolf, "Mr. Bennett and Mrs. Brown" [1924], in *Collected Essays* (London: Hogarth Press, 1966), 320.
3. "The climax of it all—for a climax was still to come after so long a period of stimulation—shook the world far beyond the limits of Paris. It was the year 1913." Roger Shattuck, *The Banquet Years: The Origins of the Avant-Garde in France, 1885 to World War I* (New York: Anchor Books, 1958), 27.
4. Liliane Brion-Guerry, ed., *L'Année 1913. Les formes esthétiques de l'œuvre d'art à la veille de la Première Guerre mondiale*, 3 vols. (Paris: Klincksieck, 1971–1973); *1913. Exposition organisée à l'occasion du 70e anniversaire de la Fondation des Amis de la Bibliothèque Nationale* (Paris: SABN, 1983); "L'année 1913 en France," *1895*, special issue of *Societe des Amies de la Bibliothèque Nationale*, 1993; Jean-Michel Rabaté, *1913. The Cradle of Modernism* (Oxford: Blackwell, 2007); Florian Illies, *1913, der Sommer des Jahrhundert* (Frankfort: Fisher Verlag, 2012); Colette Camelin and Marie-Paule Berranger, eds., *1913: cent ans après. Enchantements et désenchantements* (Paris: Hermann, 2015).
5. Jacques Rivière, "Le roman d'aventure," *Nouvelle Revue Française* 53–55 (May–July 1913).
6. Jean-Pierre Camard and Lynne Thornton, *L'Art et la vie en France à la Belle Epoque* (Bendor: Fondation Paul Ricard, 1971).
7. Béatrice Joyeux-Prunel, *Les Avant-gardes artistiques 1848–1918: une histoire transnationale* (Paris: Gallimard, 2015).
8. Claude Roy, *Descriptions critiques* (Paris: Gallimard, 1949), 206.
9. Paul Valéry, *Crisis of the Mind* [1919], trans. Denis Folliot and Jackson Mathews. Wikisource.
10. François Azouvi, *La Gloire de Bergson. Essai sur le magistère philosophique* (Paris: Gallimard, 2007).
11. Marcel Proust, "Vacances de Pâques," *Le Figaro*, March 25, 1913.
12. *Paris du temps perdu. Eugène Atget, Marcel Proust*, introduction by Arthur D. Trottenberg (Paris: Hoebecke Editions, 2012).
13. Jeanne Beausoleil and Pascal Ory, eds., *Albert Kahn. Réalités d'une utopie, 1860–1940* (Boulogne: Musée Albert Kahn, 1995).
14. Pascal Cordereix, "Les Archives de la parole," *Culture et recherche* 124 (2010–2011): 31.

15. E. Gentile, *L'Apocalypse de la modernité*; see also the chapters dedicated to the "imagined war" in Jean-Jacques Becker et al., eds., *Guerre et cultures, 1914–1918* (Paris: A. Colin, 1994), 49–63.

16. Jacques-Emile Blanche, unpublished diary, Bibliothèque de l'Institut, quoted in Jérôme Neutres, *Du côté de chez Jacques-Émile Blanche: un salon a la Belle Epoque* (Paris: Flammarion, 2012), 19.

"NOTHING MATTERED AS LONG AS WE WERE DANCING"

1. André Warnod, *Visages de Paris* (Paris: Firmin-Didot, 1930), 313.

2. André de Fouquières, *Cinquante ans de panache* (Paris: Horay, 1951), 58.

3. Hervé Guillemain and Stéphane Tison, *Du front à l'asile 1914–1918* (Paris: Alma, 2013), 352.

4. Cited in Emilio Gentile, *L'Apocalypse de la modernité: La Grande Guerre et l'homme nouveau*, trans. Stéphanie Lanfranchi (Paris: Editions Aubier, 2011), 20.

5. Warnod, *Visages de Paris*, 311.

6. André Warnod, *Fils de Montmartre. Souvenirs* (Paris: Fayard, 1955), 220–221.

7. Fouquières, *Cinquante ans de panache*, 165.

8. Warnod, *Visages de Paris*, 311–312.

9. Sophie Jacotot, *Danser à Paris dans l'Entre-deux-guerres* (Paris: Nouveau Monde, 2013).

10. Fabrice Montebello, *Le Cinéma en France depuis les années 1930* (Paris: Armand Colin, 2005) 22; Dimitri Vezyroglou, *Le Cinéma en France à la veille du parlant* (Paris: CNRS Editions, 2011).

11. Jean-Michel Guieu, *Gagner la paix. 1914–1929* (Paris: Seuil, 2015); Pascale Goetschel, "La 'Crise du théâtre': une histoire de controverses, de goûts et de représentations (milieu Crise siècle-fin des années 1930)" PhD diss., Université Paris 1, 2016, 31–32.

12. Ludovic Tournes, "L'Électrification des sensibilités: le disque, l'enregistrement électrique et la mutation du paysage sonore en France (1925–1939)," *French Cultural Studies* 16, no. 2 (2005), 135–149.

13. Sisley Huddleston, *Bohemian Literary and Social Life in Paris: Salons, Cafes, Studios* (London: Harrap, 1928).

14. BNF, Arts du spectacle, WNA-216, 1924, programme de la revue New-York Montmartre, quoted by Mathilde Terral, "Paris à la Belle Epoque: deux études sur la construction d'un imaginaire" (master's thesis, Université Paris 1 Panthéon-Sorbonne, 2014), 17.

15. Marcel de Bare, "Les Meunières du Moulin Rouge. Anecdotes et souvenirs inédits sur le bal célèbre," *Les Oeuvres libres* (June 1925): 330, 356, quoted in Terral, "Paris à la Belle Epoque," 31.

16. Yvette Guilbert, *La Chanson de ma vie: mes mémoires* (Paris: Grasset, 1927).

17. BNF, Arts du spectacle, WNA-216, 1927–29, quoted by Terral, *Paris à la Belle Epoque*, 30.

18. BNF, Arts du spectacle, WNA-216, 1927–29, quoted by Terral, *Paris à la Belle Epoque*, 30.

19. Léon Werth, *Danse, danseurs, dancings* (Paris: Rieder, 1924), 92.

20. Alice Bravard, *Le Grand monde parisien, 1900–1939. La persistance du modèle aristocratique* (Rennes: PUR, 2013).

21. Guieu, *Gagner la paix.*

22. Emmanuelle Retaillaud, *La Parisienne. Histoire d'un mythe. Du siècle des Lumières à nos jours* (Paris: Seuil, 2020).

23. Maurice de Waleffe, *Quand Paris était un paradis. Mémoires 1900–1939* (Paris: Denoël, 1947), 480; Fouquières, *Cinquante ans de panache*, 240.

24. Limore Yagil, *Au nom de l'art, 1933–1945. Exils, solidarités et engagements* (Paris: Fayard, 2015).

25. André Warnod, *Fils de Montmartre. Souvenirs* (Paris: Fayard, 1955), 259–260.

26. "1930. We stop here these memories, which we may continue one day." Warnod, *Fils de Montmartre*, 286.

27. Camille Mauclair, *La Farce de l'Art vivant*, vol. 1: *Une campagne picturale 1928–1929;* vol. 2: *Les Métèques contre l'art français* (Paris: Éd. de la Nouvelle Revue Critique, 1929–1930).

28. Gertrude Stein, *Paris France* (New York: Norton & Cie, 1940), 24.

29. Nancy Green, *The Other Americans in Paris: Businessmen, Countesses, Wayward Youth, 1880–1941* (Chicago: University of Chicago Press, 2014), 37.

30. Maria Delapérrière and Antoine Marès, eds., *Paris capitale culturelle de l'Europe centrale. Les échanges intellectuels entre la France et les pays de l'Europe médiane, 1918–1939* (Paris: Institut d'études slaves, 1997).

31. Warnod, *Visages de Paris*, 321.

32. Title of one of the sections of his *Souvenirs des milieux littéraires, politiques, artistiques et médicaux* (Paris: Nouvelle librairie nationale, 1920–1926).

33. I follow here Samuel Miloux-Comte's master's thesis, "Entre-deux-siècles, entre l'hier et l'aujourd'hui. La Belle Epoque dans les romans de l'entre-deux-guerres" (Université Paris 1 Panthéon-Sorbonne, 2012).

34. Maurice Leblanc, "La dame à la hache," in *Les Huit coups de l'horloge* (Paris: Lafitte, 1923).

35. Charles Morice, *Par le sang de la France* (Paris: Plon, 1921), 55, translated into English as *Babels, Balloons, Innocent Eyes*, trans. Brian Stableford (Snuggly Books, 2019).

36. Félicien Champsaur, *Nuit de fête* (Paris: Nouvelle revue critique, 1926), 112.

37. Camille Marbo, *La Revue du mois*, November 10, 1919; Fernand Vandérem, "Le temps perdu de M. Marcel Proust," *La Revue de Paris* (1919): 429–431; Binet-Valmer, *Comoedia*, October 5, 1919. Quoted by Léo Mahé, "Marcel Proust et la Belle Epoque" (master's thesis, Université Paris 1, 2016).

38. Blaise Cendrars, *Moravagine, a novel*, trans. Alan Brown (London: Owen, 1968).

39. Robert Desnos, *Le Soir*, February 26, 1927.

40. Jean Prévost, "Roger Martin du Gard romancier," *Europe* 73 (1929): 104.

41. Daniel Aranda, "Maurice Leblanc et la résurgence de la 'série' dans la littérature romanesque française," *Revue d'histoire littéraire de la France* 103 (2003): 111–121.

42. Francis Carco, *La Belle Epoque au temps de Bruant* (Paris: Gallimard, 1954), 162.

43. Catherine Dutheil-Pessin, *La Chanson réaliste, sociologie d'un genre* (Paris: L'Harmattan, 2004).

44. Nicole et Alain Lacombe, *Fréhel* (Paris: Belfond, 1990), 159–163.

45. "Où est-il donc?," lyrics by André Decaye and Lucien Carol, music by Vincent Scotto (Paris: Fortin, 1926).

46. Léopold Flameng, *Paris qui s'en va et Paris qui vient* (Paris: Cadart, 1860); Charles Virmaître, *Paris qui s'efface* (Paris: Savine, 1887); Paul Bellon and Georges Price, *Paris qui passe* (Paris: Savine, 1883).

47. Elie Richard, *Paris qui meurt. Saint-Julien-le-Pauvre. Le Roman de la Bièvre. La Cité et Notre-Dame* (Paris: Figuière, 1923).

48. Y. Guilbert, *La Chanson de ma vie*; Mayol, *Mes Mémoires* (Paris: Louis Querelle, 1929); Fursy, *Mon petit bonhomme de chemin. Souvenirs de Montmartre et d'ailleurs* (Paris: Louis Querelle, 1929).

49. Francis Carco, *De Montmartre au Quartier Latin* (Paris: Albin Michel, 1927), 11–12.

50. Carco, *De Montmartre au Quartier Latin*, 91.

51. Fursy, *Mon petit bonhomme de chemin*, 97.

52. Ruth Fiori, *L'Invention du vieux Paris. Naissance d'une conscience patrimoniale dans la capitale* (Wavre: Mardaga, 2012).

53. Christine Bard, *Les Garçonnes. Modes et fantasmes des années folles* (Paris: Flammarion, 1998).

54. Léo Malet, *Le Soleil nait derrière le Louvre* [1954] (Paris: Robert Laffont, 2006), 85.

THE INVENTION OF "1900"

1. André Warnod, *Visages de Paris* (Paris: Firmin-Didot, 1930), 223.

2. Warnod, *Visages de Paris*, 223–224.

3. Warnod, *Visages de Paris*, 239.

4. Warnod, *Visages de Paris*, 240.

5. *Paris-Soir*, December 1, 1930.

6. *Le Temps*, November 17, 1930.

7. Paul Poiret, *En habillant l'époque* (Paris: Grasset, 1930), 14.

8. Poiret, *En habillant l'époque*, 29.

9. Paul Morand, *1900* (Paris: Flammarion, 1931); *1900 A.D.*, trans. R. Fedden (New York: W. F. Payson, 1931), 101.

10. Morand, *1900*, 154.

11. Morand, *1900*, 141, 203.

12. Morand, *1900*, 207.

13. *Entretien avec Paul Morand,* Archives du xxe siècle, Rambouillet, enregistrement vidéo, France région 3, 1er August 1970, 53 min. 38 s.

14. Morand, *1900,* 207.

15. Morand, *1900*, 14.

16. *Le Figaro,* May 26, 1931.

17. *Le Matin,* May 24, 1931.

18. *Le Figaro,* May 24, 1931; May 18, 1931.

19. *Comoedia,* May 30, 1931.

20. *Le Temps,* May 29, 1931; *Le Petit Parisien,* June 23, 1931.

21. *Les Nouvelles littéraires,* August 22, 1931.

22. Benjamin Crémieux (*Nouvelle Revue Française* CCXIV [1931]: 151).

23. *Les Marges. Revue de littérature et d'art* 90 (June 1932).

24. Louis Chéronnet, *A Paris . . . vers 1900* (Paris: Editions des chroniques du jour, 1932).

25. Jose Shercliff, *Jane Avril of the Moulin Rouge* (London: Macrae Smith, 1952). On Jane Avril, see François Caradec, *Jane Avril* (Paris: Fayard, 2001).

26. *Paris-Midi,* August 16, 1933.

27. *Paris-Midi,* August 16, 1933.

28. *Paris-Midi,* August 7, 1933.

29. Claude-André Puget, *Valentin le désossé* (original comedy in four acts), *Les Oeuvres libres* 141 (March 1933).

30. Caroline Otéro, *Souvenirs et vie intime* (Paris: Le Calame, 1926); Yvette Guilbert, *La Chanson de ma vi: mes mémoires* (Paris: Grasset, 1927); Eugénie Buffet, *Ma vie, mes amours, mes aventures, confidences recueillies par Maurice Hamel* (Paris: Figuière, 1930).

31. Maurice de Waleffe, *Quand Paris était un paradis. Mémoires 1900–1939* (Paris: Denoël, 1947), 180; Boni de Castellane, *Comment j'ai découvert l'Amérique. Mémoires* (Paris: Crès, 1924); *L'Art d'être pauvre, Mémoires* (Paris: Crès, 1925).

32. Georges Duhamel, "Remarques sur les mémoires imaginaires," *Nouvelle Revue Française* 240 (September 1933): 382; the second part of the text was published in October 1933 (241). The two parts were gathered in a volume the following year by the *Mercure de France.*

33. Marie Scheikévitch, *Souvenirs d'un temps disparu* (Paris: Plon, 1935).

34. Jean Cocteau, *Souvenir Portraits. Paris in the Belle Époque,* trans. Jesse Browner (New York: Paragon House, 1990), 62, 56, 152.

35. Roland Dorgeles, *Quand j'étais montmartrois* (Paris: Albin Michel, 1936).

36. Alfred Sauvy, *Mythologie de notre temps* (Paris: Payot, 1965), 26.

37. Dorgeles, *Quand j'étais montmartrois,* 12.

38. Dorgeles, *Quand j'étais montmartrois,* 27.

39. Léon-Paul Fargue, *Le Piéton de Paris* (Paris: Gallimard, 1939); *D'après Paris* (Paris: Ed. de la Nouvelle Revue Française, 1931).

40. Fargue, *D'après Paris,* 247.

41. Fargue, *D'après Paris,* 30, 45.

42. Fargue, *D'après Paris,* 43, 29.

43. Louis Bourgeois-Borgex, "La fin d'un siècle," *Les Cahiers libres* 195 (September 1937): 79–124.

44. Bryher, *Paris 1900* (Paris: La Maison des amis du livre, 1938), 62.

45. Pascale Goetschel, "Le Paris du spectacle vivant," in *Imaginaires urbains, du Paris romantique à nos jours,* ed. M. Tsikounas (Paris: Le Manuscrit, 2011), 101.

46. Francis Carco, *La Belle Epoque au temps de Bruant* (Paris: Gallimard, 1954), 162.

47. Samuel Miloux-Comte, "Entre-deux-siècles, entre l'hier et l'aujourd'hui. La Belle Epoque dans les romans de l'entre-deux-guerres" (master's thesis, Université Paris 1 Panthéon-Sorbonne, 2012).

48. Roger Martin du Gard, *Les Thibault,* vol. 3: *La Belle Saison* [1923] (Paris: Gallimard, 1972), 150.

49. R. Martin du Gard, *Summer 14* [1936], trans. Stuart Gilbert (London: John Lane The Bodley Head, 1940), 671.

50. Jules Romains, *The Men of Good Will,* vol. 1: *The 6th of October* [1932] (New York: Knopf, 1934), 123.

51. Louis Aragon, *Residential Quarter* [1936], trans. H. M. Chevalier (New York: Harcourt Brace, 1938), 505–506.

52. *La Revue des vivants* 1 (1935): 89.

53. Preface, *Cloches de Bâle,* in *Oeuvres romanesques croisées d'Elsa Triolet et de Louis Aragon,* vol. VII (Paris: Robert Laffont, 1965), 23.

54. Eugène Dabit, "Compte rendu des *Cloches de Bâle,*" *Europe* 14 (February 1935): 297–299.

55. Cocteau, *Souvenir Portraits,* 110.

56. Céline, *Death on the Installment Plan* [1936], trans. Ralph Manheim (New York: New American Library, 1966), 308.

57. Cocteau, *Souvenirs Portraits,* 5.

58. Dorgeles, *Quand j'étais montmartrois,* 10. (Translation modified.)

59. Juliette Rennes, "L'Argument de la décadence dans les pamphlets d'extrême droite des années 1930," *Mots. Les langages du politique* 58 (1999): 153–164.

60. Bryher, *Paris 1900,* 20.

61. Robert Musil, *The Man Without Qualities* [1930] (New York: Capricorn Books, 1965), 13.

62. *Les Marges. Revue de littérature et d'art* 90 (June 1932): 9.

63. *Nobel Lectures. Including Presentation Speeches and Laureates' Biographies. Literature 1901–1967* (Singapore: World Scientific, 1999), 350.

64. Jean Valdois, "1900 vu par 1933," *Cinémagazine* (February 1933).

65. Henri Duvernois and André Barde, *La Poule* (operetta in three acts and four scenes), music by Henri Christiné (Paris: impr. Dorel, 1936).

66. Henri Duvernois, *La Poule, roman* (Paris: Grasset, 1931); *La Poule*, by René Guissart, featuring Dranem, Arlette Marchal, Marguerite Moreno, André Luguet, released on May 20, 1933.

67. The expression is from Jean Bourbon, *Lyrica*, January 1, 1936.

68. A file "Paradise Lost," composed of clippings and reviews published after the film's release, is available in the Rondel collection at the Bibliothèque Nationale de France.

OCCUPIED PARIS, "BELLE EPOQUE" PARIS?

1. Hervé Le Boterf, *La Vie parisienne sous l'Occupation* (Paris: France-Empire, 1974), 235.

2. *Où sortir à Paris? Le Guide du soldat allemand*, with an introduction by Laurent Lemire (Paris: Alma, 2014).

3. Stéphanie Corcy, *La Vie culturelle sous l'Occupation* (Paris: Perrin), 240. See also André Halimi, *Chantons sous l'Occupation* (Paris: Orban, 1976), and Myriam Chimènes, ed., *La Vie musicale sous Vichy* (Brussels: Complexes, 2001).

4. Gérard Régnier, *Jazz et société sous l'Occupation* (Paris: L'Harmattan, 2009), 83; Boterf, *La Vie parisienne*, 235.

5. Alan Riding, *And the Show Went On: Cultural Life in Nazi-Occupied Paris* (New York: Knopf, 2010), 9.

6. Agnès Callu, "Les music-halls et cabarets ou les petites entreprises du 'Gai Paris,'" in *Culture et médias sous l'Occupation: des entreprises dans la France de Vichy*, ed. Agnes Callu, Patrick Eveno, and Herve Joly (Paris: Ed. du CTHS, 2009), 217–232.

7. Boterf, *La Vie parisienne*, 236–238.

8. Hélène Eck, ed., *La Guerre des ondes. Histoire des radios de langue française pendant la Deuxième guerre mondiale* (Paris: Colin, 1985).

9. Myriam Chimènes and Yannick Simon, eds., *La Musique à Paris sous l'Occupation* (Paris: Fayard, 2013).

10. *Les Ondes* 25 (May 25, 1941).

11. AN, F21 8106: Déclaration devant le Comité national d'épuration des professions d'artistes dramatiques, lyriques et musiciens exécutant, November 20, 1945.

12. *Le Figaro*, February 18, 1938.

13. *Les Ondes* 26 (October 19, 1941).

14. *Les Ondes* 25 (May 25, 1941).

15. M. Defleury, in *Les Ondes* 74 (September 27, 1942).

16. *Les Ondes* 104 (April 25, 1943).

17. *Les Ondes* 104 (April 25, 1943); 133 (November 14, 1943); 148 (February 27, 1944). On Radio-Paris strategy, see Cécile Meadel, "Pauses musicales ou les éclatants

silences de Radio-Paris," in *La Vie musicale sous Vichy*, ed. Myriam Chimènes (Brussels: Complexes, 2001), 242–243.

18. Riding, *And the Show Went On*, 92.

19. *Le Figaro*, November 10, 1941.

20. Halimi, *Chantons sous l'Occupation*, 318.

21. *Le Petit Parisien*, November 15–16, 1941.

22. *La Semaine à Paris* 998 (February 4–10, 1942).

23. *Le Matin*, November 24, 1941.

24. BNF Arts du spectacle, WNA 331, programme, quoted by Mathilde Terral, "Paris à la Belle Epoque: deux études sur la construction d'un imaginaire (master's thesis, Université Paris 1 Panthéon-Sorbonne, 2014), 34.

25. *Paris-Soir*, November 25, 1941.

26. Roger Sardou, *La Semaine à Paris* 990 (November 26–December 2, 1941).

27. *L'Oeuvre*, November 20, 1941.

28. *Le Petit Parisien*, March 23, 1943.

29. *Le Matin*, June 15, 1943; *La Semaine à Paris* 1016–1026 (March 24–April 6, 1943; August 25–September 7, 1943).

30. *Le Matin*, March 16, 1944.

31. *Le Petit Parisien*, August 7, 1943.

32. Boterf, *La Vie parisienne*, 236.

33. Maurice de Waleffe, *Quand Paris était un paradis. Mémoires 1900–1939* (Paris: Denoël, 1947), 535.

34. Serge Added, "Le Succès du théâtre dans Paris occupé," in *La Vie culturelle sous Vichy*, ed. Jean-Pierre Rioux (Brussels: Complexe, 1990), 315–350; Julian Jackson, *France: The Dark Years, 1940–1944* (Oxford: Oxford University Press, 2001), 210.

35. Halimi, *Chantons sous l'Occupation*, 81.

36. Régnier, *Jazz et société*, 85.

37. René-Gustave Nobécourt, *Les Secrets de la propagande en France occupée* (Paris: Fayard, 1962), 65.

38. Quoted by Karine Le Bail, "Radio-Paris ou Radio-Vichy? Le Milieu artistique français face au nouveau marché des ondes," in *Culture et médias sous l'Occupation: des entreprises dans la France de Vichy*, ed. Agnès Callu, Patrick Eveno, and Hervé Joly (Paris: Ed. du CTHS, 2009), 333.

39. The program is reproduced in Isabelle Magne, "Le Music-hall à Paris sous l'occupation allemande" (master's thesis, Université Paris 1, 2003), 206.

40. *Les Ondes* 168 (July 16, 1944), quoted by Terral, *Paris à la Belle Epoque*.

41. Quoted by Jean Defrasne, *L'Occupation allemande en France* (Paris: PUF, 1985), 113.

42. Germaine Tillion, *Une opérette à Ravensbrück* [1944] (Paris: La Martinière, 2005).

43. Isabelle Backouche, *Paris transformé, le Marais 1900–1980. De l'îlot insalubre au secteur sauvegardé* (Paris: Créaphis, 2016).

44. Riding, *And the Show Went On,* 119.
45. See Rita Thalmann, *La Mise au pas. Idéologie et stratégie sécuritaire dans la France occupée* (Paris: Fayard, 1992).
46. Riding, *And the Show Went On,* 34.

LIBERATED PARIS, BELLE ÉPOQUE PARIS

1. Gilles Schlesser, *Le Cabaret "rive gauche" (1946–1974)* (Paris: L'Archipel, 2006), 25.
2. Peter Novick, *The Resistance Versus Vichy: The Purge of Collaborators in Liberated France* (New York: Columbia University Press, 1968), 222.
3. AN, F21 8106, dossier Alléhaut, Comité national d'épuration des professions d'artiste dramatique, lyrique et musicien exécutant, November 20, 1945.
4. AN, F21 8106, dossier Alléhaut.
5. AN, F21 8106, dossier Alléhaut.
6. http://www.radioscope.fr/grilles/inter/inter1951.htm; http://andrelimoges.unblog .fr/2010/02/25/la-troupe-de-radio-alger/.
7. Rosemary Wakeman, *The Heroic City: Paris, 1945–1958* (Chicago: University of Chicago Press, 2009).
8. Ferran Canyameres, *Joseph Ollier: l'homme de la Belle Epoque* (Paris: Editions Universelles, 1946).
9. Canyameres, *Joseph Ollier,* quotations: 11, 70, 142.
10. Lucien François, *Les Elégances de Paris* (Paris: Commissariat Général au Tourisme, 1946), unpaginated.
11. Nicole Védrès, in Georges-Michel Bovay, *Cinéma, un œil ouvert sur le monde* (Paris: La Guilde du Livre, 1952).
12. Nicole Védrès, *Un siècle d'élégance française* (Paris: Ed. du Chêne, 1943); *Images du cinéma français* (Paris: Ed. du Chêne, 1945).
13. Quoted by Annick Peigné-Giuly, "Nicole Védrès, de *Paris 1900* à nos jours," *Images documentaires* 63 (2008): 9–13.
14. André Bazin, "Paris 1900. À la recherche du temps perdu," *L'Écran français,* September 30, 1947, reprinted in *Qu'est-ce que le cinéma?,* vol. I (Paris: Cerf, 1958), and *Le Cinéma français de la libération à la Nouvelle Vague (1945–1958)* (Paris: Cahiers du cinéma, 1983), 167–168.
15. "Marker mémoire," *Cinémathèque française,* January 7–February 1, 1998, 5.
16. Peigné-Giuly, "Nicole Védrès."
17. Pascal Ory, *L'Aventure culturelle française* (Paris: Flammarion, 1989), 135.
18. Carl Einstein, *Die Kunst des 20. Jahrhunderts* (Berlin: Propyläen, 1926); Laurence Campa, "1913 en abyme," in eds., *1913: cent ans après. Enchantements et désenchantements,* ed. Colette Camelin and Marie-Paule Berranger (Paris: Hermann, 2015), 369.

19. Serge Guilbaut, "Comment la ville lumière s'est fait voler l'idée d'art moderne," in *Paris 1944–1954. Artistes, intellectuels, publics: la culture comme enjeu*, ed. Philippe Gumplowicz and Jean-Claude Klein (Paris: Autrement, 1995), 45–60.

20. Pascal Ory, *L'Aventure culturelle française* (Paris: Flammarion, 1989), 134–135.

21. André Salmon, *L'Air de la Butte. Souvenirs sans fin* (Paris: Éd. de la nouvelle France, 1945). These memories continue until 1961; Blaise Cendrars, *L'Homme foudroyé* (Paris: Denoël 1945); *La Main coupée* (Paris: Denöel, 1946).

22. Fernand Gregh, *L'Age d'or. Souvenirs d'enfance et de jeunesse* (Paris: Grasset, 1948). Later would come *L'Age d'airain (Souvenirs 1905–1925)* (Paris: Grasset, 1951).

23. Claude Coste, "1913: un mythe musical," in Camelin and Berranger, *1913*, 482.

24. L. V., "Le Sacre du printemps de M. Strawinsky [*sic*]," *Revue Française de Musique*, July 1913, 601–603.

25. Maurice Brillant and Bernard Champigneulle, *L'Art du ballet: des origines à nos jours* (Paris: Ed. du Tambourinaire, 1952); Lynn Garafola, "The Legacies of the Ballets Russes," *Experiment* 17 (2011): 31–46.

26. André Breton, *Entretiens avec André Parinaud* [1952] (Paris: Gallimard, 1969), 22.

27. Michael Kelly, *The Cultural and Intellectual Rebuilding of France after the Second World War* (Basingstoke: Palgrave Macmillan, 2004).

28. Robert Frank, *La Hantise du déclin. La France de 1914 à 2014* [1994] (Paris: Belin, 2014); René Girault and Robert Frank, *La Puissance française en question (1945–1949)* (Paris: Publications de la Sorbonne, 1988).

29. Pascal Ory, "Introduction à l'ère du doute. La puissance française dans les représentations culturelles vers 1948," in Girault and Frank, *La Puissance française en question*, 409.

30. Philip H. Gordon, *A Certain Idea of France. French Security Policy and Gaullist Legacy* (Princeton, N.J.: Princeton University Press, 1993), 15.

31. Charles de Gaulle, *War Memoirs: The Call to Honor, 1940–1942* [1954] (New York: Viking, 1955), 4.

32. Nadine Nieszawer, *Peintres juifs à Paris 1905–1939* (Paris: Denoël, 2000); Willi Jaspers, *Hotel Lutétia. Ein deutsches Exil in Paris* (Munich/Vienna: Hanser Verlag, 1994).

33. Quoted by Limore Yagil, *Au nom de l'art, 1933–1945. Exils, solidarités et engagements* (Paris: Fayard, 2015), 21.

34. Denis Peschanski, "Les Camps français d'internement (1938–1946)" (PhD diss., Université Paris 1 Panthéon-Sorbonne, 2000).

35. Arthur Koestler, *Scum of the Earth* (London: Jonathan Cape, 1941).

36. Yagil, *Au nom de l'art*; Serge Guilbaut, "Comment la ville lumière s'est fait voler l'idée d'art moderne," in *Paris 1944–1954. Artistes, intellectuels, publics: la culture comme enjeu*, ed. Philippe Gumplowicz and Jean-Claude Klein (Paris: Autrement, 1995), 45–60.

37. Marie Scot, "L'impérialisme des idées et de la culture française," in *La Vie intellectuelle en France*, vol. 2: *De 1914 à nos jours*, ed. C. Charle and L. Jeanpierre (Paris: Seuil, 2016), 360.

38. Elisa Capdevila, *Des Américains à Paris. Artistes et bohèmes dans la France d'après-guerre* (Paris: Armand Colin, 2017).

A LIVELY MID-CENTURY

1. The term "mid-century" comes from Albert Keim, *Le Demi-siècle: Souvenirs de la vie littéraire et politique, 1876–1946* (Paris: Albin Michel, 1950).
2. *L'Aurore*, June 23–34, 1951.
3. Hugo, *Vingt ans maître d'hôtel chez Maxim's* (Paris: Amiot-Dumont, 1951), 15.
4. BNF Arts du S, WNA-216n 1948–1951, quoted by Mathilde Terral, "Paris à la Belle Epoque: deux études sur la construction d'un imaginaire" (master's thesis, Université Paris 1 Panthéon-Sorbonne, 2014).
5. Archives du Moulin Rouge, programmes 1926–1955, quoted by Terral, "Paris à la Belle Epoque," 64.
6. *La Presse-Magazine*, October 26, 1954.
7. *Libération*, April 5–6, 1952.
8. *La Presse-Magazine*, October 26, 1954.
9. *La Presse*, November 21, 1951; *La Presse-magazine*, October 22, 1950; *Franc-Tireur*, April 11, 1956.
10. Anne de Bercy and Armand Ziwes, *À Montmartre le soir: cabarets et chansonniers d'hier* (Paris: Grasset, 1951).
11. This is the case with *Histoire du music-hall*, by l'Académie du cirque et du music-hall (Paris: Editions de Paris, 1954), or Jean Charles, *Cent ans de music-hall. Histoire générale du music-hall des origines à nos jours* (Genèva: Editions Jeheber, 1956). See Jacques Cheyronnaud, "De quoi nos histoires du music-hall sont-elles l'histoire?," in *Les Mondes du music-hall*, ed. J. Cheyronnaud, S. Hureau, and V. Read (Marseille: Centre national du patrimoine de la chanson, des variétés et des musiques actuelles, 2011).
12. Pierre la Mure, *Moulin Rouge* (Paris: Presses de la Cité, 1951).
13. Jean Renoir, interview by François Truffaut, *Cahiers du cinéma* 78 (December 25, 1957).
14. André Salmon, *L'Air de la Butte. Souvenirs sans fin* (Paris: Éd. de la nouvelle France, 1945), 178.
15. André Warnod, *Ceux de la Butte* (Paris: Julliard, 1947), 105.
16. Warnod, *Ceux de la Butte*, 95.
17. Max Aghion, *Hier à Paris* (Paris: Marchot, 1947), 71.
18. André Warnod, *Fils de Montmartre. Souvenirs* (Paris: Fayard, 1955), 29.
19. Aghion, *Hier à Paris,* 70.
20. Salmon, *L'Air de la Butte,* 31.
21. Salmon, *L'Air de la Butte,* 183.
22. Warnod, *Fils de Montmartre,* 72.
23. Roland Dorgelès, *Au beau temps de la butte* (Paris: Albin Michel, 1963), 60–61.

24. André Billy, *La Terrasse du Luxembourg* (Paris: Fayard, 1945), 265.

25. Salmon, *L'Air de la Butte*, 58.

26. Aghion, *Hier à Paris*.

27. Warnod, *Ceux de la Butte*, 92.

28. André de Fouquières, *Cinquante ans de panache* (Paris: Horay, 1951), 6.

29. Fouquières, *Cinquante ans de panache*, 164.

30. Robert Montesquiou, *Les Pas effacés, Mémoires* (Paris: Emile-Paul, 1923); Philippe Jullian, *Robert de Montesquiou: un prince 1900* (Paris: Perrin, 1965). Montesquiou was painted by Boldini and became a subject of Julian Barnes's *The Man in the Red Coat* (2019).

31. Fouquières, *Cinquante ans de panache*, 469.

32. Fouquières, *Cinquante ans de panache*, 57–58.

33. Fouquières, *Cinquante ans de panache*, 92.

34. Pauline de Pange, *Comment j'ai vu 1900. Confidences d'une jeune fille* (Paris: Grasset, 1965).

35. Eric Mension-Rigau, *Aristocrates et grands bourgeois. Éducation, traditions, valeurs* (Paris: Plon, 1994).

36. Nicole Pellegrin, ed., *Histoires d'historiennes* (Saint-Etienne: Publications de l'Université Saint-Étienne, 2006), 339–340.

37. Cléo de Mérode, *Le Ballet de ma vie* (Paris: Horay, 1955), 155–156.

38. Fouquières, *Cinquante ans de panache*, 261.

39. Maurice de Waleffe, *Quand Paris était un paradis. Mémoires 1900–1939* (Paris: Denoël, 1947), 136.

40. Fouquières, *Cinquante ans de panache*, 211.

41. Waleffe, *Quand Paris était un paradis*, 136.

42. Georges de Lauris, *Souvenirs d'une belle époque* (Paris: Amiot-Dumont, 1948).

43. Lauris, *Souvenirs d'une belle époque*, 146.

44. Lauris, *Souvenirs d'une belle époque*, 255.

45. Gabriel-Louis Pringué, *Trente ans de diners en ville* (Paris: Ed. Revue Adam, 1948).

46. Maurice Donnay, *J'ai connu 1900* (Paris: Fayard, 1951).

47. Maurice Chevalier, *Ma route et mes chansons* (Paris: Julliard, 1946), 108.

48. Fouquières, *Cinquante ans de panache*, 23.

49. Mérode, *Le Ballet de ma vie*, 191.

50. Stefan Zweig, *The World of Yesterday* (London: Cassel & Co., 1943), 4.

51. Mérode, *Le Ballet de ma vie*, 192.

52. Warnod, *Fils de Montmartre*, 158–159. Belleville and Ménilmontant are working-class areas in the 20th arrondissement.

53. Mérode, *Le Ballet de ma vie*, 193.

54. Francesco Dorigo, "Nostalgia per la Belle Epoque," *L'Altro cinema: rivista del cinema d'amatore* 73 (February 1960): 83–91.

55. A list of the principal French movies appeared in an appendix to the French edition.

56. *L'Aurore*, May 24, 1950.

57. *L'Aurore*, March 12, 1951.

58. *Positif* 13 (March–April 1955).

59. *L'Express*, September 18, 1954.

60. *L'Aurore*, June 27, 1951; *Le Canard Enchaîné*, December 3, 1958.

61. *France-Soir*, September 30, 1950.

62. Dossier Sadoul 454 B30, filmography 195, IDHEC, archives of the Cinémathèque in Bercy, quoted by Alice Simon, "La Belle Epoque cinématographique des années 1950" (master's thesis, Université Paris 1, 2013).

63. Alain Ferrari, "La Belle Epoque du vaudeville et de la chanson," *Positif* 548 (October 2006).

64. *L'Aurore*, December 1, 1951.

65. Jean-Louis Bory, "Au cinéma Frou-Frou," *L'Express*, December 7, 1955.

66. *L'Humanité*, September 2, 1953.

67. Title of the film Jacques Rivette dedicated to Renoir in 1966.

68. *Positif* 14–15 (1955).

69. Geneviève Sellier, "The 'Belle Époque' Genre in Post-War French Cinema: A Woman's Film à la Française?," *Studies in French Cinema* 3, no. 1 (2003): 47–53.

70. Martin O'Shaughnessy, "The *Belle Époque* films of Jean Renoir," in *New Perspectives on the Fin de Siècle in Nineteenth- and Twentieth-Century France*, ed. Kay Chadwick and Timothy Unwin (Lewiston, N.Y.: The Edwin Mellon Press, 2000), 215–228.

71. *Le Canard Enchaîné*, May 4, 1955.

72. *Renoir on Renoir, Interviews, Essays and Remarks* [1979] (Cambridge: Cambridge University Press, 1989), 219.

73. Quoted by Valérie Vignaux, *"Casque d'or" de Jacques Becker* (Neuilly: Atlande, 2009), 132.

74. "Pavane pour des apaches défunts," *Cahiers du cinéma* 13 (June 1952): 71.

75. Woody Allen would use the same device in *Midnight in Paris* (2011).

76. Noel Herpe, "La Belle époque cinématographique de Feydeau (1945–1955)," in *Feydeau. La plume et les planches*, ed. Violaine Heyraud (Paris: Presses Sorbonne nouvelle, 2014), 160–166.

77. *L'Aurore*, May 26, 1950.

78. Rémy Pawin, "Retour sur les 'Trente Glorieuses' et la périodisation du second xxe siècle," *Revue d'histoire moderne et contemporaine* 60–61 (2013): 155–175.

79. *L'Express*, March 29, 1957.

80. The Italian Renato Castellini also shot a *Zaza* in 1942.

81. Vanessa Schwartz, "The Belle Époque That Never Ended," in *It's so French! Hollywood, Paris and the Making of Cosmopolitism Film Culture* (Chicago: University of Chicago Press, 2007), 19–53.

82. I am following Schwartz's analysis.

83. Jacques Chastenet de Castaing, *La France de M. Fallières. Une époque pathétique* (Paris: Fayard, 1949).

84. Jacques Chastenet, *La Belle Époque: la société sous M. Fallières* (Paris: Fayard, 1951). More books of that kind followed: *Histoire politique de la Troisième République,* vol. III: *La République triomphante 1893–1906* (Paris: Hachette, 1955); vol. IV: *Jours inquiets et sanglants 1906–1918* (Paris: Hachette, 1957).

85. Robert Burnand, *Paris 1900* (Paris: Hachette, 1951).

86. Jacques Castelnau, *Belle Époque* (Paris: Librairie académique Perrin, 1962).

87. Gilbert Guilleminault, ed., *Le Roman vrai de la IIIe République* (Paris: Denoël, 1956–1965). Followed by *Roman vrai de la IVe République,* then by *Roman vrai de la Ve République* (Paris: Laffont, 1991).

88. Charles-Olivier Carbonnel, *Histoire et historiens, une mutation idéologique des historiens français, 1865–1885* (Toulouse: Privat, 1976).

89. Jacques Banville, *La Troisième République* (Paris: Fayard, 1935).

90. André Siegfried, *Tableau politique de la France de l'Ouest sous la IIIe République* (Paris: Colin, 1913); Siegfried, *Tableau des partis en France* (Paris: Grasset, 1930); Auguste Soulier, *L'Instabilité ministérielle sous la IIIe République (1871–1938)* (Paris: Librairie du Recueil Sirey, 1939).

91. Robert de Jouvenel, *La République des camarades* (Paris: Grasset, 1914); Daniel Halévy, *La République des comités: essai d'histoire contemporaine (1895–1934)* (Paris: Grasset, 1934); Alexandre Zévaès, *Histoire de la Troisième République de 1870 à 1925* (Paris: Éd. Georges Anquetil, 1926).

92. Joseph Reinach, *Histoire de l'affaire Dreyfus* (Paris: Ed. de la Revue blanche, 1901–1911); Emile Bourgeois, *Les Origines et les responsabilités de la Grande Guerre: preuves et aveux* (Paris: Hachette 1922); Pierre Renouvin, *Les Origines immédiates de la guerre* (Paris: Costes, 1925).

93. Charles Seignobos, *L'Evolution de la IIIe République 1875–1914* (Paris: Hachette, 1921), which is the eighth volume of Lavisse's *Histoire de France contemporaine*; Georges Bourgin, *La Troisième République* (Paris: Colin, 1939).

94. Pierre Renouvin, *La Crise européenne et la Grande Guerre (1904–1918)* (Paris: Alcan, 1934); Maurice Baumont, *L'Essor industriel et l'impérialisme colonial (1878–1904)* (Paris: PUF, 1937); Pierre Renouvin, Edmond Préclin, and Gaston Hardy, *La Paix armée et la grande guerre (1871–1919)* (Paris: PUF, 1939); Georges Bourgin, *La Troisième République* (Paris: Colin, 1939).

95. Olivier Dumoulin, "L'histoire contemporaine," in André Burguière, ed., *Dictionnaire des sciences historiques* (Paris: PUF, 1986), 154–156.

96. Jules Isaac, *1914. Le problème des origines de la guerre: un débat historique* (Paris: Rieder, 1933).

97. Georges Bonnefous (André Daniel), *Histoire politique de la Troisième République* (Paris: PUF, 1955); Jacques Gouault, *Comment la France est devenue républicaine* (Paris: Colin, 1955); Pierre Renouvin, ed., *Histoire des Relations internationales,* vol. VI: *1871–1914* (Paris: Hachette, 1955).

98. André Billy, *L'Epoque 1900. 1885–1905* (Paris: Tallandier, 1951).

99. *1900: La Belle Epoque à Bordeaux et dans le Sud-Ouest,* exhibition held from October 19 to November 19, 1957, catalogue by Jean-Gabriel Lemoine (Bordeux: Musée des Beaux-Arts de Bordeaux, 1957), 1.

100. *Le Figaro littéraire*, July 22, 1961.
101. Alfred Sauvy, *Mythologie de notre temps* (Paris: Payot, 1965), 27.
102. Gérard Baüer, "La Belle Epoque," *Réalités* 54 (July 1950).
103. Fouquières, *Cinquante ans de panache*, 57–58.
104. "La Belle époque. Panorama et réhabilitation des années 1900," *Le Crapouillot* 29 (1955).
105. Paul Prist, *1900. Souvenirs littéraires* (Brussels: Office de publicité, 1949), 46.
106. Waleffe, *Quand Paris était un paradis*, 243.
107. Chastenet, *La Belle Époque*; Aghion, *Hier à Paris*, 23.
108. Alain Corbin, "Paris-Province," in *Realms of Memory: Rethinking the French Past*, ed. L. Kritzman and P. Nora, trans. Arthur Goldhammer (New York: Columbia University Press, 1996), 1: 427–464.
109. Caroline Otéro, *Souvenirs et vie intime* (Paris: Le Calame, 1926), 159.
110. Paul Poiret, *En habillant l'époque* (Paris: Grasset, 1930), 73.
111. Zweig, *The World of Yesterday*, 151.
112. Hugo, *Vingt ans maître d'hôtel chez Maxim's*, 8.
113. Francis de Miomandre, "Heureuse Epoque! . . . ," *Le Temps*, January 14, 1942.
114. Armand Lanoux, *Amours 1900* (Paris: Hachette, 1961), 141.
115. Chéronnet, *A Paris . . . vers 1900*.
116. *Le Crapouillot* (1955): 54.
117. M. Durant, *Le Canard Enchaîné*, December 3, 1958.
118. Christian Corvisier, *Cléo de Mérode et la photographie. La première icône moderne* (Paris: Ed. du patrimoine, 2007).
119. Michael D. Garval, *Cléo de Mérode and the Rise of Modern Celebrity Culture* (Farnham: Ashgate, 2012), 185.
120. Lanoux, *Amours 1900*, 361.
121. Hugo, *Vingt ans maître d'hôtel chez Maxim's*, 132.
122. "Viens, Poupoule!" song by Adolf Spahn, 1902.
123. Warnod, *Fils de Montmartre*, 158–159.
124. Waleffe, *Quand Paris était un paradis*, 154.
125. Fouquières, *Cinquante ans de panache*, 57–58.

THE "BELLE ÉPOQUE" ISN'T WHAT IT USED TO BE

1. François Truffaut, "A Certain Tendency of the French Cinema" [1954], in *Movies and Methods. An Anthology*, ed. Bill Nichols (Berkeley: University of California Press, 1976), 224–236.
2. Georges Darien, *Le Voleur* [1997] (Paris: Gallimard Folio, 1990), 339. Then Darien wrote *La Belle France*, the most violent pamphlet ever published against the society of this time (Paris: Savine, 1900).
3. Anne Wiazemsky, *Un an après* (Paris: Gallimard, 2015).
4. François Guérif, *Le Cinéma policier français* (Paris: H. Veyrier, 1983), 145.

5. See Dominique Kalifa, *Biribi: Les bagnes coloniaux de l'armee français* (Paris: Éditions Perrin, 2009).

6. Isabelle Veyrat-Masson, *Quand la télévision explore le temps. L'histoire au petit écran, 1953–2000* (Paris: Fayard, 2000).

7. Adeline Cordier, *Post-War French Popular Music: Cultural Identity and the Brel-Brassens-Ferré Myth* (Farnham: Ashgate, 2014).

8. *Libération,* February 1, 1961, quoted by Cordier, *Post-War French Popular Music,* 124.

9. *Le Canard Enchaîné,* April 26, 1950.

10. *Les Lettres françaises,* October 20, 1966.

11. Maurice Rheims, *L'Objet 1900* (Paris: Arts et Métiers Graphiques, 1964), 9.

12. Jean Mollet, *Les Mémoires du baron Mollet* (Paris: Gallimard, 1963).

13. Hervé Lauwick, *Jupons et hauts-de-forme. La vie secrète de la Belle Epoque* (Paris: Plon, 1964).

14. *Les Grandes énigmes de la belle époque . . . ,* TV series presented by Bernard Michal (Paris: Éd. de Saint-Clair, 1966–1967).

15. John Ashbery, "Toulouse-Lautrec," October 13 1964, in *Reported Sightings: Art Chronicles 1957–1987* (Manchester: Carcanet, 1989), 131.

16. André Warnod, *Fils de Montmartre. Souvenirs* (Paris: Fayard, 1955), 272.

17. For a first and concise history of the modern Paris, see Bernard Marchand, *Paris. Histoire d'une ville, XIXe–XXe siècles* (Paris: Seuil, 1993).

18. Philippe Thiébaut, *Guimard. L'Art Nouveau* (Paris: Gallimard/RMN, 1992), 110.

19. Letter of René Clair to Marcel Allain, May 21 1969, quoted in P. Souvestre and M. Allain, *Fantômas* (Paris: Laffont, 1987), vol. 1, 1013.

20. Louis Chevalier, *The Assassination of Paris* [1977], trans. David P. Jordan (Chicago: University of Chicago Press, 1994), 18.

21. Henri Mendras, *La Fin des paysans* (Paris: Sedes, 1967); *La Seconde Révolution française* (Paris: Gallimard, 1988) ; *The Vanishing Peasant: Innovation and Change in French Agriculture* (Cambridge, Mass.: MIT Press, 1971).

22. Archives INA, http://www.ina.fr/contenus-editoriaux/articles-editoriaux/georges-pompidou/.

23. Hubert Juin, *Le Livre de Paris 1900* (Paris: Belfond, 1977), 13.

24. Gil Delannoi, *Les Années utopiques, 1968–1978* (Paris: La Découverte, 1990).

25. Some examples: Robert Brécy, *Le Mouvement syndical en France, 1871–1921* (Paris-La Haye: Mouton, 1963); Georges Lefranc, *Le Mouvement socialiste en France sous la troisième République* (Paris: Payot, 1963); Claude Willard, *Le Mouvement socialiste en France (1893–1905): les guesdistes* (Paris: Ed. sociales, 1965); Rolande Trempé, *Les Mineurs de Carmaux, 1848–1914* (Paris: Ed. ouvrières, 1971); Jacques Julliard, *Fernand Pelloutier et les origines du syndicalisme d'action directe* (Paris: Seuil, 1971); Michelle Perrot, *Les Ouvriers en grève* (Paris: Mouton, 1973); Madeleine Rebérioux, *Jaurès et la Classe ouvrière* (Paris: Maspero, 1975); Yves Lequin, *Les ouvriers de la région lyonnaise (1848–1914)* (Lyon: PUL, 1977).

26. Jean-Pierre Babelon, *La Belle Epoque, 1900–1910,* preface by Guy Duboscq (Paris: Archives Nationales, 1972).

27. Isaac de Première, *Naissance du monde moderne (1848–1914)*, 1961.

28. *Histoire 1848–1914*, senior year textbook (Paris: Bordas, 1978).

29. Marcel Gauchet. *La Condition historique. Entretiens avec François Azouvi et Sylvain Piron* (Paris: Stock, 2003), 294–295.

30. Jean Maitron, dir., *Dictionnaire biographique du mouvement ouvrier français* (Paris: Editions ouvrières, 1964–1997); volumes 10 to 15 (1973–1977) refer to the turn of the century. His older *Histoire du mouvement anarchiste en France (1880–1914)* [1951] was republished by Maspero in 1975.

31. Marcel Merle, *L'Anticolonialisme européen de Las Casas à Karl Marx* (Paris: Colin, 1969); Charles-Robert Ageron, *L'anticolonialisme en France de 1871 à 1914* (Paris: PUF, 1973).

32. Daniel Guérin, *Ni Dieu, ni Maître. Anthologie de l'anarchisme* (Paris: Maspero, 1965); *L'Anarchisme. De la doctrine à l'action* (Paris: Gallimard, 1965).

33. Jean-Paul Crespelle, *Les Maîtres de la Belle Epoque* (Paris: Hachette, 1966).

34. Jean-Pierre Camard and Lynne Thornton, *L'Art et la vie en France à la Belle Epoque* (Bendor: Fondation Paul Ricard, 1971).

35. Élisabeth et Michel Dixmier, *L'Assiette au beurre: revue satirique illustrée, 1901–1912* (Paris: Maspero, 1974); *La Belle Epoque et son envers. Quand la caricature écrit l'histoire* (Monte-Carlo: André Suret, 1980).

36. Anaëlle Angebaud, "Exposer les illustrations de presse des années 1900, la construction d'un patrimoine" (master's thesis, Université Paris 1, 2014).

37. Rachel Mesch, *Having It All in the Belle Époque: How French Women's Magazines Invented the Modern Woman* (Stanford, Calif.: Stanford University Press, 2013).

38. Jennifer Waelti-Walters, *Feminist Novelist of the Belle Époque: Love as a Lifestyle* (Bloomington: Indiana University Press, 1990).

39. Steven C. Hause, *Hubertine Auclert: The French Suffragette* (New Haven, Conn.: Yale University Press, 1987).

40. Christine Bard, *Les Filles de Marianne. Histoire des féminismes, 1914–1940* (Paris: Fayard, 1995); H. Ollion, "Le Féminisme et le vote des femmes," *Revue Apologétique* (1925): 346.

41. Claude Maignien and Charles Sowerwine, *Madeleine Pelletier: une féministe dans l'arène politique* (Paris: Les Éditions ouvrières, 1992); Christine Bard, *Madeleine Pelletier (1874–1939). Logique et infortunes d'un combat pour l'égalité* (Paris: Côté-Femmes, 1992).

42. Paul Lorenz, *Sapho 1900. Renée Vivien* (Paris: Julliard, 1977); Nicole G. Albert, "De la topographie invisible à l'espace public et littéraire: les lieux de plaisir lesbien dans le Paris de la Belle Époque," *Revue d'histoire moderne et contemporaine* 80–84 (2006): 87–103.

43. *Le Crapouillot* 29 (1955): 39–42.

44. Pierre Masson, *Le disciple et l'insurgé, roman et politique à la Belle Epoque* (Lyon: PUL, 1987).

45. William Kenneth Cornell, *The Symbolist Movement* (New Haven, Conn.: Yale University Press, 1951) and *The Post-Symbolist Period: French Poetic Currents,*

1900–1920 (New Haven, Conn.: Yale University Press, 1958). In the same year were published Alfred E. Carter, *The Idea of Decadence in French Literature, 1830–1900* (Toronto: University of Toronto Press, 1947) and the seminal book by Roger Shattuck, *The Banquet Years. The Arts in France, 1885–1918. Alfred Jarry, Henri Rousseau, Erick Satie, Guillaume Apollinaire* (New York: Harcourt, Brace, 1958).

46. Michel Decaudin, *La Crise des valeurs symbolistes: vingt ans de poésie française (1895–1914)* (Toulouse: Privat, 1960); Jacques Lethevé, "Le Thème de la décadence dans les lettres françaises à la fin du 19e siècle," *Revue d'histoire littéraire de la France* LXIV (1963); Bonner Mitchell, *Les Manifestes littéraires de la Belle Epoque, 1896–1914: anthologie critique* (Paris: Seghers, 1966); Emilien Carassus, *Le Snobisme et les lettres françaises de Paul Bourget à Marcel Proust 1884–1914* (Paris: Colin, 1966); Noël Richard, *Le Mouvement décadent: dandys, esthètes et quintessents* (Paris: Nizet 1968).

47. Jean Pierrot, *L'imaginaire décadent (1880–1900)* (Paris: PUF, 1977).

48. Only four volumes published: Béatrix Dussane, *Dieux des planches*, 1964; Simon Arbellot, *La Fin du boulevard*, 1965; René Jeanne, *Cinéma 1900*, 1965; Jacques Charles, *Caf Conc'*, 1966.

49. (Paris: Seghers, 1972).

50. Pascal Ory, *L'Entre-deux-mai. Histoire culturelle de la France, mai 68-mai 81* (Paris: Seuil, 1983), 118.

ALL OF FRANCE IN THE BELLE ÉPOQUE

1. Pascal Ory, *L'entre-deux Mai. Histoire culturelle de la France, mai 68–mai 81* (Paris: Seuil, 1983), 107.

2. D. Fabre, ed., *Emotions patrimoniales* (Paris: Ed. de la MSH, 2013), 13–98.

3. Jean-Luc Bodiguel, *L'Implantation du ministère de la culture en région. Naissance et développement des directions régionales des affaires culturelles* (Paris: Comité d'histoire du ministère de la culture, 2000).

4. Alban Bensa and Daniel Fabre, eds., *Une histoire à soi. Figuration du passé et localités* (Paris: Ed. de la MSH, 2001), 2.

5. Bensa and Fabre, eds., *Une histoire à soi*, 11.

6. Ory, *L'entre-deux Mai*, 108; Ory, *L'Aventure culturelle française* (Paris: Flammarion, 1989), 225–227; Mathias Bernard, *Les Années Mitterrand. Du changement socialiste au tournant libéral* (Paris: Belin, 2015), 211–253.

7. Ludivine Bantigny, *La France à l'heure du monde. De 1981 à nos jours* (Paris: Seuil, 2013), 341.

8. Nicolas Offenstadt, *14–18 aujourd'hui. La Grande Guerre dans la France contemporaine* (Paris: Odile Jacob, 2010).

9. Roger d'Arteuil, *Nancy à la Belle Époque* (Nancy: impr. G. Thomas, 1960); Paul-Henri Paillou, *Mon village à la Belle Époque* (Aurillac: Éditions du Centre, 1962);

André Canivez, *Escaudain, mon village, petite histoire et souvenirs de jeunesse et de la Belle Époque* (Douai: G. Sannier, 1966).

10. Annie Fettu et Yves Lecouturier, *Découvrir la Normandie à la Belle Époque* (Cully: Orep, 2011).

11. Serge Zeyons, *La Belle Epoque. Les années 1900 par la carte postale* (Paris: Larousse, 1990).

12. Ado Kyriou, *L'âge d'or de la carte postale* (Paris: Balland, 1966); Daniel Bénard, Bruno Guignard, and Alan Sutton, *La Carte postale: des origines aux années 1920* (Saint-Cyr-sur-Loire: Mémoires en images, 2010), 144.

13. Naomi Schor, "'Cartes Postales': Representing Paris 1900," *Critical Inquiry* 18, no. 2 (1992): 217.

14. *Le Figaro illustré* 175 (October 1904).

15. *Images de la Belle Époque, regard d'aujourd'hui* (Albi: Éd. Grand Sud, 2013).

16. Joëlle and Gérard Neudin, *Argus international des cartes postales* (self-pub., 1975). Then came André Fildier, *Catalogue des cartes postales anciennes de collection* (self-pub., 1978); Annie and François Baudet, *Encyclopédie internationale de la carte postale illustrée* (self-pub., 1978); Serge Zeyons, *Guide de la carte postale* (Paris: Hachette, 1979).

17. Aline Ripert, Claude Frère, and Sylvie Forestier, *La Carte postale: son histoire, sa fonction sociale* (Paris: CNRS Editions, 1983).

18. J. and G. Naudin, "Une bonne année cartophile," *Le Collectionneur français* (January 1985): 13–14; Yves di Maria, *Le Guide pratique de la carte postale*, special issue of *Collectionneur français* (self-pub., 1981).

19. Claude Frere Michelat, "En voyant ces merveilles . . . Les Collectionneurs de cartes postales," *Ethnologie française* 13, no. 3 (1983): 283–290.

20. Beatrix Forissier, *25 ans d'actualités à travers la carte postale: 1889–1914* (Paris: Ed. de l'Amateur, 1976).

21. Serge Zeyons, *La France paysanne: les années 1900 par la carte postale* (Paris: Larousse, 1992); Vincent Brugere Trelat, *C'était la France. Chronique de la vie quotidienne des Français avant 1914 racontée par la photographie* (Paris: Chêne-Camara, 1976); James Eveillard, *Insolites images d'une France disparue* (Rennes: Ed. Ouest-France, 2013).

22. Eveillard, *Insolites images*, 8.

23. René-Charles Plancke, *Brie-Comte-Robert et le Val d'Yerres à la Belle Epoque* (Le Mée-sur-Seine: Ed. Lys Presse/Ed. Amattéis, 1993), 10–11.

24. *Le Soir*, December 10, 1982.

25. Victor Segalen, *Essay on Exoticism. An Aesthetics of Diversity*, trans. Yaël Rachel Schlick (Durham, N.C.: Duke University Press, 2002).

26. Bensa and Fabre, eds., *Une histoire à soi*, 24.

27. Liane de Pougy, *Mes cahiers bleus* (Paris: Plon, 1977).

28. Lucien A. Bouly de Lesdain, *Souvenirs de la Belle époque et de ses lendemains, 1894–1924* (self-pub., 1972); *Moi, Jules Couasnault, syndicaliste de Fougères. Le contrat social dans la capitale française de la chaussure à la "Belle Epoque"*

(Rennes: Apogée, 1995); Marcel Voisin, *C'était le temps de la "Belle Epoque."* *Une enfance pénible—une vie de lutte* (Claix: La Pensée sauvage, 1978); Pierre Trimbach, *Quand on tournait la manivelle ou les mémoires d'un opérateur à la Belle Epoque* (Paris: CEFAG, 1970); Paul Dimoff, *La Rue d'Ulm à la Belle Époque, 1899–1903, mémoires d'un normalien supérieur* (Nancy: impr. G. Thomas, 1970); *Un amour bigouden ou On l'appelait Marlène* (Brest: Ed. de la Cité, 1972).

29. Voisin, *C'était le temps de la "Belle Epoque,"* 2.

30. Jean Contrucci, *Ça s'est passé à Marseille*, 5 vols. (Marseille: Autres temps, 1992–1999); *Marseille de la Belle Epoque* (Marseille: Autres temps, 2005).

31. Gérard Guicheteau, *Histoire anecdotique de la Belle Epoque* (Paris: Le Pré-aux Clercs, 1984); *Les Années 1900* (Paris: Sélection du Reader's Digest, 1991); Jean-Claude Simoën, *Histoires vraies du XXe siècle. 1. Les années d'enthousiasme 1895–1909; 2. Les années radieuses (1909–1914); 3. Les années sanglantes (14–18)* (Paris: Fayard, 2005).

32. Bruno Fuligni, *Les frasques de la Belle Epoque: les plus belles unes du Petit journal* (Paris: Albin Michel, 2012).

33. Javier Figueiro and Marie-Hélène Carbonel, *La Véritable biographie de la Belle Otéro et de la Belle Epoque* (Paris: Fayard, 2003); Christiane Peugeot, *On a retrouvé le journal d'une cocotte de la Belle Epoque, Madame Steinheil, ma grand-tante* (Unicité, 2012); François Caradec, *Jane Avril* (Paris: Fayard, 2001); Claude Dufrene, *Trois grâces de la Belle Epoque* (Paris: Bartillat, 2003).

34. Nigles Gosling, *Paris 1900–1914: The Miraculous Years* (London: Weidenfield & Nicolson, 1978); Franco Borsi and Ezio Godoli, *Paris 1900* (New York: Rizzoli, 1977), 9; Raymond Rudorff, *Belle Époque. Paris in the Nineties* (London: Hamilton, 1972).

35. *Belle Époque? Le chaudron de l'apocalypse*, presented by Jean-Pierre Guéno (Paris: Triartis, 2014).

36. Mary McAuliffe, *Dawn of the Belle Époque: The Paris of Monet, Zola, Bernhardt, Eiffel, Debussy, Clemenceau, and Their Friends* (Lanham, Md.: Rowman & Littlefield, 2011); *Twilight of the Belle Époque: The Paris of Picasso, Stravinsky, Proust, Renault, Marie Curie, Gertrude Stein, and Their Friends Through the Great War* (Lanham, Md.: Rowman & Littlefield, 2014).

37. Patrick Waldberg, *Eros Modern Style* (Paris: Pauvert, 1964).

38. The title of a naughty weekly published from February to April 1897.

39. Philippe Sollers, *Photos licencieuses de la Belle Epoque* (Paris: Les Editions 1900, 1987), 7.

40. Jean Pierre Bourgeron, Christian Bourdon, and Jean Agélou, *De l'académisme à la photographie de charme* (Paris: Éditions Marval, 2006); Jo and Paul Richardson, *Quand la femme pose . . . L'Âge d'or de la photographie érotique* (Boulogne-Billancourt: Éd. du May, 2009).

41. Martin Stevens, *French Postcards: An Album of Vintage Erotica* (New York: Rizzoli International, 2006); *French Vintage Nude. Cartes postales érotiques des années 1900* (Neuilly: Ragage, 2008).

42. Robert Lebeck, *Die erotische Postkarte* (Schaffhausen: Stemmle, 1988); Paul Hammond, *French Undressing: Naughty Postcards from 1900–1920* (London: Bloomsbury, 1988); Farina Ferruccio, *Die verbotene Venus. Erotische Postkarten 1895–1925* (Stuttgart: Parkland Verlag, 1989).

43. *La Casa de Cita: Mexican Photographs from the Belle Époque* (New York: Quartet Books, 1986).

44. Maxence Rodemacq, "L'Industrie de l'obscénité à Paris (1855–1930)," *Romantisme* 167 (2015): 13–20.

A VERY BROAD "BELLE ÉPOQUE"

1. The "Belle Époque" rooms formerly on view at the Belvue Museum in Brussels once had their own URL: http://www.belvue.be/sites/default/files/pedagogical tool/pdf/Mus%C3%A9e%20BELvue%20%20histoire%20de%20la%20Belgique%20%20textes%20des%20salles.pdf.

2. Paul Prist, *1900. Souvenirs littéraires* (Brussels: Office de publicité, 1949).

3. Yolande Oostens-Wittamer, ed., *Les Affiches de la Belle Epoque* (Brussels: Association royale des demeures historiques et jardins de Belgique, 1961).

4. Christophe Verbruggen, Daniel Laqua, and Gita Deneckere, "Belgium on the Move: Transnational History and the Belle Époque," *Revue Belge de Philologie et d'Histoire* 90, no. 4 (2012) : 1213–1326.

5. Hermann Schreiber, *Die Belle Epoque: Paris 1871–1900* (Munich: Paul List, 1990); Roger Shattuck, *Die Belle Epoque. Kultur und Gesellschaft in Frankreich, 1885–1918* (Munich: Piper, 1963).

6. Mike Jay and Michael Neve, eds., *1900. A Fin-de-siècle Reader* (London: Penguin, 1999). Some French authors also use the notion of "fin de siècle" until 1914. For instance, Jean Roman, *Paris fin de siècle* (Paris: Robert Delpire, 1958).

7. Raymond Rudorff, *Belle Époque: Paris in the Nineties* (London: Hamilton, 1972), 13.

8. Jill Forbes and Michael Kelly, *French Cultural Studies. An Introduction* (Oxford : Oxford University Press, 1995), 37–38.

9. Suzanne Gourdon, *La* Jugend *de Georg Hirth: la Belle Epoque munichoise entre Paris et Saint-Pétersbourg* (Strasbourg: Centre d'Etudes germaniques, 1997); Bernard Michel, *Prague Belle Époque* (Paris: Aubier, 2008); Jacques Le Rider, *Arthur Schnitzler ou la Belle Époque viennoise* (Paris: Belin, 2003).

10. Angiolo Biancotti, *Ai tempi di Addio Giovinezza: cronache e profili della "Belle Epoque"* (Milano: Gastaldi, 1954).

11. Giuseppe Chiassi, *La Roma dei miei vent'anni: La nostra "Belle Epoque"* (Rome: Fratelli Palombi, 1957).

12. Francesco Dorigo, "Nostalgia per la Belle Epoque," *L'Altro cinema: rivista del cinema d'amatore* 73 (February 1960): 83–91.

13. Manlio Miserocchi, *Un personaggio della Belle Epoque* (Venice: Alfieri, 1961).

14. Tom Antongini, *La Belle Epoque* (Milan: Longanesi, 1965).

15. Bruno Coceani, *Trieste della belle époque* (Trieste: Libreria Universitas, 1971); Bruno De Cesco, *Una città con le ghette: Verona Belle Epoque (1882–1914)* (Verona: Bertani, 1981); Livio Jannattoni, *Roma Belle Epoque* (Rome: Multi-grafica, 1986); Alfredo Giovine, *Bari Belle Epoque* (Fasano: Schena, 1989); Lucio Lami, *Le Passioni del dragone: cavalli e donne: Caprilli campione della Belle Epoque* (Milano: Mursia, 2009); Ursula Salwa, ed., *La Belle Epoque a Milano* (Naples: Intra moenia, 2011); Roberta Cordani, ed., *Milano verso il Sempione: la città di Napoleone e della Belle Epoque: viaggio nella storia, nell'arte e nel paesaggio* (Milan: CELIP, 2006); Franco Fava, ed., *Milano nella Belle Epoque* (Genoa: De Ferrari, 2003); Fosco Rocchetta, ed., *Riccione estivo: agosto 1894, origini del turismo riccionese al tempo della Belle Epoque* (Riccione: Comune, 2009).

16. Vittorio Paliotti, *Il Salone Margherita e la belle époque: Napoli tra fine Ottocento e primo Novecento* (Rome: Benincasa, 1975); Paolo Sommaiolo, *Il café-chantant: artisti e ribalte nella Napoli belle époque* (Naples: Tempolungo, 1998); Vittorio Paliotti, *Salone Margherita: una storia napoletana: il primo café chantant d'Italia: dalle follie della belle époque all'avanspettacolo e oltre* (Naples: Altra-stampa, 2001).

17. Luigi Persone, *Il teatro italiano della belle époque. Saggi e studi* (Florence: L. S. Olschki, 1972); Francesca Cagianelli and Dario Matteoni, eds., *La Belle Époque: arte in Italia, 1880–1915* (Milan: Silvana, 2008); Lucia Monacis, *Genio, follia e criminalita nella belle époque* (Lecce: Pensa multimedia, 2009); Stefano Pivato, *La bicicletta e il Sol dell'avvenire: sport e tempo libero nel socialismo della Belle Epoque* (Florence: Ponte alle Grazie, 1992); Giovanni Ansaldo, *Gli anarchici della Belle Epoque* (Florence: Le lettere, 2010).

18. Daniela Rossini, *Le Americane. Donne e immagini di donne fra Belle Epoque e fascismo* (Rome: Biblink, 2008), 17.

19. Nino Valeri, *Dalla belle époque al fascismo: momenti e personaggi* (Bari: Laterza, 1975); *Il Tirolo e l'Italia: dall'invasione napoleonica alla Belle Epoque,* studio seminar, ed. Mario Allegri, Rovereto, October–December 1999.

20. Valeri, *Dalla belle époque al fascismo,* 3.

21. Willy Haas, *Die Belle Epoque* (Munich: Kurt Desch, 1967).

22. Dorigo, "Nostalgia per la Belle Epoque."

23. Franco Fava, ed., *Milano nella Belle Epoque* (Genoa: De Ferrari, 2003), 9.

24. Giovanni Castelani, *La Belle Epoque: storia segreta* (Milano: Pan, 1977).

25. Eleonora Bairati, Philippe Jullian, Malcolm Falkus, Paolo Monelli, Jànos Riesz, and Brunello Vigezzi, *La Belle époque: L'ingannevole euforia di un quindicennio della storia d'Europa* (Milan: Mondadori, 1977), soon translated into English: *La Belle Epoque: Fifteen Euphoric Years of European History* (New York: William Morrow, 1978).

26. Carlos Maul, *O Rio da Bella Epoca* (Rio de Janeiro: Sao Jose, 1967); Jaime Larry Benchimol, *Pereira Passos: um Hausmann tropical* (Rio de Janeiro: Biblioteca Carioca, 1990).

27. Jeffrey D. Needell, *A Tropical Belle Époque. Elite Culture and Society in Turn-of-the-Century Rio de Janeiro* (Cambridge: Cambridge University Press, 1987); Marcia Camargos, "Uma Republica nos moldes franceses," *Revista USP* 59 (2003): 134–143.
28. Conde Maite, *Consuming Visions. Cinema, Writing, and Modernity in Rio de Janeiro* (Charlottesville: University of Virginia Press, 2012).
29. Amara Silva de Souza Rocha, "A seduçao da luz. Electrificaçao e imaginario no Rio de Janeiro da Belle Epoque," http://www.revistas2.uepg.br/index.php/rhr/article/viewFile/2042/1524.
30. Diana Dorothea Danon and Benedito Lima de Toledo, *São Paulo "Belle Epoque"* (São Paulo: Companhia Editora Nacional, 1974).
31. Sebastião Rogério Ponte, *Fortaleza belle époque: reformas urbanas e controle social, 1860–1930* (Fortaleza: Fundaçao Democrito Rocha, 1993).
32. Sandra Jatahy Pesavento, "Um novo olhar sobre a cidade: a nova historia cultural e as representacoes do urbano," in *Porto Alegre na virada do veculo 19: cultura e sociedade* (Porto Alegre: Ed. UFRGS, 1994).
33. Ana Maria Daou, *A belle époque amazônica* (Rio de Janeiro: Jorge Zahar Editor, 2000).
34. Sidney Chalhoub, *Trabalho, lar e botequim: o cotidiano dos trabalhadores no Rio de Janeiro da Belle Epoque* (São Paulo: Brasiliense, 1986); Monica Pimenta Velloso, *As tradicoes populares na Belle Epoque* (Rio de Janeiro: Funarte, 1988); Hermengarda Leme Leite Takeshita, *Um grito de liberdade: uma família paulista no fim da belle-époque* (São Paulo: Alvorada, 1998).
35. André Luiz Paulilo, *Os artificios da metropole: anotacoes sobre a transformacao de vida urbana depois da Belle Epoque* (Campinas: Educação & Sociedade, 2004).
36. Ary Vasconcelos, *Panorama da música popular brasileira na "belle époque"* (Rio de Janeiro: Liv. Sant'Anna, 1977).
37. Danielle Kiffer, "O Rio de Janeiro da Belle Époque é retratado em vídeos-documentários para estudantes," http://www.faperj.br/?id=2880.2.5.
38. Elias Thome Saliba, *Raizes do Riso. A representacao humoristica na historia brasileira: da Belle Epoque aos primeiros tempos do radio* (Rio de Janeiro: Companhia das Letras, 2002).
39. Rachel Soihet, *A subversao pelo riso: o carnaval carioca da belle epoque ao tempo de Vargas* (Rio de Janeiro: Fundação Getulio Vargas, 1998).
40. R. J. Oakley, *The Case of Lima Barreto and Realism in the Brazilian "Belle Époque"* (Lewiston, N.Y.: The Edwin Mellen Press, 1998).
41. Vicente de Paula Araújo, *A bela epoca do cinema brasileiro* (São Paulo: Perspectiva, 1976); *A Belle Epoque Carioca em revista*, 9e Coloquio de Modan, Universidade Federal do Rio de Janeiro, 2013.
42. Juan Somolinos, *La "Belle Époque" en Mexico* (Mexico: Sep/Setentas, 1971).
43. María Eugenia Aragón Rangel, *Casas escasas: el art nouveau en la ciudad de México* (Mexico: Instituto Nacional de Antropología e Historia, 2011).

44. Jose Maria Rivarola Matto, *La Belle Epoque y otras hodas* (Asunción: Arte Nuevo, 1980).

45. Alfredo Castellanos, *La "Belle Époque" montevideana. Vida social y paisaje urbano* (Montevideo: Arca, 1981).

46. Alberto Sanchez, *Valdelomar o la belle época* (Mexico: Fondo de cultura económica, 1969); José Ochoa Montero, *La pluma en la Belle Epoque* (Lima: Universidad de San Martín de Porres, 1999).

47. Pedro José Muñoz, *Imagen afectiva de Caracas: la "Belle Époque" caraqueña* (Caracas: Municipalidad de Caracas, 1972); Cristian G. Werckenthien, *El Buenos Aires de la belle époque: su desarrollo urbano 1880–1910* (Buenos Aires: Vinciguerra, 2001); Leandro Losada, *La Alta sociedad en la Buenos Aires de la belle époque: sociabilidad, estilos de vida e identidades* (Buenos Aires: Siglo XXI, 2008); Alberto Roa Saldarriaga and Benjamín Villegas Jiménez y Antonio Castañeda Buraglia, *Casa Republicana: Colombia's Belle époque* (Bogotá: Villegas Editores, 1996); Manuel Vicuña Urrutia, *La Belle époque Chilena: alta sociedad y mujeres de elite en el cambio de siglo* (Editorial Sudamericana, 2001); Jorge Salomo Flores, *La Belle époque viñamarina: a través de la caricatura de Mundo* (Valparaíso: Pontificia Universidad Católica de Valparaíso, 2011).

48. José Montero Alonso, *Madrid y su "Belle Epoque"* (Madrid: Editorial Master, 1994), describes the happy Madrid, 1913–1930, that discovered flappers and architectural modernity (Circulo de Bellas Artes, Palacio de Comunicaciones, Ramal). For the Portuguese case, see Luis Vidigal, *O jovem Aquilino Ribeiro: ensaio biografico e antoloogico na Lisboa da "belle époque" (1903–1908)* (Lisbon: Livros Horizonte, 1986).

49. Arthur Schärli, *Höhepunkt des schweizerischen Tourismus in der Zeit der "Belle Epoque" unter besonderer Berücksichtigung des Berner Oberlandes: kulturgeschichtliche Regionalstudi* (Bern/New York: Peter Lang, 1984); Anita Ulrich, *Bordelle, Straßen Dirnen und bürgerliche Sittlichkeit in der Belle Epoque: eine sozialgeschichtliche Studie der Prostitution am Beispiel der Stadt Zürich* (Zürich: Antiquarische Gesellschaft, 1985); Werner Ross, *Bohemiens und Belle Epoque. Als Munchen leuchtete* (Berlin: Siedler, 1997); Jerzy S. Majewski, *Warszawa niedobudowana: metropolia belle époque* (Warsaw: Wydawn Veda, 2003); Giannēs Spandōnēs, *Stēn Athēna tēs "Bel Epok"* (Athens: Informecanica, 2007).

50. Mercedes Volait, "La 'Belle Époque': registres, rhétoriques et ressorts d'une invention patrimoniale," *Égypte/Monde arabe* 3, nos. 5–6 (2009), http://ema.revues.org/2891; Trevor Mostyn, *Egypt's Belle Époque: Cairo 1869–1952* (London and New York: Quartet Books, 1989).

51. Amanda Mackenzie Stuart, *Empress of Fashion. A Life of Diana Vreeland* (London: Thames & Hudson, 2013).

52. *La Belle Époque* (New York: The Metropolitan Museum of Art, 1982), 3.

53. First published in Bairati et al., *La Belle Époque*.

54. John Duka, "La Belle Europe Reigns Again at Met Museum," *New York Times,* December 7, 1982; Charlotte Curtis, "Diana Vreeland's Way," *New York Times,* September 14, 1982.

55. *Paris Belle Époque: 1880–1914. Faszination einer Weltstadt* (Recklinghausen: Aurel Bongers, 1994).

56. Some examples: Ebria Feinblatt and Bruce Davis, *Toulouse-Lautrec and His Contemporaries: Posters of the Belle Époque from the Wagner Collection,* Los Angeles County Museum of Art, 1985; Constance Schwartz and Franklin Hill Perrel, *La Belle Époque and Toulouse-Lautrec,* Nassau County Museum of Art, Roslyn Harbor, N.Y., 2003; *Toulouse-Lautrec and Montmartre,* National Gallery of Arts, Washington, D.C., March–May 2005, then Chicago; *Toulouse-Lautrec and the Belle Époque in Paris and in Athens,* Herakleidon Museum, Athens, 2008.

57. *Schilderkunst uit la belle époque,* July 4–September 16, 1964, ed. Maria van Es and C. J. M. van Pampus (Laren: Singer Memorial Foundation, 1964).

58. *Europa 1900,* June 3–September 30, 1967 (Ostend Kursaal: Éd. de la connaissance, 1967).

59. *La Belle Époque: Belgian Posters, Watercolors, and Drawings from the Collection of L. Wittamer-De Camps,* introduction and catalogue by Yolande Oostens-Wittamer, preface by Emile Langui (New York: Grossman, 1970).

60. *Affiches "Belle Epoque"* (Antwerp: Museum Vleeshuis, 1979).

61. *The Belle Époques. Fashionable Life in Paris, London and New York, 1870–1914,* catalogue designed and edited by Bohdan-Hamilton and Associates, November–December 1981 (New York: Stair's Incurable Collector, 1981); *La Belle Époque: Masterworks by Combaz, Leo Jo and Livemont. A Loan Exhibition from the collection of L. Wittamer-De Camps,* intro. and catalogue by Yolande Oostens-Wittamer, preface by Alan Fern, circulated by International Exhibitions Foundation, 1970–1971 (New York: Grossman, 1980–1981); *Masterpieces of the Poster from the Belle Époque,* 45 full-color plates selected and edited by Hayward and Blanche Cirker (New York: Dover, 1983); Constance Schwartz and Franklin Hill Perrel, *La Belle Époque* (Roslyn Harbor, N.Y.: Nassau County Museum of Art, 1995); *1900: la belle époque des arts,* London Royal Academy of Art, January 16–April 3, 2000; *Portraits of the Belle Époque,* CaixaForum de Barcelona, then Valencia, 2011; Tomás Llorens Serra, *Portraits of the Belle Époque,* Consorci de Museus de la Comunitat Valenciana/fundación "la Caixa" (Valencia: El Viso, 2011); *Affiches de la Belle Epoque. Entre plaisirs et spectacles* (Ixelles: 2015).

62. Nikola Doll, *Signes des temps: œuvres visionnaires d'avant 1914* (Brussels: Racine, 2014).

63. W. Boyd Rayward, *Information Beyond Borders. International Cultural and Intellectual Exchange in the Belle Époque* (Farnham: Ashgate, 2014).

64. Hebe Dorsey, *The Belle Époque in the Paris Herald* (New York: Thames and Hudson, 1986), 52.

65. Dorsey, *The Belle Époque in the Paris Herald,* 14.

EVERYTHING IS CULTURAL IN THE ERA OF THE VINTAGE

1. *Encyclopedia of the Age of Imperialism, 1800–1914* (Westport, Conn.: Greenwood Press, 2008), 1: 79–80.

2. "La Belle Epoque," syllabus of Professor Thomas Ertman, New York University, 2012.

3. Philippe Thiébaut, ed., *1900* (Paris: RMN, 2000).

4. Jeanne Geyer, *Belle Epoque à l'affiche, 1885–1914* (Strasbourg: Musée des Beaux-arts, 1981).

5. Respectively, Michel Boisrond in 1991, Luc Béraud in 1995, Ange Casta in 1980, Jean-Daniel Verhaeghe in 2005, Daniel Jeannau in 2011.

6. *Les Lautrec de Lautrec. Toulouse-Lautrec: les estampes et affiches de la Bibliothèque nationale,* Queensland Art Gallery, Brisbane; National Gallery of Victoria, Melbourne (Paris: BNF, 1992), 18.

7. *Un Amour de Swann*, by Volker Schlöndorff (1984); *Le temps retrouvé* by Raul Ruiz (1999); *Le Grand Meaulnes* by Jean-Daniel Verhaeghe (2006); *Jean de Florette,* then *Manon des sources* by Claude Berri (1986); *La Gloire de mon père* and *Le Château de ma mère* by Yves Robert (1990); *Les Thibault* by Jean-Daniel Verhaeghe (2003).

8. Kolleen M. Guy, "Wine, Champagne and the Making of French Identity in the Belle Époque," in *Food and Identity in Europe,* ed. Peter Scholliers (Providence: Berg Press, 2000), 163–177; *When Champagne Became French: Wine and the Making of a National Identity* (Baltimore: Johns Hopkins University Press, 2002).

9. Kali Argyriadis and Sandra Le Menestrel, *Une culture guinguette? Analyse d'une revitalisation esthétique,* Rapport d'enquête, Mission du patrimoine ethnologique, 2000.

10. Catherine Dutheil-Pessin, *La Chanson réaliste, sociologie d'un genre* (Paris: L'Harmattan 2004), 309–310.

11. *Formidable,* the centenary show, was broadcast on TV channel France 3 on December 31, 1992, and the books followed: Jacques Pessis and Jacques Crépineau, *Le Moulin Rouge* (Paris: Hermé, 1989/La Martinière, 2002); Françoise Dorin, *Nini pattes en l'air* (Paris: Laffont, 1990); Evane Hanska, *La Romance de la Goulue* (Paris: Librairie générale française, 1990); Michel Souvais, *Moi, la Goulue de Toulouse-Lautrec* (Publibook, 2008); Jacques Habas, *Les Secrets du Moulin Rouge* (Paris: Belle Gabrielle, 2010); Jean Casterede, *Le Moulin Rouge, reflet d'une époque* (Paris: France-Empire, 2001); François Caradec and Jean Nohain, *Le Pétomane au Moulin Rouge* (Paris: Mazarine, 2000); François Caradec, *Jane Avril* (Paris: Fayard, 2001); Christophe Mirambeau, *Moulin Rouge* (Paris: Assouline, 2003); Alain Weil, *120 ans de Moulin Rouge* (Paris: Ed Seven, 2010).

12. Quoted by Mathilde Terral, "Paris à la Belle Epoque: deux études sur la construction d'un imaginaire" (master's thesis, Université Paris 1 Panthéon-Sorbonne, 2014), 92.

13. Some examples: Michelle Roy describes in *Ils étaient une fois,* 3 vols. (St-Georges d'Orques: Ed. Causse, 1998) the amorous life of Clémentine de Malhois, aged

twenty-one in 1900, in the corrupted designer milieu of the Belle Époque. Written in collaboration with François Truffaut in the perspective of a film, *Belle Époque* by Jean Gruault (Paris: Gallimard, 1996) traces the story of Lucien Lachenay (the inventor of the 1900 moving sidewalk) to give an overview of the period. With *Le Maudit de la Belle Époque* (Paris: Seuil, 2013), Catherine Guigon retraces the descent into hell of Max Lebaudy, the tragic heir of a great manufacturer.

14. Anne-Marie Garat, *Dans la main du diable* (Paris: Actes Sud, 2006), whose action takes place in 1913, opens a trilogy that extends to the aftermath of World War Two.

15. Kate Cambor, *Gilded Youth. Three Lives in France's Belle Epoque* (New York: Farrar, Straus and Giroux, 2009), retraces the lives of Jeanne Hugo, Léon Daudet, and Jean-Martin Charcot in the years preceding the Great War.

16. Jean-Christophe Sarrot and Laurent Broche, *Le Roman policier historique* (Paris: Nouveau Monde, 2009), 315.

17. Quoted in Sarrot and Broche, *Le Roman policier historique*, 87.

18. Jean Contrucci, *Les Nouveaux mystères de Marseille* (Paris: Lattès, 2001–2015); Jacques Neireynck, *Le Crime du prince de Galles; La Mort de Pierre Curie; La Faute du Président Loubet* (Paris: 10/18, 2007–2008); Renée Bonneau, *Nature morte à Giverny* (Quimper: Quadri Signe, 1999); *Sanguine sur la Butte* (Quimper: Quadri Signe, 2002); *Danse macabre au Moulin Rouge* (Paris: Nouveau Monde, 2007); *Piège de feu à la Charité* (Arles: Actes Sud, 2008); *Meurtre au cinéma forain* (Paris: Nouveau Monde, 2011); Marc Rolland, *Le Sioux des grands boulevards* (Paris: Éd. du 28 août, 2008); Hervé Jubert, *La Trilogie de Blanche* (Paris: Albin Michel, 2005–2007).

19. Jacques Tardi, *The Most Extraordinary Adventures of Adèle Blanc-Sec*, trans. Randy and Jean-Marc Lofficier (New York: NBM Publishing, 1990–1992).

20. Gradimir Smudja, *Vincent et Van Gogh* (Paris: Delcourt, 2003); Gradimir Smudja, *Le Cabaret des muses*, 4 vols. (Paris: Delcourt, 2004–2008); Julie Birmant and Clément Oubrerie, *Pablo*, 4 vols. (Paris: Dargaud, 2012–2014); Olivier Bleys and Yomgui Dumont, *Toulouse-Lautrec* (Toulouse: Glénat, 2015).

21. *Bandes dessinées* (graphic novels) include Florent Calvez and Fred Duval, *L'Homme de l'année 1894: l'Homme à l'origine de l'Affaire Dreyfus* (Paris: Delcourt, 2014); Leo Henry and Stéphane Perger, *Sequana*, 3 vols. (Paris: Emmanuel Proust, 2008–2010); Gité and Perc, *Les aventures d'Alex Médoc et Belle Époque*, 2 vols. (Ed. Tarmeye, 1987); Olivier Bocquet and Julie Rocheleau, *La colère de Fantômas*, 3 vols. (Paris: Dargaud, 2013–2015).

22. Christian Lacroix, preface to John Peacock, *20th Century Fashion* (London: Thames & Hudson, 1993), 6.

23. Tom Tierney, *Great Fashion Designs of the Belle Époque: Paper Dolls in Full Color* (New York: Dover, 1982).

24. Stephen Gundle, "Mapping the Origins of Glamour: Giovanni Boldini, Paris and the Belle Époque," *Journal of European Studies* 23, no. 3 (1999): 269–295.

25. Claude Conyers, "Courtesans in Dance History: les belles de la Belle Epoque," *Dance Chronicle* 26, no. 2 (2003) : 219–243.

26. Maurice Donnay, *J'ai connu 1900* (Paris: Fayard, 1951), 119.

27. Colette Windish, "Arsène Lupin, une certaine idée de la France," *French Cultural Studies* 12, no. 35 (2001): 149–160.

28. Evelyne Saez, *Cafés, restaurants et salons de thé de la Belle Epoque à Paris* (Rennes: Ouest-France, 2013).

29. "Montmartre bute sur Starbucks," *Libération*, January 18, 2013.

30. Gault-Millau, *La Belle Epoque à table* (Paris: Ed. Jour d'azur/Gault-Millau, 1981); Shirley King, *Dining with Marcel Proust. A Practical Guide to French Cuisine of the Belle Époque* (London: Thames and Hudson, 1979).

31. *La Belle Époque: Twenty-Six Paintings of Parisian Life* (New York: Sotheby Parke Bernet, 1979); *Sotheby's Belle Époque Sculpture and Furniture* (London, 1991); *La belle époque paintings and sculptures, Sotheby's* (New York, 1999); *Sotheby's New York la Belle Époque, Including "the Age of Innocence"* (New York, 2000).

32. "Questionnaire on the Belle Epoque in the antiques market," carried out by Sophie Lhermitte (Centre d'histoire du XIXe siècle, Université Paris 1, 2015).

33. In 2020 Arsène Lupin was played in a Netflix TV series by the Black actor Omar Sy.

34. Respectively: Francis Valéry, *La Cité entre les mondes* (Paris: Denoël, 2000); Fabrice Colin and Mathieu Gaborit, *Confession d'un automate mangeur d'opium* (Paris: Ed. du Rocher, 1999); Johann Heliot, *La Lune seule le sait* (Paris: Mnemos, 2000); Fabien Clavel, *Feuillets de cuivre* (Paris: Actu SF, 2015).

35. On historical role-playing games, see Olivier Caïra, *Jeux de rôle. Les Forges de la fiction* (Paris: CNRS éditions, 2007); Olivier Caïra and Jérôme Larré, eds., *Jouer avec l'histoire* (Villecresnes: Pinkerton Press, 2009).

EPILOGUE: TANGLED TIMES

1. Malcolm Chase and Christopher Shaw, "The Dimensions of Nostalgia," in *The Imagined Past: History and Nostalgia* (Manchester: Manchester University Press, 1989), 1.

2. For a recent point on these issue, see Henry Rousso, *Face au passé. Essai sur la mémoire contemporaine* (Paris: Belin, 2016).

3. Armand Lanoux, *Amours 1900* (Paris: Hachette, 1961), 11.

4. Christophe Léribault, "Au comptoir de la fantaisie," in *La véritable histoire de la Belle Époque*, ed. Dominique Kalifa (Paris: Fayard, 2017), 17; Claude Dufrene, *Trois grâces de la Belle Epoque* (Paris: Bartillat, 2003), 7.

5. Adrien Genoudet, *Dessiner l'histoire. Pour une histoire visuelle* (Paris: Le Manuscrit, 2015), 184.

6. Ann Colley, *Nostalgia and Recollection in Victorian Culture* (Basingstoke/New York: Macmillan and St. Martin's, 1998); Kate Mitchell, *Victorian Afterimages. History and Cultural Memory in Neo-Victorian Fictions* (London: Palgrave, 2012).

7. Roland Dorgelès, *Quand j'étais montmartrois* (Paris: Albin Michel, 1936), 38.
8. Walter Benjamin, "On the Concept of History" [1935–1937], in *Selected Writings* (Cambridge, Mass.: The Belknap Press of Harvard University Press, 1996), 389–400; Françoise Proust, *L'Histoire à contretemps. Le Temps historique chez Walter Benjamin* (Paris: Cerf, 1994).
9. J. Neutres, "Neutre, du côté de chez Jacques-Émile Blanche," in *Jacques-Emile Blanche: portraitiste de la Belle Epoque* (Paris: Editions de Falaises, 2016), 19.
10. Marc Gaillard, *Paris à la Belle Epoque. Au temps de Proust* (Etrepilly: Presses du village), 5.
11. René-Charles Plancke, *Brie-Comte-Robert et le Val d'Yerres à la Belle Epoque* (Le Mée-sur-Seine: Ed. Lys Presse/Amattéis, 1993), 5.
12. Giorgio Agamben, *The Man Without Content* (Stanford, Calif.: Stanford University Press, 1999), 109–110.

POSTSCRIPT: THE BELLE ÉPOQUE AND THE GILDED AGE

1. See Vanessa R. Schwartz, *It's So French: Hollywood, Paris and the Making of Cosmopolitan Film Culture* (Chicago: University of Chicago Press, 2007).
2. *Les lieux de mémoire* (3 vols.), ed. Pierre Nora (Paris: Gallimard, 1984–1982); *Realms of Memory*, ed. Lawrence D. Kritzman, trans. Arthur Goldhammer (New York: Columbia University Press, 1996–1998).
3. Willa Silverman, "Fin de Siècle," in *Les Noms d'époque: De "Restauration" à "années de plomb,"* ed. Dominique Kalifa (Paris: Gallimard, 2020), 119–142.
4. Indeed, when economist Thomas Piketty wrote his *Capital in the Twenty-First Century*, both the English and French editions distinguished between a European Belle Époque and an American Gilded Age: Venita Datta, "Gilded Age," in *Les Noms d'époque: De "Restauration" à "années de plomb,"* ed. Dominique Kalifa (Paris: Gallimard, 2020), 97–117.
5. Some historians put the end of the Gilded Age at 1901, with the accession of Theodore Roosevelt to the presidency. As of this writing, interest in the Gilded Age was sharpened by a drama series by that title, set in 1880s New York City, produced by HBO.
6. Datta, "Gilded Age," 105, 112. Historian Alan Lessoff is currently working on a book-length project that examines the origins of the term "Gilded Age."
7. Not only in the 2017 French edition of this book but also in a collective volume of essays published in 2019, entitled *Les Noms d'époque* (The names of a period), in which he tasked fourteen historians to examine the history of a variety of chrononyms. See Kalifa's introduction to the volume, pp. 7–24.
8. Henry Rousso, *The Vichy Syndrome: History and Memory in France Since 1944*, 2nd ed., trans. Arthur Goldhammer (Cambridge, Mass.: Harvard University Press, 1994).

BIBLIOGRAPHY

Angenot, Marc. *Le Cru et le faisandé: sexe, discours social et littérature à la Belle Époque.* Brussels: Labor, 1986.

Barjot, Maurice, Jean-Pierre Chaine, and André Encrevé, *La France au XIX siècle, 1814–1914.* Paris: PUF, 1995.

Barnes, Julian. *Man in the Red Coat.* New York: Knopf, 2020.

Benjamin, Walter. "On the Concept of History" [1935–1937]. In *Selected Writings.* Cambridge, Mass.: The Belknap Press of Harvard University Press, 1996.

Berlanstein, Leonard. "Selling Modern Femininity: *Femina*, a Forgotten Feminist Publishing Success in Belle-Epoque France." *French Historical Studies* 30 (Fall 2007): 623–650.

Burnham, Helen. *Toulouse-Lautrec and the Stars of Paris.* Boston: Museum of Fine Arts Publications, 2019.

Cambor, Kate. *Gilded Youth: Three Lives in France's Belle Epoque.* New York: Farrar, Straus and Giroux, 2009.

Carco, Francis. *La Belle Epoque au temps de Bruant.* Paris: Gallimard, 1954.

Carter, Alfred E. *The Idea of Decadence in French Literature, 1830–1900.* Toronto: University of Toronto Press, 1947.

Cate, Philip Dennis. *The Spirit of Montmartre: Cabarets, Humor and the Avant-Garde 1875–1950.* New Brunswick, N.J.: Rutgers University Press, 1996.

Charle, Christophe. *Discordance des temps. Une brève histoire de la modernité.* Paris: Colin, 2011.

——. *Paris fin de siècle: Culture et politique.* Paris: Seuil, 1998.

Cocteau, Jean. *Souvenir Portraits: Paris in the Belle Époque.* Trans. Jesse Browner. New York: Paragon House, 1990.

Corbin, Alain. *Les Filles de Noce*. Paris: Aubier, 1978.

Cordier, Adeline. *Post-War French Popular Music: Cultural Identity and the Brel-Brassens-Ferré Myth*. Farnham: Ashgate, 2014.

Crain, Esther. *The Gilded Age in New York: 1870–1910*. New York: Black Dog & Leventhal, 2016.

Cronin, Vincent. *Paris on the Eve 1900–1914*. New York: St. Martin's Press, 1990.

Darien, Georges. *La Belle France*. Paris: Savine, 1900. Republished for Kindle in 2015.

Datta, Venita. *Heroes and Legends of Fin-de-Siècle France*. Cambridge: Cambridge University Press, 2011.

Gordon, Philip H. *A Certain Idea of France: French Security Policy and Gaullist Legacy*. Princeton, N.J.: Princeton University Press, 1993.

Gosling, Nigel. *Paris 1900–1914: The Miraculous Years*. London: Weidenfeld & Nicolson, 1978.

Green, Nancy. *The Other Americans in Paris: Businessmen, Countesses, Wayward Youth, 1880–1941*. Chicago: University of Chicago Press, 2014.

Holmes, Diana, and Carrie Tarr. *A Belle Epoque? Women in French Society and Culture 1890–1914*. New York: Berghahn Books, 2006.

Jay, Mike, and Michael Neve, eds. *1900: A Fin-de-Siècle Reader*. London: Penguin, 1999.

Kalifa, Dominique. *La Culture de masse en France 1860–1930*. Paris: La Découverte, 2001.

——. *Crime et culture au XIX siècle*. Paris: Perrin, 2005.

——. *L'Encre et le sang: Récits de crimes et société à la Belle Epoque*. Paris: Fayard, 1995.,

——, ed. *Noms d'epoque: Chrononymes de "Restauration" à "Années de Plomb"* (Paris: Gallimard, 2019), especially Willa Silverman's "Fin-de-Siecle" and Venita Datta's "The Gilded Age."

——. *Vice, Crime, and Poverty: How the Western Imagination Invented the Underworld*. Trans. Susan Emanuel. New York: Columbia University Press, 2019.

Lévesque, Jean-Jacques. *Les Années de la Belle Epoque*. Paris: ARC editions, 1991.

McAuliffe, Mary. *Dawn of the Belle Epoque: The Paris of Monet, Zola, Bernhardt, Eiffel, Debussy, Clemenceau, and Their Friends*. Lanham, Md.: Rowman & Littlefield, 2011.

——. *Twilight of the Belle Epoque: The Paris of Picasso, Stravinsky, Proust, Renault, Marie Curie, Gertrude Stein, and Their Friends Through the Great War*. Lanham, Md.: Rowman & Littlefield, 2014.

Mendras, Henri. *La Fin des paysans*. Paris: Sedes, 1967. In English: *The Vanishing Peasant: Innovation and Change in French Agriculture*. Trans. Jean Lerner. Cambridge, Mass.: MIT Press, 1971.

——. *La Seconde Révolution française*. Paris: Gallimard, 1988. In English: *Social Change in Modern France: Towards a Cultural Anthropology of the Fifth Republic*. Trans. Alistair Cole. Cambridge: Cambridge University Press, 2011.

Mesch, Rachel. *Having It All in the Belle Époque: How French Women's Magazines Invented the Modern Woman*. Stanford, Calif.: Stanford University Press, 2013.

Mitchell, Kate. *Victorian Afterimages. History and Cultural Memory in Neo-Victorian Fictions*. London: Palgrave, 2012.

Morand, Paul. *1900*. Paris: Flammarion, 1931. In English: *1900 A.D.*, trans. R. Fedden. New York: W. F. Payson, 1931.

Nora, Pierre, and Lawrence Kritzman. *Realms of Memory: Construction of the French Past*, vol. 3: *Symbols (Lieux de Memoire)*. Trans. Arthur Goldhammer. New York: Columbia University Press, 1989.

Nordau, Max. *Degeneration* [1892]. London: William Heinemann, 1989.

Ory, Pascal. *L'Aventure culturelle française*. Paris: Flammarion, 1989.

———. "Le mythe de Paris, Ville-Lumière, dans les années 1900." In *La Puissance française à la Belle Epoque: Mythe ou réalité?*, ed. P. Milza and R. Poidevin. Paris: Complexe, 1992.

Prochasson, Christophe. *Les Années électriques, 1880–1910*. Paris: La Découverte, 1991.

———. *Paris 1900. Essai d'histoire culturelle*. Paris: Calmann-Lévy, 1999.

Rayward, W. Boyd. *Information Beyond Borders: International Cultural and Intellectual Exchange in the Belle Époque*. Farnham: Ashgate, 2014.

Rearick, Charles. *Paris Dreams, Paris Memories: The City and Its Mystique*. Stanford, Calif.: Stanford University Press, 2011.

———. *Pleasures of the Belle Epoque: Entertainment and Festivity in Turn-of-the-Century France*. New Haven, Conn.: Yale University Press, 1988.

Rebérioux, Madeleine *La Republique Radicale? 1898–1914*. Vol. 11 of Nouvelle Histoire contemporaine. Paris: Seuil, 1975.

Retaillaud, Emmanuelle. *La Parisienne: Histoire d'un mythe. Du siècle des lumières à nos jours*. Paris: Seuil, 2020.

Riding, Alan. *And the Show Went On: Cultural Life in Nazi-Occupied Paris*. New York: Knopf, 2010.

Rousso, Henry. *The Latest Catastrophe: History, the Present, the Contemporary*. Trans. Jane Marie Todd. Chicago: University of Chicago Press, 2016.

Schwartz, Constance, and Franklin Hill Perrel. *La Belle Epoque and Toulouse-Lautrec*. Roslyn Harbor, N.Y.: Nassau County Museum of Art, 2003.

Schwartz, Vanessa. *Spectacular Realities: Early Mass Culture in Fin-de-Siècle Paris*. Berkeley: University of California Press, 1998.

Shapiro, Barbara Stern. "Paris Capital of the 19th Century." In *Pleasures of Paris: From Daumier to Picasso*. Boston: David R. Godine, 1991.

Shattuck, Roger. *The Banquet Years. The Origins of the Avant-Garde in France: 1885 to World War I*. New York: Anchor Books, 1958.

Veyrat-Masson, Isabelle. *Quand la télévision explore le temps: L'histoire au petit écran, 1953–2000*. Paris: Fayard, 2000.

Visages de Paris 1900: 100 photos de legende. (On the Exposition Universelle, collectively authored.) Paris: Parigramme, 2014.

Waelti-Walters, Jennifer. *Feminist Novelist of the Belle Époque: Love as a Lifestyle.* Bloomington: Indiana University Press, 1990.

Warnod, André. *Visages de Paris.* Paris: Firmin-Didot, 1930.

Weber, Eugen. *France Fin-de-Siècle.* Cambridge, Mass.: Harvard University Press, 1986.

Winock, Michel. *La Belle Epoque: La France de 1900 à 1914.* Paris: Perrin, 2002 and 2003.

INDEX

Hélène Cixous, *Portrait of Jacques Derrida as a Young Jewish Saint*

Theodor W. Adorno, *Critical Models: Interventions and Catchwords*

Julia Kristeva, *Colette*

Gianni Vattimo, *Dialogue with Nietzsche*

Emmanuel Todd, *After the Empire: The Breakdown of the American Order*

Gianni Vattimo, *Nihilism and Emancipation: Ethics, Politics, and Law*

Hélène Cixous, *Dream I Tell You*

Steve Redhead, *The Jean Baudrillard Reader*

Jean Starobinski, *Enchantment: The Seductress in Opera*

Jacques Derrida, *Geneses, Genealogies, Genres, and Genius: The Secrets of the Archive*

Hélène Cixous, *White Ink: Interviews on Sex, Text, and Politics*

Marta Segarra, ed., *The Portable Cixous*

François Dosse, *Gilles Deleuze and Félix Guattari: Intersecting Lives*

Julia Kristeva, *This Incredible Need to Believe*

François Noudelmann, *The Philosopher's Touch: Sartre, Nietzsche, and Barthes at the Piano*

Antoine de Baecque, *Camera Historica: The Century in Cinema*

Julia Kristeva, *Hatred and Forgiveness*

Roland Barthes, *How to Live Together: Novelistic Simulations of Some Everyday Spaces*

Jean-Louis Flandrin and Massimo Montanari, *Food: A Culinary History*

Georges Vigarello, *The Metamorphoses of Fat: A History of Obesity*

Julia Kristeva, *The Severed Head: Capital Visions*

Eelco Runia, *Moved by the Past: Discontinuity and Historical Mutation*

François Hartog, *Regimes of Historicity: Presentism and Experiences of Time*

Jacques Le Goff, *Must We Divide History Into Periods?*

Claude Lévi-Strauss, *We Are All Cannibals: And Other Essays*

Marc Augé, *Everyone Dies Young: Time Without Age*

Roland Barthes: *Album: Unpublished Correspondence and Texts*

Étienne Balibar, *Secularism and Cosmopolitanism: Critical Hypotheses on Religion and Politics*

Ernst Jünger, *A German Officer in Occupied Paris: The War Journals, 1941–1945*

Dominique Kalifa, *Vice, Crime, and Poverty: How the Western Imagination Invented the Underworld*